Photography and memory in Mexico: Icons of revolution

MANCHESTER
1824

Manchester University Press

Photography and memory in Mexico

Icons of revolution

Andrea Noble

Manchester University Press

Manchester and New York

distributed in the United States exclusively by Palgrave Macmillan

The right of Andrea Noble to be identified as the author of this work has been asserted by her in accordance with the Copyright, Designs and Patents Act 1988.

Published by Manchester University Press
Oxford Road, Manchester M13 9NR, UK
and Room 400, 175 Fifth Avenue, New York, NY 10010, USA
www.manchesteruniversitypress.co.uk

Distributed in the United States exclusively by
Palgrave Macmillan, 175 Fifth Avenue, New York,
NY 10010, USA

Distributed in Canada exclusively by
UBC Press, University of British Columbia, 2029 West Mall,
Vancouver, BC, Canada V6T 1Z2

British Library Cataloguing-in-Publication Data
A catalogue record for this book is available from the British Library

Library of Congress Cataloging-in-Publication Data applied for

ISBN 978 0 7190 7842 2 hardback

First published 2010

The publisher has no responsibility for the persistence or accuracy of URLs for any external or third-party internet websites referred to in this book, and does not guarantee that any content on such websites is, or will remain, accurate or appropriate.

Typeset in Dante MT
by Servis Filmsetting Ltd, Stockport, Cheshire
Printed and bound in Great Britain by the MPG Books Group

Contents

List of figures

Acknowledgements

Three people have been generous and supportive mentors to me. They are Alex Hughes, John King and Ian MacDonald, and I would like to acknowledge here their important presence in my academic formation. Thanks to fellow members of the Durham Centre for Advanced Photography Studies, Ed Welch, Jonathan Long and David Campbell for making the study of photography stimulating and fun. Over the years, many colleagues have discussed icons with me, provided help and guidance, answered email queries, etc. I'd like to thank Claire Lindsay and Nuala Finnegan, Rosa Casanova, Alberto del Castillo Troncoso, Rebeca Monroy Nasr, John Mraz, César Avilés Icedo, Mike Thompson, Sam Brunk, John Lear, Alan Knight, Leonard Folgarait, Teresa Matabuena Peláez, Rob Buffington, Armando Cristeto Patiño, Dolores Tierney. I learnt much from my former PhD student Alexia Richardson's own project on photographic icons in relation to Argentina and Peru; and from Pippa Oldfield's MA dissertation on *Soldaderas*. I'd like to thank all those who assisted me with archival work in Mexico, including staff at the Biblioteca Lerdo Tejada; Mayra Mendoza and staff at the Fototeca Nacional in Pachuca were incredibly swift and efficient with assistance with copyright permissions; and I am indebted to Lorena Gutiérrez Schott at the Hemeroteca de la UNAM for her flexibility at very short notice. I have been immensely grateful for invitations to present papers at a range of seminars and conferences over the years and for the comments and suggestions received there. In particular, I'd like to thank my colleagues Guy Thomson, Rebecca Earle and John King (again) at the University of Warwick, where I gave the first paper related to this project in 1997 – before I knew it was a book – and also, this time knowingly, the last paper, by neat symmetry in 2007. Thanks to Jens Andermann and Sasha Schell for selecting my paper for presentation at their 'Icons of Power' conference at Birkbeck College: in hindsight, the methodological core of this book started to take shape there. Thanks as well to Erica Segre for invitations to present my work at Cambridge. Special thanks also to Daniel Escorza for the invitation to attend and present at the thirtieth anniversary of the Fototeca Nacional in Pachuca in 2006 and the opportunity to meet fellow students of the photography of the revolution, Marion Gautreau and Carlos Alberto Barboso.

I am grateful to students on my final-year module on Visual Culture in Mexico who, once they overcame their fear of photographs, engaged thoughtfully with the material, providing me with a lively forum in which to explore and get my ideas straight with them.

At Manchester University Press, thanks to Emma Brennan and Kim Walker for keeping the book on track, and to George Pitcher for his meticulous copyediting and for keeping the photographs in view in the process.

An earlier version of Chapter Four was published as 'Photography, Memory, Disavowal: The Casasola Archive', in Jens Andermann and William Rowe (eds), *Images of Power: Iconography, Culture and the State in Latin America*, New York and Oxford: Berghahn Books, and sections of Chapter Five are based on earlier versions of 'Casasola's *Zapatistas en Sanborns* (1914): Women at the Bar', *History of Photography* 22 (1998), and 'Gender in the Archive: María Zavala and the Drama of not Looking' in Alex Hughes and Andrea Noble (eds) *Phototexualities: Intersections of Photography and Narrative*, Albuquerque: University of New Mexico Press.

This book could not have been researched and completed without the financial support of the British Academy for funding for two archival visits to Mexico and to the Arts and Humanities Research Council for a research leave grant that gave me valuable time away from teaching and administrative duties to finish off. Finally, as ever, thanks to Lalo for help with managing the pictures, and to Alma, who is still a little puzzled about why anyone should be so interested in photographs of the Mexican revolution . . .

TRANSLATIONS

For longer quotations in Spanish, an English translation is provided in-text and the Spanish original appears in a footnote. For short quotations, an English translation appears parenthetically in-text. Unless otherwise stated, translations are my own.

List of abbreviations

CND	Convención Nacional Democrática (National Democratic Convention)
EZLN	Ejército Zapatista de Liberación Nacional (Zapatista Army of National Liberation)
INAH	Instituto Nacional de Antropología e Historia (National Institute of Anthropology and History)
NAFTA	North American Free Trade Agreement (= TLC)
PAN	Partido de Acción Nacional (National Action Party)
PNR	Partido Nacional Revolucionario (National Revolutionary Party)
PRD	Partido de la Revolución Democrática (Party of the Democratic Revolution)
PRI	Partido Institucional Revolucionario (Institutional Revolutionary Party)
PRM	Partido Revolucionario Mexicano (Mexican Revolutionary Party)
SINAFO	Sistema Nacional de Fototecas (National System of Photographic Libraries)
TLC	Tratado de Libre Comercio (Free Trade Agreement) (= NAFTA)

Part I Panoramas

1
Icons of revolution

For better or for worse, human beings establish their collective identity by creating around them a second nature composed of images which do not merely reflect the values consciously intended by their makers, but radiate new forms of value formed in the collective, political unconscious of their beholders. (Mitchell 2005: 105)

On 16 March 1999, eight members of the Ejército Zapatista de Liberación Nacional (EZLN, Zapatista Army of National Liberation) entered Sanborns in the heart of Mexico City to take light refreshment in the department-store's famous restaurant. Once installed at the bar, they were snapped by scores of waiting photographers (See Figure 8.5). This was no ordinary photo opportunity, however. It was the recreation of one of the best-known images of the Mexican revolution, recording the moment when, in December 1914, troops from Emiliano Zapata's Ejército Libertador del Sur (Liberation Army of the South) similarly took their places at the bar of Sanborns and were immortalised in sepia (see Figure 6.2). In this way, the modern-day Zapatistas signalled that in the age of globalised neo-liberalism, the basic revolutionary principle of social justice remains a far from realised goal. At the same time, that this performance was readily legible to its late twentieth-century viewers confirms that, on the eve of the centenary of the outbreak of the revolution, photographs of the conflict – or more to the point, a select handful thereof – continued to exert their presence in the Mexican social imaginary.[1]

It has been estimated that Mexico's foremost repository of photographs, the Casasola Archive, holds some 37,661 images made during the armed phase of the conflict between 1910 and 1923, out of an overall total of 484,004 photographic items (both positives and negatives).[2] Nevertheless, even as more images are coming to light thanks to the valuable archival and historical research that is being carried out in conjunction with Mexico's national network of Fototecas, the same circumscribed assortment continues to be endlessly repeated, appropriated and reworked. In some cases, this process was set in motion from the moment

3

that the images were first produced. So, for example, versions of the classic image of Zapata (see Figure 8.2) – cartridge belts across his chest, rifle in one hand, the other grasping the hilt of a sword – were repeatedly reproduced in the print press during the revolution. In other instances, the process of iconisation occurred in a post hoc fashion across the domains of official and popular culture.

In the decades after the struggle, the Mexican muralists worked from photographs of the revolution in their monumental visual essays that came to adorn the walls of the nation's public buildings, providing 'the polish for the muddied boots of the "backwoods" military generals who ruled postrevolutionary Mexico', and who 'sorely needed this cultural capital to negotiate with the outside world.'(Vaughan and Lewis 2006: 14) In time, images of the conflict also came to be appropriated and reworked by a range of national and foreign artists, including Arnold Belkin, Alberto Gironella (see Figure 7.6), Felipe Ehrenberg and photographer Héctor García (see Figure 7.5). Meanwhile, school children in Mexico become acquainted with them in their state-issued, grade-four history textbook, in which a familiar selection of images is used to illustrate the chapters devoted to the conflict, still a crucial event in the narrative of their civic education. As José Luis Barrios (2001: 42) argues 'The heroic, mythical iconography of these books permeates official discourse and dominates the country's historical, cultural, and social imaginaries.'

Similarly, in the everyday sphere, this select handful of images is to be seen on the walls of restaurants; emblazoned on tee-shirts; in the form of picture post-cards, fridge magnets, commemorative desk diaries and calendars; they are sold as posters on Mexico's thriving informal market; one can even have one's photograph taken in the style of a revolutionary combatant in the *Bazar de Fotografía* in the heart of Mexico City's *Centro Histórico*, owned by descendants of the Casasolas. At various points, images of revolutionary leaders, especially Emiliano Zapata, have featured on postage stamps. And, until 1992, when it was withdrawn, a drawing based on another classic photographic portrait of Zapata featured on the ten-peso note (Figures 1.1 and 1.2).[3] Indeed, the ten-peso note is itself richly emblematic of the iconic photograph as a social and cultural phenomenon: such images are everyday objects that circulate widely across semiotic forms and across media; as objects of exchange, they are embedded in broader visual economies; they are at once singular and repeated; they have socially ascribed currency that is subject to fluctuation. In short, instantly recognisable, iconic photographs have by now become so familiar that they barely warrant a second glance, let alone serious scholarly attention.

In 'Notas sobre la historia de la fotografía en México' (Notes on the History of Photography in Mexico), cultural commentator Carlos Monsiváis lists images from this privileged group. In a direct address to his reader, he states:

> You already know them [Usted ya los conoce]: a group of Zapatistas with an indecipherable expression on their faces having breakfast in the Porfirian palace,

1.1 Emiliano Zapata, Retrato/Emiliano Zapata, Portrait, c.1914.

Sanborns/a *Soldadera* [woman combatant/camp follower] looking at us from a train/a man facing the firing squad with a look of premeditated contempt or refined irony/Zapata and Villa get comfortable in the seat of power/Carranza distributing his maturity and gravity amongst a bunch of youngsters/Obregón observing the manoeuvres of a regiment/Villa entering Torreón on horseback/Eufemio, Emiliano and their wives attest to the survival of the couple in the turmoil of revolution.[4] (Monsiváis 1980: unnumbered pages)

A number of the key images that appear in Monsiváis' inventory will return in the chapters that follow. For now, we might simply note that the photographs

1.2 Ten Peso Note, Banco de México.

themselves are conspicuous by their absence as illustrations to Monsiváis's essay. Their presence would, of course, be superfluous, for the reader 'ya los conoce'. It is one thing, however, to acknowledge that, as constantly recycled artefacts, certain photographs have insinuated themselves into the cultural imaginary or, as Monsiváis (1980) suggestively puts it, have become 'impresas en el inconsciente colectivo' / 'imprinted on the collective unconscious'. It is another to explore the terms and conditions of photographic iconicity. We may think that we know an iconic photograph when we see one.[5] And Monsiváis certainly thinks he does. Yet, when we attempt to define photo iconicity, it soon becomes clear that this is a cultural phenomenon that does not lend itself to easy explanation.

In fact, the genesis of this book illustrates the slippery phenomenon that it seeks to analyse. The photographic representation of the revolution first piqued my curiosity in the mid-1990s, while conducting research for my PhD on the Italian-American photographer Tina Modotti (1896–1942) who, like many for-eigners, arrived in Mexico in the 1920s, attracted by the cultural renaissance that was taking place in the immediate post-revolutionary period. Foraging among the dusty bookshelves of the Librería Gandhi in Mexico City's Coyoacán district, I came across a book that at that time I did not know would loom large in my engagement with Mexican cultural history and identity: *Jefes, héroes y caudillos: Fondo Casasola* (1986), featuring images made during the revolution selected by Pablo Ortiz Monasterio, with an introductory text by Flora Lara Klahr. And then, by chance, I received as a gift an old, battered copy of volumes 6 to 10 of the 1942 edition of *Historia gráfica de la revolución*, also based on a selection of images from the Casasola Archive. At this point, I was making my way into a new area of research on Mexican cinema; as a satellite project, I started to prepare a series of conference and seminar presentations – in essence, analyses of a number of individual images that had aroused my curiosity in these books. It was some years later, when I stepped back and paused to reflect on the images I had chosen for examination in these, at the time, one-off papers – for example, *Villa en la silla presidencial* (see Figure 4.1), *Zapatistas en Sanborns* (see Figure 6.3) – that I realised that, serendipitously, I had been attracted to the most famous, iconic images of the revolution. Or was it serendipity? What was it about these images that had drawn me to them? Had I been drawn to them precisely because I had seen them so often, or was there something singular about the images themselves?

These questions crystallised further in the summer of 2006 when, riding in the back of a taxi in Mexico City, I fell into conversation with the driver, who asked what an English woman was doing in the capital. Explaining that I was a researcher, working on a project related to the iconic photographs of the revolution, the driver immediately knew the ones I meant: *Sí, señorita*, the one of Villa on horseback, the one of Villa and Zapata together in the Presidential Palace, ah yes, and Zapata with hand on sword and cartridge belts. Clearly, he as a Mexican citizen and I as a foreign student of Mexico shared a common set of photographic images of the revolution that came to our minds' eye: images that we would have unconsciously encountered in our interactions with the visual cultures of Mexican everyday reality; and, in my case, in the numerous academic books on Mexico that mediate my scholarly relationship with my long-distance object of study.

A class of image that does not lend itself to easy definition, for a start, the terms 'icon' and 'iconic' are ubiquitous in contemporary vernacular parlance. One might denominate a range of things and persons as icons. One speaks of iconic buildings (e.g. the Eiffel Tower or the Torre Latinoamericana); of popular celebrities, such as film stars, as iconic (e.g. Marlene Dietrich or María Félix); of iconic films (e.g. *Citizen Kane* or *Nosotros los pobres*); and even of periods of time (e.g. the 1960s as the 'iconic decade' of the twentieth century). In each of these examples, the iconic person or thing is invested with cultural salience – we might say aura – that transcends the ordinary and that is collectively recognised as a form of shorthand for a series of condensed qualities and meanings by a broad constituency of subjects in a given place and at a given time.

In some instances, the icon has metonymic status, where the part stands in for the whole: the Eiffel Tower stands in for Paris and, in turn, for France more generally. The Eiffel Tower, we might go further, is a global icon, enjoying wide international recognition, unlike its Mexican counterpart, the Torre Latinoamericana. But if the Eiffel Tower, the Torre Latinoamericana, Dietrich and Félix are icons, it is because they circulate in the form of still and moving images in a mass-mediated visual economy, with specific geopolitical coordinates. Or to put this otherwise: *Citizen Cane* is an icon – meaning here, classic or seminal text – of the international cinema; *Nosotros los pobres*, an example of 'world cinema', is a classic of Mexican and Hispanic cinema.

In other instances, as icons of the screen, Dietrich and Félix embody certain qualities, namely, feminine glamour and sophistication; at the height of their fame, their star status rendered them objects of admiration and imitation. Now,

7

however, the meanings associated with them have shifted, and they are icons of nostalgia for the golden ages in Hollywood and Mexican cinemas respectively. Nevertheless, figures of veneration of a bygone age, screen icons remind us, beyond contemporary vernacular use, of the religious connotations of the word icon. From Latin *icon* and Greek *eikon* – meaning likeness, image, portrait, semblance, similitude, simile – icons were originally memorial images made by early Christians of dead persons, which came to be embraced as cult images. As Philip Ethington and Vanessa Schwartz (2006: 10) explain in the excellent introduction to their 'urban icons project': 'These pictures were imagined as authentic copies of the "original images" of Christ, the Virgin Mary, the saints or biblical scenes rather than objects created by human hands'. What, though, of specifically photographic icons?

Until recently, the iconic photograph had received little sustained critical attention. On the one hand, picture books such as Lorraine Monk's *Photographs that Changed the World* (1989), and Hans-Michael Koetzle's *Photo Icons* (2005) present a selection of salient twentieth-century photographic images, providing journalistic-style stories behind the images. On the other, a number of academic articles have appeared that explore individual iconic photographs – for example, Sally Stein (2003) on Dorothea Lange's *Migrant Mother*; Holly Edwards (2007) on Steve McCurry's *Afghan Girl* – and series of iconic photographs related to specific historical events – for example, Marianne Hirsch (2001) and Cornelia Brink (2000) on Holocaust images; Patrick Hagiopan (2006) on Vietnam. With the 2007 publication of *No Caption Needed: Iconic Photographs, Public Culture, and Liberal Democracy*, Robert Hariman and John Louis Lucaites offer the first extended discussion of this photographic phenomenon anchored in the context of US public culture.

In an introductory chapter, the US-based scholars of communication and culture pick up on the ubiquity of the term 'icon', which encompasses 'a wide range of images ranging from smiley buttons to the crucifix', before clarifying that their book focuses on

> a class of photographic images that occur initially in the public news media and then circulate there and more widely to become familiar markers of a distinctively public subjectivity. 'Icon' is a familiar term among photojournalists and commentators on the public media. Our use of the term is consistent with theirs. To make that common usage both explicit and more focused, we define photojournalistic icons as those *photographic images appearing in print, electronic, or digital media that are widely recognized and remembered, are understood to be representations of historically significant events, activate strong emotional identification or response, and are reproduced across a range of media, genres, or topics.* (Hariman and Lucaites 2007: 27, emphasis in original)

With the aim of offering an account of the rhetorical power of iconic photographic images in US public culture, Hariman and Lucaites advance five assumptions about their modes of appeal, which I set out in synoptic form here.

First, iconic photographs are conventional images, drawing in a straight-forward fashion on the visual codes and conventions of the culture that produces them: 'The iconic image is a moment of visual eloquence, but it is never obtained through artistic experimentation. It is an aesthetic achievement made out of thoroughly conventional materials.' (30) *Second*, they enable modes of 'civic performance'. As framed entities that are reproduced many times over and across a conventionalised range of settings, iconic photographs are 'special acts of display' (31) that work performatively on their audiences through the repetition of ritual grounded in the social. Highlighting the 'deeply repetitive features of social life' (33), their performance is civic in that they are 'particularly well suited to communicate . . . social knowledge that is the foundation for political affiliation'. (34) But this is not to state that they are univocally-coded artefacts. *Third*, then, iconic photographs present multiple 'semiotic transcriptions', where their available artistic, social and political codes are coordinated in a manner that 'provides aesthetic management of the tensions within the frame. Through dense yet instantaneous articulation of the codes defining a historical event, the image can represent complexity and appeal to a large audience.' (34) *Fourth*, as emotional scenarios that play out between the viewer and the people in the picture, they invite a powerful affective response: 'the image activates available structures of feeling within the audience, keys the emotional dimension of an event, bonds an audience, artistic practice, representational object, and social context affectively'. (36) And finally, *fifth*, they allow for contradictions and crises: 'Because all societies, and particularly democratic societies, are grounded in conflict, there is continual need for performances that can manage conflict.' (37)

I have chosen to gloss Hariman and Lucaites at some length because *at a generic level*, their definition of the formal qualities of the iconic photograph and the assumptions regarding its modes of appeal provide a helpful starting point from which to approach the images that are the subject of this study.[6] Documenting a historically significant event, namely the 1910 revolution, the images under discussion in this book were produced by photojournalists and appeared in the print media to inform their readers of the conflict as it played out around them. Some sense of the original context of production and, where possible, reproduction informs the analyses of the photographs. Although sometimes displayed in these media in ways that look unconventional to twenty-first-century eyes, these photographs are aesthetically conventional images that feature human agents caught up in the struggle, from key protagonists to anonymous combatants and bystanders.

To return the images to their historical and material contexts is not, however, to freeze and fix these photographic emotional scenarios and the identifications that they engender in that distant place. Rather, it is to initiate the process of investigation in the light of what Elizabeth Edwards, drawing on anthropological approaches to material culture and the colonial archive, terms 'social biography'.[7] For Edwards (2001: 13), photographs cannot be understood at one single point in their existence, but instead 'they constantly pick up new meanings, both rework-ing the relationship between signifier and signified, and in relation to the way in which photographs are used to create and sustain meanings in people's lives'. Alongside Hariman and Lucaites's definition of the iconic photograph, the notion of 'social biography' provides another methodological starting point in this study because it is a structuring metaphor with significant performative and explana-tory force and utility. To place an emphasis on the *life*, the *afterlife* – and also, we will see, *pre-life* – of those iconic photographs that haunt the post-revolutionary landscape, is to approach them as dynamic objects, where their rhetorical power is derived from a combination of their visual eloquence and their ability to coor-dinate patterns of identification with and memories of the idea of the revolution as a foundational event in Mexican history.

But photographs, of course, are not just any objects. If the images of the revolu-tion under discussion in this book have rhetorical and affective power – if they are imbued with a life force – this is in part a function of their status as *photographic* images. Following the work of Charles Peirce, who developed a philosophy of signs in the nineteenth century, commentators on the medium have insisted on the photograph's unique combination of iconic and indexical signs. For Peirce, iconic signs resemble the object they stand for; indexical signs, meanwhile, bear the trace of the encounter with that object. In short, photographs look like what they represent: that which, in turn, imprinted itself onto the light-sensitive emulsion. Or as Tom Gunning (2008: 35) puts it, 'photographs do seem to point beyond themselves in a curious manner, and this is part of the reason the index does seem to explain part of its power'. A photograph of Francisco 'Pancho' Villa weeping at the burial of the remains of Francisco I. Madero in 1914 is moving not so much because Villa is crying (melodramatically) into a large white handker-chief; rather because 'a photograph puts us in the presence of something' (ibid.). The epistemological promise of the photograph resides in the way in which it is the product of an encounter between the historical personage Villa and the pho-tographer. Semiotics then, as Gunning also signals, only go so far in accounting for the compelling fascination of photographic images, which 'are more than just pictures. Or rather, they are pictures of a special sort, ones whose visual reference invites us to a different sort of observation, to ask different questions and think different thoughts' (ibid.).

SHAPE OF THE BOOK

This book aims to tell the life stories of some of the famous photographic images made during the Mexican revolution and repeatedly reproduced in its aftermath. It is concerned with the forms of knowledge and affect associated with the pho-tographic iconography of an event that has been constructed as foundational in modern Mexican memory. It aims to address a series of questions. Which photographs have become icons of the conflict and why these particular images and not others? How do images become iconic? How do we construct a critical framework for addressing the issues raised by iconic photographs? How do their contexts of reproduction and reception effect change on these meanings? Who, moreover, owns the meanings? What claim do iconic images make on their viewers? What is their mode of address, and how do viewers respond to claims such images make upon them? As referential images that provided the contemporary viewers – who encountered them in, for example, the print press or indeed in the form of 'wanted' posters – with knowledge about the conflict, they continue to bring us 'news' from a distant time and space. By bringing these ubiquitous but overlooked objects into focus, I hope to reflect more broadly upon what their biographies can tell us about Mexican cultural memory and identity in the twentieth century and into the twenty-first century.

After a lead-in second chapter, which offers an overview of the revolution as historical event and an account of the work of the Casasola family in making and archiving photographs of this cataclysmic moment in Mexican history, the book is structured around a series of topoi, which together constitute a form of photographic iconography of the revolution. Chapter 3 is an exploration of one of the modern period's foremost iconic figures – iconic in the loose, vernacular sense of the word – Porfirio Díaz, who embodies the age of order and progress, and its other side, violence and impoverishment of the masses. The President was an astute manipulator of the modern media of photography and latterly cinema, using them to project an image of his powerful presence in Mexican political life over the course of his rule, reaching an apogee in the centenary celebrations of independence in 1910. Homing in on two famous photographs of Díaz – posing at the foot of the 'Calendar Stone' and presiding over a ceremony in honour of his predecessor and erstwhile nemesis Benito Juárez – which were reproduced in the illustrated press, Chapter 3 contends that the camera not only documented a vision of the pomp and power embodied in the figure of the president; careful attention to his photographic iconography reveals the limits of Porfirian vision that was blind to events that existed beyond its circumscribed frame of reference.

Porfirio Díaz's relationship to the photographic image in many ways stands as a precursor to that enjoyed by the caudillos who overthrew the aged president, who similarly took care to have their campaigns photographically documented for posterity. Although lacking the careful stage-management that characterised Díaz's repertoire, Chapter 4 examines an impromptu photo opportunity taken in the National Palace in December 1914. *Villa en la silla presidencial*, featuring a jocose Pancho Villa seated on the presidential chair, beside him a solemn-faced Emiliano Zapata, has been multiply reproduced in myriad forms since its making and is arguably one of the most iconic photographs of the revolution. Locating the photograph in the first instance in its original historical and material contexts of production and reproduction, the chapter then foregrounds the relationship between photography and memory of the conflict in the post-revolutionary period to argue that this is an image that is shot through with crises and contradictions. On the one hand, one explanation for its longevity is that it activates structures of feeling and identification that chime with hegemonic post-revolutionary constructions of national identity. On the other, drawing on psychoanalytic notions of the compulsion to repeat, it becomes possible to argue that this photograph contains within its frame a vision of another radical notion of polity, one which has the potential to call into question the very hegemonic project it has been used to shore up.

Iconic photographs are not inert or passive; rather, they are entities with lively biographical trajectories that intersect with those of others; they have pasts and futures; they migrate across space, time and media, their meanings mutating in the process. The longevity and transatlantic life story of the photograph of the short-lived Fortino Sámano that is the focus of Chapter 5 illustrates this facet of iconic photographs. Executed by firing squad on Thursday 1 March 1917, the image of Sámano awaiting his death was particularly prized by French photographer Henri Cartier-Bresson, and, as reported in *Le Monde* of 24 December 2004, was 'une des deux seules que Cartier-Bresson guardait dans son atelier'/'one of only two photographs that Cartier-Bresson kept in his studio' (Monroy Nasr 2006: 11). The French photographer's ownership of a copy of the image, and his nomination of it as one of his 'photographs of the century', at once is evidence of the photograph's iconic status and participates in the ongoing process of iconisation. To grasp the full force of the life story of this particular image, however, we must trace the way in which it becomes entangled with the future-anterior, post-revolutionary elevation of the death cult to the status of national symbol; and also trace how it resonates with another photograph of a firing squad, namely the composite image of the execution of Emperor Maximilian of Hapsburg. Reading Fortino Sámano through the execution of Maximilian is, further, to consider photography's materiality and its relationship to questions of temporality; it prompts us to reconsider the ways in which photographs have the power to call into question the linearity of the historical narratives in which they are embedded.

The role of women in the historiography of the revolution has, until recent developments in women's and gender studies, been occluded from view by traditional historians. Chapter 6 explores how the considerable corpus of images featuring the presence of women – both engaged actively as *soldaderas* or as bystanders going about their everyday life – might help us to 'see' women in the conflict. The straightforward alignment of historical accounts with photographic evidence that documents women's presence and participation in the struggle can, however, prove problematic. Focusing on two case studies – *Zapatistas en Sanborns* capturing the moment in December 1914 when Zapatista troops took up their place at the bar at the famed department store, and the mysterious *María Zavala* made in 1923 – this chapter brings to bear feminist scholarship on our understanding of women and visual representation in the revolution. It argues that it is only when we foreground issues of vision and sexual difference that we can start to see women more critically in the photographic record of the revolution.

Chapter 7 returns to the theme of death and is a detailed exploration of the famous image of Zapata's death mask, taken on Thursday 10 April 1919 to prove to his enemies and supporters alike that the reviled and revered revolutionary leader had indeed finally been despatched. Inserting the photograph back into the historical narrative of Zapata's ambush and assassination and locating it in the pages of the Constitutionalist daily *El Demócrata*, it becomes clear that in April 1919 this was a trophy photograph, freighted with forensic evidence testifying to the death of its subject. Nevertheless, within a few years of Zapata's assassination he was transformed into a secular saint and admitted into the pantheon of revolutionary heroes. In this light, it is worth taking another look at the revolutionary's death mask, where its visual eloquence derives from its striking activation of iconographic codes associated with the passion of Christ.

Iconic photographs are all about repetition. Chapter 8 is a form of repetition insofar as it returns to two photographs explored in earlier chapters of this book, namely *Villa en la silla presidencial* and *Zapatistas en Sanborns*, to focus on their performative appropriation by the EZLN in the movement's engagement with civil society. Demonstrating how revolutionary photographs still carry enormous rhetorical and symbolic force in the context of this counter-hegemonic movement, this chapter establishes the mythical figure of Votán Zapata as a template for the Neo-Zapatistas' astute ritualistic performances of these iconic photographs in their demands for ethnic citizenship in the heart of the nation, Mexico City.

NOTES

1 My understanding of the concept of the social imaginaries is informed by the work of Gaonkar (2002: 4) writing in the introduction to the special issue of *Public Culture*, 'Toward New Imaginaries': 'social imaginaries are ways of understanding the social that become social entities themselves, mediating collective life . . . They are embedded in the habitus of a population or are carried in modes of address, stories, symbols and the like. They are imaginary in a double sense: they exist by virtue of representation or implicit understandings, even when they acquire immense institutional force; and they are the means by which individuals understand their identities and their place in the world.'

2 The figures relating to the images made during the conflict are derived from an early version of the website of the Sistema Nacional de Fototecas (SINAFO) www.cnca. gob.mx/cnca/inah/acervos/sinfpag3 (accessed 13 February 2007). The overall total figure of images that belong to the Casasola Archive is taken from Rosa Casanova and Adriana Konzevik's masterful book *Luces sobre México* (2006). SINAFO's up-to-date site can be accessed at www.sinafo.inah.gob.mx/main.html. I discuss the SINAFO in more detail in the next chapter. The cut-off date of 1923 takes the conflict up to the Adolfo de la Huerta rebellion of that same year. The revolution is more conventionally dated either 1910–17 or 1910–20. I address the question of the periodisation of the

conflict in the historical sketch in Chapter 2; it also arises at various points throughout this book.

3 See Gilbert (2003) for a study of the elevation of Zapata's status as textbook hero, which he dates to the regime of Lázaro Cárdenas (1934–40) and the turn to socialist principles in education. I return to the appropriation of Zapata in a number of the chapters of this study.

4 'Usted ya los conoce: unos Zapatistas con expresión indescifrable desayunan en el palacio porfirista de Sanborns/una soldadera nos mira desde un tren/un fusilable atiende con meditado desprecio o refinada ironía al pelotón/Zapata y Villa se acomodan en las sillas del poder/Carranza distribuye su madurez y su gravedad entre un tropel de jóvenes. Obregón ve maniobrar a un regimiento/Villa entra a caballo a Torreón/Eufemio, Emiliano y sus mujeres dan fe de la sobrevivencia de la pareja en el torbellino de la revolución. . .'

5 In this sense, as my colleague Jonathan Long reminded me, they are not unlike pornography as (not) defined by Justice Potter Stewart in the 1964 Jacobellis vs Ohio case.

6 I stress *at a generic level*, for the idea of the 'public sphere' and 'liberal democracy' in a US context is very different from the Mexican case. Nevertheless, the notion that all societies are grounded in conflict certainly holds good. See Knight (2001) for a discussion of democratic and revolutionary traditions in Latin America, and Lomnitz (2001) on the 'geographies of the public sphere' in Mexico.

7 See for example essays in Appadurai (1986); and Gell (1998).

2
History through photography

In a 1999 review essay of recently published works on Mexico and its revolution, Eric Van Young (144) observes that the 1910 uprising has cast a long 'teleological shadow' over the historiography of modern Mexico. Not only does this shadow loom large over accounts of the post-revolutionary period, it is also manifest in writings on the nineteenth-century struggles for independence, and even the Bourbon reforms of the eighteenth century whereby 'one failed or partial revolution gives way to another, and the Great Event is somehow immanent in all of them' (Van Young 1999a: 145). Acknowledging the difficulty of stepping outside this teleological framework, Van Young asserts that

> [O]ne major reason for the centrality of the Revolution of 1910 to interpretations of Mexico's national history is that the groups that emerged triumphant from the revolution and their legatees managed to seize the levers of not only political, economic, and social reproduction but also cultural reproduction. The nation builders were thus assured access to the symbolic coordinates by which citizens locate themselves in their social surroundings as well as to the historical memory by which they construct a meaningful past. (Van Young 1999a: 145)

Although rarely acknowledged by historians of the revolution – as we will see later in this chapter – nation builders and their proxies deployed photographs taken during the conflict as symbolic coordinates to etch the war into the public consciousness; at the same time, these images have always been subject to appropriations and interpretations that exceed the officially sanctioned meanings ascribed to them.

Before, however, turning our attention more fully to the iconic photographs of the revolution and their place in 'the fashioning of multiple nation views' (Stephen 2002: xxxvi), we must adopt a more panoramic focus. First, notwithstanding the powerful ideological charge of the myth of the revolution in the national imaginary with its attendant perils and pitfalls, it is expedient to establish a historical overview of the revolutionary process and its historiography in order to anchor ensuing chapters of this book. Second, a significant number of the images under discussion in this study belong to the Casasola Archive. Drawing on the valuable work of Mexico's historians of photography, this chapter concludes with a brief introduction to this national institution, from its origins as an agency formed to supply a news media hungry for contemporary views of the civil war, to its establishment as an archive, purveyor of potent memorial mediations of the historical past. Focusing on figures, episodes and issues that will become salient later, the synoptic approach adopted throughout this chapter is designed to set the scene for the close-up detail triggered by the analysis of specific photographs in the pages that follow.

ABOUT 1910

In September 1910, a mere two months prior to the official outbreak of the revolution on 20 November, Mexico was in the throes of lavish celebrations to mark the centenary of the initiation of its struggles for independence from Spain.[1] Achieved in 1821, the aftershocks from the independence process reverberated long past this milestone, because 'Like many peripheral nations, Mexico emerged as the result of the collapse of an empire more than because of an overwhelmingly popular desire for national independence' (Lomnitz 2001: 126). As a result, throughout a significant portion of the nineteenth century, Mexico was dominated by political turmoil, as Conservatives and Liberals fought for power, reaching its apogee during the violent paroxysms of the Reform period (1857–1861).

While the Conservatives favoured the preservation of Catholic and Hispanist traditions – a continuation of the colonial-style, corporate order – the Liberals 'asserted individualism and popular sovereignty' (Servín et al 2007: 6) and were, moreover, fervently secularist. The bitter civil wars that raged through the Reform period eventually saw the triumph of the liberal cause emblematised in the figure of Benito Juárez, who first acceded to the presidency in 1861. What is more, despite the fragility of Mexico's institutional structures at this time, the cornerstones on which the liberal future rested were established in the form of the Constitution of 1857 and the 1860 Reform Laws. The Constitution instituted liberal policies, including freedom of speech, conscience, press and assembly; guarantees of civil liberties; the secularisation of education; the abolition of slavery; and the abolition of colonial-era military and church court systems. Meanwhile, the Reform Laws explicitly set out to separate the State and Church by, for example, nationalising Church property, establishing a civil registry system and prohibiting official attendance at Church functions. Although the primary aim of such legislation was to undercut the pervasive power of the Catholic Church, changes to property law also targeted communal land held by indigenous groups, whom the Liberals wished to prise from traditional social and cultural practices and thereby induct them into the larger body politic. That larger body politic was, however, a contradictory entity. François Xavier Guerra (2007: 134) characterises the epoch: 'the idea of a nation formed by citizen-individuals coexisted with, and often conflicted with, a nation formed by bodies of all kinds . . . The existence of a unique

Mexican nation, a historical community with a well-defined identity, was not questioned. Its political structure, however, was not unitarian. It was pluralistic: a conglomerate of pueblos, states, cities, and villages of varying importance but with equal rights and engaging the government through multiple acts'.

As the battles for power raged, the nation suffered two traumatic foreign interventions, the first of which 'should not be underestimated as an ideological crucible for the forging of widely diffused idioms of Mexican nationalism' (Van Young 2007: 51). During the Mexican-American war (1846–48), Mexico City was captured by US troops in 1847, culminating in the loss of half of national territory to the United States under the 1848 Treaty of Guadalupe Hidalgo. Then, in 1861, Louis Napoleon Bonaparte, determined to extend his empire and influence with the aid of a puppet proxy, sent a French expeditionary force of 270,000 troops with the aim of installing Austrian archduke Maximilian of Hapsburg as emperor of Mexico. After nearly two years of fighting and with the support of the Conservatives, Maximilian was duly enthroned in 1864. If the Mexican-American war spurred the forging of idioms of nationalism, after the totemic execution of Maximilian by firing squad in 1867, according to Claudio Lomnitz (2001: 87) 'Mexico earned its "right" to exist as a nation. Until that time, no strong central state had existed, and the country's sovereignty was severely limited.' If the bullet that ended Maximilian's life induced the birth of the sovereign nation-state, and if the principles governing that entity were enshrined during the Reform period and symbolically associated with Benito Juárez, it was, however, the presidency of Porfirio Díaz that finally ushered in an epoch of (relative) political and social stability.

Ascending to the premiership for the first time in 1876 and remaining there for thirty-five years – with one four-year hiatus from 1880 to 1884 – under Díaz, the country experienced the dramatic and vertiginous changes wrought by his administration's pursuit of economic modernisation. Aided and abetted by his technocratic advisors, the *ciéntificos*, and influenced by currents in social Darwinism, Díaz set out to restore order in the violent and divided national territory. Combining strong-arm tactics with social engineering, during the Porfiriato, as the period was known after the president, the nation's architects sought to bring about a cultural revolution, thereby to ameliorate Mexico's tarnished international image and attract foreign investment. In this process, it was hoped, Mexicans would abandon the still persistent colonial-era coordinates of identification mediated by family, Church and local community, and switch allegiance to a more abstract, bureaucratic (and modern) concept of the nation-state. The results of these policies were, of course, less than clear cut. To be sure, once deterred by reports of banditry and marauding Apache Indians, Díaz's more coercive strategies succeeded and Mexico did indeed become a magnet for foreign investors so that '[by] 1900, foreign investors held some 90 percent of the incorporated value of Mexican industry. Americans alone held 70 percent. Foreigners also held 150 million of Mexico's 485 million acres' (Hart 2000: 435).

17

The hallmarks of modernity in the form of roads, railways, telegraph and telephone systems, streetcars and electricity started to extend across the Republic as the century drew to a close. In 1876, for example, Mexico was traversed by 640 km of rail track; by 1898, it boasted 12,172 km (Tenorio-Trillo 1996: 33). In time, these innovations began to transform people's lives.

Ensconced in Mexico City, Díaz allowed political abuse and endemic corruption in the provinces to go unchecked – indeed he even encouraged it – in the name of tightening central control. A consummate manipulator, he practised a politics of divide and rule, playing off different elite interest groups against one another. Against this backdrop, wealth in the form of land remained in the hands of a few privileged families – by 1910 half the country's rural population lived in the boundaries of a hacienda (Buffington and French 2000: 418) – and the production of staple crops was scaled back in preference for crops for export, pushing up the price of food. French culture was *à la mode* among the Mexican aristocracy: one of the major thoroughfares in Mexico City, the Paseo de la Reforma underwent a 'make-over' in intimation of the Champs Elysées; and French cuisine was *de rigueur* in the capital. Meanwhile sanitation and diet among the masses was so poor that average life expectancy at birth hovered at around thirty years (McCaa 2003: 392).

In November 1910, with the celebrations to commemorate the centenary barely over, and an ageing Díaz well into the third decade of his rule, Francisco I. Madero drafted the Plan de San Luis Potosí, calling for the nation to rise up in revolution. A wealthy landowner from the northern state of Coahuila, Madero's campaign was largely couched in political rather than social terms – 'No re-elección y sufragio efectivo' (No re-election and effective suffrage) – and, in the face of economic stagnation, reflected the growing frustrations of key regional elites who, under Díaz, were locked out of power. But his call to arms resonated profoundly across the social spectrum, tapping into the grievances of urban and rural workers alike, who were equally vulnerable to the economic downturn that afflicted Mexico, hit hard by the 1907–08 world recession. The ensuing civil war was violent and protracted; lasting ten years, with a death toll in the region of one million, out of a population of some 13.5 million. But for all that the human stakes of participation in the revolution were high, what it ultimately achieved and how it was to be classified and interpreted have been the subject of intense and prolific debate.

The one undisputed accomplishment of the revolution was the toppling of Díaz. Many of the other achievements, however, are rather less easy to define, for the revolution was not a clear-cut struggle between liberators and oppressors. Rather, it was a bitter factional strife of shifting allegiances and political agendas, in which the chief protagonists – Francisco I. Madero, Emiliano Zapata, Francisco (Pancho) Villa, Venustiano Carranza and Álvaro Obregón – fell victim to political assassination at the behest of their rivals. Indeed, death will become a thematic thread weaving throughout many of the chapters of this book, from the representation of the firing squad during the revolution, back to the execution of Maximilian on the Cerro de Campanas (Hill of Bells) in Querétaro, through the use of political assassination as favoured tactic for the elimination of political opponents, to the associations between femininity and death as the twin sites of alterity par excellence.

The first protagonist to lose his life to the revolution was Madero himself. Although he had managed to galvanise broad-based support for his campaign against Díaz, as the wily ex-president predicted on embarking for exile in France in 1911, Madero ultimately failed to tame the tiger he had unleashed. Elected president in the autumn of that same year, Madero could count on the continuing support from northern caudillos with a similar elite social profile to his own, key among them Carranza and Obregón. But he soon alienated erstwhile adherents to his cause. Most notably, his lacklustre attitude toward agrarian reform lost him the support of Zapata in the south, leading the latter to draft the Plan de Ayala which, proclaimed on 25 November 1911, set out a radical vision for land redistribution to communes and cooperatives. Through 1912, Zapata won grass-roots peasant sympathy that extended far beyond his home state of Morelos, his supporters calling themselves Zapatistas. Meanwhile, through 1913, to the north a militarily powerful rural insurgency gathered pace under the leadership of Pancho Villa who, although he remained loyal to Madero, nevertheless, like Zapata, represented the grass-roots, more radical end of the revolution. For these men and their followers, haciendas and foreign-owned business interests were perceived as a tangible threat to their way of life and were duly targeted for attack. At the same time, in the capital, the urban working classes also grew disillusioned with Madero's failure to act in their interests. While Madero faced mounting opposition on a number of fronts, the role of intellectual author of his assassination lay elsewhere, namely with Victoriano Huerta, the man whom the incumbent president had placed in charge of the federal army and made responsible for his protection. At the culmination of the Decena Trágica or Ten Tragic Days on 21 February 1913, Madero and his vice-president José María Pino Suárez were murdered after a series of insurrections and double-crosses. Huerta acceded to the presidency; the civil war intensified significantly.

Although united in their opposition to the usurper Huerta, in broad terms, the revolution split down two lines at this point: a loose alliance between Zapata and Villa on the one hand versus the northern caudillos on the other. After the North American intervention of April 1914, when US troops occupied the port of Veracruz, Huerta's position was severely weakened and he was forced into exile in the summer of that year. Recognising the superior combined military might of the peasant leaders Villa and Zapata, the northern caudillos engineered a meeting with the Villistas and Zapatistas, which took place on 10 October 1914 in Aguascalientes. The Conventionists, thus named after the Convention of Aguascalientes and comprising the Villistas and Zapatistas, demanded that

19

the northern caudillos led by Carranza accept the Plan de Ayala with its radical programme for land reform. Carranza's Constitutionalists meanwhile espoused a rather less radical social agenda and duly refused this demand. Nationalists who appealed to the masses in the name of federalism, democracy and an end to the foreign ownership of Mexican assets, they backed reforms that respected private property overseen by strong central government.

The Convention of Aguascalientes ultimately failed to bring about an accord between the bitterly opposed factions. The jockeying to and fro to broker deals between the various parties did, however, buy the Constitutionalists some time. More to the point, it provided Obregón with the opportunity to garner crucial working-class support from among the radicals of the Casa del Obrero Mundial, and time also for the North American government to side with Carranza and supply him with much-needed arms. Their numbers swollen by workers from the Casa del Obrero Mundial and equipped with US munitions, the Constitutionalist forces confronted Villa's División del Norte at the decisive Battle of Celaya in 1915. The resounding defeat of the fabled and feared División del Norte marked the end of large-scale military action in the north, where the revolution was downgraded into small-scale, guerrilla warfare, including Villa's legendary attack on the North-American town Columbus in a last-ditch attempt to impose his authority.

Similarly, in the south, by 1916 Zapatismo was starting to make the transition from conventional army to guerrilla status, reduced in numbers, based in remote mountain camps, with hit-and-run raids as its favoured military tactic. Nevertheless, Zapatismo still had a tenacious hold over rural communities of Morelos that was fast becoming a thorn in the side of the nearly, but not quite, triumphal Constitutionalists, for whom dealing with the Zapatistas was 'like dealing with an inflated balloon' (Knight 1986, Vol. 2: 366). Just as they were squeezed out of one zone, they would pop up in another, much to the consternation of the Constitutionalists who vented their spleen in racially tinged references to Zapatista atrocities in the national press and culminating in Zapata's assassination on the instructions of Carranza on 10 April 1919.

Riven with internecine conflict, then, the revolution ultimately saw the triumph of the middle-class Constitutionalists, who promoted national capitalism and shared a broad liberal agenda. Led first by the *Primer Jefe* Carranza, and then, once he had quietly manoeuvred to have the latter assassinated, by Obregón, the Constitutionalists fell heir to the project of taking the revolution forward, setting in motion the process of national reconstruction.[2] The guiding principles arising from the revolutionary movement were set out in the Constitution of 1917, promulgated during the presidency of Carranza. Hailed by Mary Kay Vaughan (2006: 22) as 'the Western Hemisphere's most progressive legal blueprint . . . it promised land reform to the peasantry; protection, welfare and organising rights to the working class; national control over natural resources; and liberation from Catholic control over hearts, minds, and bodies'.

Radical Constitution notwithstanding, the post-revolutionary process of national reconstruction was, however, no simple task; nor did its radicalism translate smoothly into political and social practice. The Mexican Republic that was born in 1821 had been a fragmented entity, with subject-citizens who cleaved strongly to colonial-era corporate structures; in the intervening ninety years, political and cultural coherence remained elusive, so that on the eve of the outbreak of the revolution

> Mexico of 1910 was, borrowing Lesley Simpson's phrase, 'many Mexicos,' less a nation than a geographical expression, a mosaic of regions and communities, introverted and jealous, ethnically and physically fragmented, and lacking common national sentiments; these sentiments came after the Revolution and were . . . its offspring rather than its parents. (Knight 1986, Vol. 1: 2)

If, as Knight's comments suggest, Mexico was more a collection of fragments than a coherent whole in 1910, so too was the revolution, which as we have seen was ultimately a highly factionalised and bitter civil war. For the revolution to function within the post-revolutionary political and cultural imaginary as the desired unifying foundational narrative of identity, it therefore had to be remembered and thereby *reinvented* as a unified struggle: 'Forging one official, dominant yet fraternal Revolutionary Tradition would help the revolutionaries accomplish the goals that tradition is designed to accomplish: to disseminate la Revolución in the present and transmit la Revolución to succeeding generations, in the process to inculcate beliefs, legitimize institutions, and promote social cohesion' (Benjamin 2000: 21). Given that it was the middle-class, conservative faction embodied by Carranza and Obregón that emerged as victorious (and not the *campesinos* or radicals), the revolution had to be retrospectively re-presented not only as coherent, but also (in appearance at least) as propelled by a social and political *revolutionary* agenda. Thus, if Emiliano Zapata (murdered, it will be recalled, on the orders of Carranza) came to embody the ideals of the revolution in official as well as popular revolutionary discourse, this was because, in the words of Lynn Stephen (2002: 244), 'The appropriation of the goals and symbols of the Mexican Revolution has anchored the Mexican state's twentieth-century construction of nationalism. Chief among these symbols is the figure of Emiliano Zapata and through him, the right to land.'

The political regimes that carried out the project of national reconstruction, during the so-called institutional phase of the revolution (1920–40), had to face up to another of the indisputable achievements of the conflict: the birth of the *pueblo* not as an elite, bourgeois concept, but as a popular construct embodied in the masses. Indeed, the deposal of Díaz and the subsequent struggles to define the future direction of the revolution had involved a level of mass mobilisation unheard of in Latin American history. And with it 'came new popular forces, manifested in social banditry, guerrilla and conventional armies, sindicatos and mutualist societies, peasant leagues and embryonic political parties of both

Right and Left' (Knight, 1994: 393). To the degree that the revolution engendered unprecedented mass mobilisation, the Díaz dictatorship gave way not to liberal democratic politics, but rather to a one-party dictatorship. That party came into existence in the first instance in 1929, when it was known as the Partido Nacional Revolucionario (PNR, National Revolutionary Party); it then became the Partido Revolucionario Mexicano (PRM, Mexican Revolutionary Party) in 1938, before being rebaptised as the oxymoronically titled Partido Revolucionario Institucional (PRI, Institutional Revolutionary Party) in 1946. The PRI governed Mexico uninterrupted for seventy-one years, until it was ousted from power in the historic election of 2000 that ushered in the reign of the right-wing Partido de Acción Nacional (PAN, National Action Party).

Nevertheless, the new, self-perpetuating political class – the presidency passed to anointed successors in six-yearly terms or *sexenios* – harboured few illusions concerning what was in the best interests of the masses.[3] In the eyes of its representatives, the unleashed power of the masses needed to be harnessed to the strongly centralist project of nation-state. The masses required education. They needed to be secularised and to learn to identify with the 'nation', whose manifestations, in turn, had to reflect the masses back to themselves. Furthermore, the masses had to leave behind their traditional practices and allegiances to local community and, like their nineteenth-century forebears, to be inducted into the ways of the modern nation in pursuit of capitalist development with its associated social forms. In short, they had to be *modernised*. Perhaps these last points are the ultimate paradoxes underpinning the outcome of the revolution, paradoxes that historians Gil Joseph and Daniel Nugent (1994: 15) phrase in the following terms: 'Understanding how such a regulated set of social forms of life – i.e. capitalism – emerged in so strong a form in Mexico is not an easy task, particularly since that historical outcome is frequently masqueraded as the result of a popular, peasant war.'

HISTORIES OF THE REVOLUTION

The historical literature devoted to this pivotal event in national history is by now immense. Understandings of the revolution and the relationship between the new forms of mass participation and politics to which it gave rise have, as we would expect, undergone a series of transformations over the course of the twentieth and into the twenty-first century. For a start, as Joseph and Nugent (1994: 5) have noted, the revolution is 'variously described as having occurred between 1910 and 1917, 1910 and 1920, or 1910 and 1940, and the debates about how to periodize [it] not only highlight its complexity as historical process during which popular resistance figured significantly, but also point to another process simultaneous in space and time: revolutionary and post-revolutionary state formation.' In the first decades after the end of the armed phase, historians and commentators – many of whom had been personally involved – offered romanticised accounts of the revolution as a spontaneous agrarian insurrection, propelled by unified, socially oriented aims in the form of land redistribution and the nationalisation of foreign assets. Smoothing out ideological tensions and conflicts, and notably glossing over the shortcomings in the social agenda of the triumphant faction, these accounts chimed neatly with the version of events promoted by the post-revolutionary state. First-generation commentators shared a vision of the revolution as a progressive force for good: a vision that also played out, for example, in feature films of Mexico's so-called cinematic Golden Age such as *Flor Silvestre* (Emilio Fernández, 1943), and *Enamorada* (Emilio Fernández, 1946), and the fascinating *Memorias de un mexicano* (Carmen Toscano, 1950), based on early footage captured by Salvador Toscano.[4]

The year 1940, as Joseph, Rubenstein and Zolov (2001: 8) note, is held as a turning point in the historical literature, marking 'the beginning of the end to the revolutionary promise, embodied particularly in the now mythic figure of Lázaro Cárdenas . . . [A] convenient historical signpost of the shift in revolutionary politics away from Cárdenas's radical redistribution of wealth toward Ávila Camacho's policy of intensive capital accumulation'. To be sure, the 1940s constituted a period of accelerated industrialisation and urbanisation, coupled with strong economic growth and political stability, which by the late 1950s came to be hailed as the Mexican 'Miracle'.[5] At the same time, however, the more authoritarian hues of the post-revolutionary project of nation-state became manifest, starting with the suppression of labour strikes in the capital (1958–59) and culminating in the watershed year 1968, when government-backed paramilitaries were sent to suppress student demonstrations in the Plaza de las Cuatro Culturas, leading to the massacre of several hundred.

In turn, revisionist interpretations of the revolution started to appear, particularly in the aftermath of the student massacre of 1968, challenging the prevailing notion that the revolution had been a popular struggle which sought emancipation from backwardness and social inequalities and whose goals were achieved through post-revolutionary state policies.[6] Post-1968 historiography placed an emphasis instead on the state as a monolithic, centralised entity that brokered power via the co-option of the popular masses. If the revisionists offered an important corrective to earlier celebratory interpretations of the revolution, their work has subsequently come under critical scrutiny. More recently, a post-revisionist historiography has emerged that challenges this heavy-handed approach, seeking instead to understand the revolution and post-revolutionary politics and power as a negotiation between state and society, rather than as a simply 'top-down' imposition.

At the same time, this post-revisionist historiography has been undergoing a hotly contested cultural turn, the so-called new cultural history. Eschewing teleological, grand narratives, cultural history is an interpretive matrix that draws on anthropological approaches to notions of community and identity, and shares an interest in issues of textuality with literary scholarship. It is attentive to the way

23

in which representations frame the way in which individuals and collectivities make sense of and interact with the world that surrounds them. In the words of one of the contributors to the 1999 special issue of the *Hispanic American Historical Review*, dedicated to debating the polemics surrounding this field of inquiry, and writing specifically of the nineteenth century, new cultural historians are interested 'in "imagining" or perhaps more accurately, in "imaginings". That is, they seek to understand how the nation has been imagined, how subjectivity has been imagined and, in some of their most provocative work, how the imaginings and thus construction of nation and subjectivity have been (and are) implicated in each other' (French 1999: 249).[7]

PHOTOGRAPHY AND HISTORY

To the degree that the new cultural historians are precisely interested in culture – 'to the process of meaning formation, the codes by which meanings are stabilized and transmitted, and the ideas in people's minds' (Van Young 1999b: 216) –visual artefacts such as film and art have, for some time, registered on their critical radar. By contrast, the photographic image as a material trace of the past largely overwhelms by its underpresence as a focus of study.[8] Needless to say, however, photographs are not absent from the work of cultural historians or, indeed, historians of Mexico more generally. They are frequently to be found gracing the pages of even the most academic (as opposed to popular) historical work. So, for example, several essays by distinguished historians of Mexico that comprise the edited volume *Cycles of Conflict, Centuries of Change*, are accompanied by photographs (Servín, Reina and Tutino 2007). The reader is, however, hard-pressed to find an in-text reference to the images, where they serve an, albeit extremely loose, illustrative function.[9] In short, their use seems to confirm Caroline Brothers's assertion (1997: 14) that '[it] is confusion over the way photographs carry their meaning, and suspicion over their teasing ambiguity, that makes scholars wary of the evidence photographs embody. At worst images, and particularly photographs, are ignored by historians altogether; at best they are used merely in illustration of other histories'.

In Mexico, by contrast, the history of photography and history through photography are booming. Supported by an exceptional institutional framework, the Sistema Nacional de Fototecas (SINAFO), under the auspices of the Instituto Nacional de Antropología e Historia (INAH), the conservation, classification, storage and (increasingly) digitisation of the nation's photographic patrimony have been assured. The SINAFO, created toward the end of 1993, – for Casanova and Konzevik (2006: 6) a crucial moment in the institutional history of photography in Mexico – coordinates approximately twenty photographic archives across the Republic from the hub of the Fototeca Nacional, located in Pachuca, Hidalgo, 88 kilometres north of Mexico City. Over the last three decades of the twentieth century, this institutional structure has seen the emergence of a generation of curators, archivists and critics, Mexican and foreign alike – among them Rosa Casanova, Olivier Debroise, Alberto del Castillo, Deborah Dorotinsky, Daniel Escorza, Marion Gautreau, Rebeca Monroy Nasr, John Mraz, Pablo Ortiz Monasterio and Carlos Alberto Sampaio Barbosa to name but a select few – who have created a thriving scholarly community devoted to the historical study of national photographic traditions. Even prominent professional historians such as Enrique Krauze and Enrique Florescano are alert to the potential of the photographic and other image forms as a category for analysis to be taken seriously in an understanding of the past. The photographic sources on which they have to draw are rich indeed. At the time of writing, the Fototeca Nacional houses some 900,000 items, consisting of forty-one different collections and covering 160 years of photographic history, of which one of the most important collections is, without doubt, the Casasola Archive.

THE CASASOLA LEGACY

If Mexico boasts a flourishing photographic culture, it can be attributed in part to the legacy of the Casasola family, whose agency turned archive has proven a rich photographic endowment to the nation. For the photo-historian and indeed the historian *tout court*, the Casasola Archive represents a valuable and unique source of photographs of the Mexican revolution and, indeed, the majority of those discussed in this book are derived from it. The archive originated in the work of three generations of photojournalists in the Casasola family, a tradition that was initiated by Agustín Víctor Casasola in conjunction with his brother Miguel. As Eduardo Ancira signals (2005: 335), it is the name of Agustín Víctor Casasola that is most widely known both at home and abroad and about whom most has been written.[10]

Born in 1874, Agustín Víctor Casasola started out professionally as a reporter working on Mexico City newspapers such as *El Liberal*, *El Correo Español*, *El Popular*, *El Universal*, *El Globo* and *El Tiempo*. It was in this capacity that he turned, in the first instance, to photography to illustrate the articles he authored. As Alberto del Castillo Troncoso (2005: 67) observes, from the mid-1880s advances in technology, including rotogravure and halftone had led to the increasing use of photographs in illustrated magazines and latterly newspapers. In such contexts, photographic images served as visual documents that reinforced textual reportage. Thus when, in 1904, Casasola started to work for the *Porfirian* mouth-piece *El Imparcial*, a daily that was conceding increasing importance to visual illustration, and particularly the photographic image, he joined a significant emerging profession, photojournalism.

The exile of the ageing Díaz in 1911 marked a pivotal year for the nation; so too it was a turning point for photojournalism. The foundation of the Asociación Mexicana de Fotógrafos de Prensa (Mexican Association of Press Photographers) – of which Casasola was director – inaugurated a new relationship between the photojournalist and power (Arroyo and Casanova 2002: 205). If previously the photojournalist occupied the position of poor relation in comparison with his counterpart the reporter, with the change of regime came a marked shift in the photographer's status. Now the newly elected President Madero posed for a picture with the photographers whose work was shown in Mexico's first exhibition dedicated to the 'art' of photojournalism. Madero, of course, was not the only revolutionary leader to court the photojournalists. In the face of a largely illiterate population and a rapidly changing political landscape, all the major caudillos, no doubt attracted to the medium's immediacy and apparent transparency, had an eye to their photographic and filmic representation. So, for example, the Zapatistas' campaign was covered by Hugo Brehme; the Obregonistas by Jésus H. Abitia; meanwhile, Pancho Villa's relationship with the North American Mutual Film Co., for whom it is alleged he staged battles and arranged for hangings to be performed by daylight, is legendary.[11]

In 1912, Casasola left *El Imparcial* and founded the *Agencia Fotográfica Mexicana* (Mexican Photography Agency), shortly afterward renamed *Agencia Mexicana de Información Gráfica* (Mexican Graphic Information Agency). Under the slogan 'Tengo o hago la foto que usted necesite' / 'I have or I'll take the photo you need', the *Agencia* advertised its activities as set out on its presentation card as follows:

> This agency
>   takes photographs by day and by night
>   in the capital and beyond
>   negotiates their publication in the press
>   provides portraits and views of the whole world
>   buys, sells and hires out cameras and lenses. (Arroyo and Casanova, 2002: 206)[12]

The creation of the *Agencia Mexicana de Información Gráfica* was an astute commercial move. As the conflict gathered momentum, demand by the national and international news media for photographic images grew apace. As a repository for the work of 483 photographers (Gutiérrez Ruvulcaba 1996: 191) whose authorship, as recent scholarship has demonstrated and sought to rectify, more often than not went unacknowledged, the *Agencia* was well placed to meet this demand. Furthermore, even after the agency ceased operation in 1913 for reasons unknown (Gutiérrez Ruvulcaba 1996: 193), this unique family business lived on long beyond the conclusion of the violent phase of the revolution, as successive generations of Casasolas and their employees continued to photograph scenes from national life for some six decades more.

Even as the Casasolas received new commissions and created a vast repository of what is frequently termed '*memoria visual*' in the post-revolutionary period, they clearly had an eye to the foundational status and monumental quality of (not to say, commercial opportunities associated with) the material they had accrued during the armed phase of the uprising. So, in the immediate aftermath of the conflict, Víctor Agustín Casasola embarked on an ambitious enterprise to produce a fifteen-volume set of photo-books charting the revolution from the dying days of the Porfiriato to the presidency of Alvaro Obregón.[13] Combining bilingual text in Spanish and English (and therefore clearly oriented to a North American as well as Mexican readership), the first and only volume of the *Álbum histórico gráfico* was duly published in 1921. Commercially unviable, critics have argued that for Mexican audiences it was simply too soon to look again at scenes from the immediate past, and thus the *Álbum* project was shelved, for the time being at least. In fact, according to Del Castillo Troncoso (2005: 77) 'A couple of decades would have to pass before the violent events could be seen through the lens of nostalgia and the photographs would be converted into key icons of the legitimacy of the new political regimes that emerged from the Mexican revolution.'[14] The market for photo-books may have been slower to emerge; as we shall see in the chapters that follow, photographs of the conflict circulated from the early 1920s on.

In due course, some four years after Agustín Víctor Casasola's death, the project was resurrected in 1942 with the publication of the *Historia gráfica de la Revolución*, under the editorial guidance of the patriarch-founder's son, Gustavo. Covering the period 1900 to 1940 and issued in instalments, this publication was richly resonant of 'la Revolución hecha gobierno' (the Revolution made government) or, as Thomas Benjamin (2000: 68) puts it, the Revolution (with a capital letter) 'was transformed into government . . . and was thus perceived as permanent and ongoing'. However much they protested that the archive simply offered an objective lens on Mexican society, the Casasolas were consistently and closely allied with the political regimes of the day, which in turn forged their legitimacy as sons and heirs in the on-going visualisation of the revolutionary process. This is nowhere more clearly evinced than in the organising principle behind the *Historia gráfica de la Revolución*, which offers a chronological visual history, in which the revolution as foundational event extends into the present and is, furthermore, structured by presidential terms or *sexenios*.

If the precocious *Álbum* received a lukewarm reception in 1921, the same cannot be said of the 1942 *Historia gráfica de la Revolución*, which clearly proved a profitable enterprise. The Casasolas went on to produce further photobooks, including the *Historia gráfica de la Revolución Mexicana* which appeared in the 1960s, and was extended again in 1973 by the publishers Trillas, taking the revolution up to 1970 and the regime of Gustavo Díaz Ordaz. The Casasola family must, in some large measure, be responsible for the salient and significant status that the photographic image and its material base the photobook enjoy in Mexican culture. Testimony to its status as an enduring item of Mexican culture, the archive was sold to the Mexican state in 1976 and is currently in the custody of the INAH.[15]

Interest in, and activities associated with the Casasola Archive and, in particular, its representation of the revolutionary years, have continued unabated. This should not surprise us. If, as Van Young (1999a) asserts, the revolution has cast a long teleological shadow over the historiography of modern Mexico, then so too the photographs taken at the height of the cataclysmic political violence loom large in the cultural imagination. In the words of one commentator, the Casasola archive is the archive that 'is most readily identified in collective memory [*memoria ciudadana*], that best conjures up for us the Mexican Revolution, and that has most infiltrated national identity' (Ochoa Sandy (1997: 11).[16] Given the archive's impact on the shaping of memory, how then might an examination of those iconic images that have become a form of visual shorthand for the conflict illuminate our understanding of the revolutionary process and its aftermath and, by extension, Mexican identity itself?

NOTES

1 Alan Knight (1986: 1) observes in the opening sentence of his seminal two-volume study: 'Histories of the Mexican Revolution traditionally begin with the Centennial celebrations of 1910.' I too have chosen to follow convention in the condensed account that follows and, in Chapter 3, I similarly focus on the centenary. I nonetheless part company with the professional historians in my focus on photographic representation. As I make the final revisions to this manuscript in Mexico City in August 2009, preparations are underway to celebrate the centenary of the revolution and the bicentenary of independence. In addition to a wealth of publications and other media – such as the Instituto Mora's *BiCentenario: El ayer y hoy de México*, or the lavishly illustrated journal *20/10: Memoria de las Revoluciones en México*, or official websites and exhibitions – the days, minutes and seconds to the official anniversary of independence on 16 September 2010 are being counted down on a special digital clock, located between the Metropolitan Cathedral, the Templo Mayor and the National Palace in the Zócalo, or central plaza, in Mexico City. See Tenorio-Trillo 2009 on Mexico's centenaries.

2 Obregón's turn came later. He was gunned down by a Catholic activist on 17 July 1928 in protest at the strong anticlerical stance of his post-revolutionary regime.

3 See Castañeda (2000) on how Mexican presidents were chosen during the reign of the PRI.

4 Like Mariano Azuela's classic novel of the revolution *Los de abajo* (1915), not all feature films were as ideologically blinkered where the reality of the revolution was concerned, and notably Fernando de Fuentes's revolutionary trilogy (*El compadre Mendoza*, 1933; *El prisionero trece*, 1933; *¡Vámanos con Pancho Villa!* 1935) presented it in a critical light. On cinema of the revolution and particularly *Memorias de un mexicano* see Noble (2005), chapter 2 and Wood (2009). On Emilio Fernández, see Tierney (2007).

5 See Cockcroft (1998) and Sherman (2000) on the Mexican 'Miracle'.

6 On the specificity of political violence in Mexico as compared to that in other Latin American nations, see Knight (1999). On Mexico's 68, see Scherer García and Monsiváis (2002 and 2004).

7 The special issue of *HAHR*, edited by Susan Deans-Smith and Gilbert M. Joseph, includes contributions by historians anti as well as pro the 'cultural turn'. For an excoriating critique of what he sees as the excesses of cultural history, see also Knight (2002).

8 See for example essays on art by Rochfort, Oles, Lowe and Zavala, and film by Hershfield, in Vaughan and Lewis (2006). The exception is the work of John Mraz (see bibliography for further details of Mraz's extensive scholarship).

9 Wilson (2004: 27) suggests by contrast, 'Textbooks, perhaps due to the commonplace assumption that each generation is more visually literate than the previous, are larded with images'. (Although his use of 'larded' is revealing.) See Wilson (2004) for an excellent discussion of some of the reasons for which historians treat visual artefacts with suspicion, ranging from the ahistorical methodological paradigms that can frame work in visual culture studies, through history's tendency toward logocentrism, to its firmly materialist analyses of social, economic and political phenomena. For an exception, see the special issue of the *Hispanic American Historical Review*, edited by Fernando Coronil (2004) and dedicated to 'Seeing History'.

10 This section is indebted to the work of Flora Lara Klahr (1986); Ignacio Gutiérrez Ruvulcaba (1996 and 1998); Sergio Raúl Arroyo and Rosa Casanova (2002) and Alberto del Castillo Troncoso (2005).

11 See De Orellana (1992) and De los Reyes (1985) on the relationship between Villa and the still and moving image.

12 Esta agencia

> se encarga de tomar fotografias de día y de noche
>
> dentro y fuera de la capital
>
> de gestionar su publicación en los periódicos
>
> de proporcionar retratos y vistas de todo el mundo
>
> compra, venta y alquiler de cámaras y lentes

13 As Mraz (2004) notes, *historia gráfica* is a thriving business in Mexico.

14 We can see parallels with the cinema where, again, there was little appetite for films that focused on the revolution until the production of the revolutionary trilogy of Fernando de Fuentes in the 1930s. 'Tendrían que pasar un par de décadas para que los hechos violentos pudieran ser vistos bajo el tamiz de la nostalgia y las fotografias se convirtieran en iconos fundamentales para la legitimidad de los nuevos regímenes políticos emanados de la Revolución mexicana.'

15 Despite the sale of the archive, Casasola Cuarta Generación S.A. (Casasola Fourth Generation PLC) is still active in the photographic business, maintaining the *Bazar de Fotografía* on Avenida 16 de Septiembre in Mexico City. Trading in the nostalgia for revolutionary memorabilia, the *Bazar* is a veritable treasure trove for the cultural tourist with a keen eye for the photographic icons of the revolution. It is difficult to establish the exact nature of the relationship between the Bazar de Fotografía Casasola and the Fondo Casasola administered by the INAH. To be sure, the former is clearly a commercial enterprise. Nevertheless, the *Bazar*'s publicity material states that it is also involved in the diffusion of graphic history in Mexico, which it claims to make 'accessible to writers, historians, researchers, editorial projects, exhibitions and governmental institutions'. Informal conversations with both employees of the *Bazar* and colleagues at the Fototeca Nacional in Pachuca have failed to shed light on the apparent blurring of functions between the *Bazar* and the Fondo Casasola.

16 'es probablemente el más identificado en la memoria ciudadana, el que más nos rememora la Revolución Mexicana, el más filtrado en la identidad nacional'.

Part II   Close-ups

Part II: Close-ups

Photography at the end of an epoch

3

Photography at the end of an epoch

OF ANECDOTES AND APHORISMS

According to an ironic anecdote that is often recycled in the historical literature devoted to the 31-year rule of Porfirio Díaz, the President's second wife Doña Carmen Romero Rubio is credited with inducting her husband into the social mores of polite society, teaching him 'not to spit on the carpet [and] not to walk through mirrors' (Buffington and French 2000: 413). This anecdote is undoubtedly an urban myth that circulated among Mexico City's elite to highlight the civilising influence of the aristocratic Doña Carmen, or Carmelita as she was popularly known, on her uncouth, provincial spouse. That the frock-coated aristocracy mockingly imagined Díaz walking through mirrors at the age of 51 (the marriage to the 18-year-old Carmen took place in 1881) not only signals the urban elite's disparaging sense of his lack of sophistication (he could not even recognise his own reflection when he saw it); it also invokes an age, characterised by its cleavage to a myth of progress and modernity, in which image was everything.

If Doña Carmen attended to her husband's dress, speech and table manners – the marriage to a devout Catholic also marking a pragmatic re-accommodation between the liberal Díaz regime and the Church – all the evidence suggests that, humble origins notwithstanding, Díaz was neither slow nor backward in grasping the important relationship between image and power. On the contrary, it was said that he was meticulous in matters of personal grooming. According to another anecdote, Díaz was wont to whiten his skin with a special cosmetic powder, in so doing erasing his mestizo origins.[1] What is more, he did not hesitate to harness the indexical media of photography (and on its arrival in Mexico in 1896, the moving image) to a project of self-aggrandisement. In photograph after photograph, we find a uniformed Díaz dripping in medals (Figure 3.1); or else we encounter an impeccably dressed, erect, frock-coated gentleman, often engaged in acts of spectatorship, promoting an image of the President as omnipotent patriarch of the Mexican nation.[2]

The Porfiriato not only provides cultural historians with a wealth of anecdotes that reveal both the racial and social politics of the era and something of the

3.1 Porfirio Díaz, Retrato/Porfirio Díaz, Portrait, c.1910.

tensions that ran between different factions of the ruling elite, of whom Díaz was a consummate manipulator, it also was the age of the aphorism, of which Díaz was a prodigious purveyor. With regard to the Republic's geopolitical location, for instance, the cliché – '¡Pobre México! Tan lejos de Dios y tan cerca de los Estados Unidos'/'Poor Mexico, so far from God and so close to the United States' – is attributed to Díaz. On his resignation on 25 May 1911, his prescience is renowned when he is reported to have said, 'Madero ha soltado al tigre, veremos si puede domarlo'/'Madero has released the tiger, let's see if he can tame it.' Meanwhile, Claudio Lomnitz (2001: xii) claims that long ago the *Oaxaqueño* Díaz recognised Mexico City as '"the balcony of the Republic." In an authoritarian country, public opinion and national sentiment were both concentrated and represented in the national capital'. True to form, Diaz's idea of Mexico City as the 'balcony of the Republic' is endowed with rich metaphorical resonances that have endured beyond the demise of the autocrat.[3] The balcony is not simply the space from which the powerful survey those who are implicitly below them; it is also the position in which they, in turn, are surveyed from below. It is, moreover, in the circuit of looks that plays out between the surveyor and the surveyed that power crystallises.[4]

Writing of the performative dimension of statecraft in his important study of Mexico's presence at the world's fairs, Mauricio Tenorio-Trillo (1996a: 31) asserts that 'one of the mandatory roles of the national state – and perhaps its ontological raison d'être – was theatrical: to invent, re-create, and manage the national mythology'. This chapter explores the specifically photographic performance of the national mythology as it was associated with and embodied in the President. In Díaz, we have a historical personage whose manipulation of the camera image in the name of perpetuating his power prefigures, indeed functions as a model for, the caudillos who toppled him. Turning on the central axis of the dialectical looking relations that play out in Mexico City as the 'balcony of the Republic', it first establishes the 'view from below', setting out examples of how the popular classes of Porfirian society understood the rhetorical power of photographic images and how, in turn, this segment of society was viewed 'from above'. It then homes in on the pivotal year 1910, to examine a select few of the profusion of images produced to celebrate the presidency of Porfirio Díaz. As his rule progressed, Díaz certainly learnt valuable lessons about the power of the image; in time, nevertheless, he became dazzled by his own (photographic) reflection. Careful attention to Diaz's photographic iconography not only alerts us to the central figure of the President in the invention, re-creation and management of the national mythology; it also leads us to a consideration of the limits of vision in Porfirian Mexico.

PHOTOGRAPHY AND PERSUASION IN PORFIRIAN MEXICO

In the late nineteenth century, the politically powerful were not the only members of society to take advantage of the persuasive powers of photography. To be sure, the commercial dissemination of the photographic image of the political personality of national standing, as we shall examine in more detail in Chapter 5, took off in Mexico in anticipation of the arrival of Maximilian of

Hapsburg and Carlota in 1864. Accordingly, images of the principal liberal leader Benito Juárez, whose presidency commenced in 1858, did not arouse much interest among collectors until that precedent had been set, with the restoration of the Republic in 1867 (Aguilar Ochoa 1996: 25). Even then, it would not be until after his death in 1872, and some time into the regime of his successor and erstwhile enemy Porfirio Díaz, that the image and concomitant idea of Juárez as the 'high priest of patriotic civil religion' (Bantjes 2006: 141) really took hold in the collective imagination. As we shall see later in this chapter, Juárez became a key ideological signifier, mobilised by Porfirians and anti-Porfirians alike in their struggles to assert their opposing political agendas. Nevertheless, as the century drew toward its close, photography fell within the means of ever greater numbers and its rhetorical force was increasingly understood and tapped by members of society other than the ruling elite.

In her study of the uses of photographic images in the 'Porfirio Díaz Collection', Teresa Matabuena Peláez (1991) demonstrates how a broad cross-section of Porfirian society used the medium in their petitions to the President. Currently in the custody of the Universidad Iberoamericana, Mexico City, this archive comprises some 600,000 documents pertaining to the personal correspondence received by Díaz between 1876 and his death in 1915, among which a noteworthy proportion contains appended or integrated photographs in a variety of formats.[5] As the title of Matabuena Peláez's study signals – 'Uses and *Concepts* of Photography during the Porfiriato' (emphasis added) – the ways in which photographs were deployed by a wide range of Mexican citizens in their letters to the President provide insights into what John Tagg (1982) terms the currency of the photographic image in this period. In his influential essay, Tagg argues for a historically and socially situated understanding of the relationship between photography and reality, whereby 'What defines and creates "truth" in any society is a system of more or less ordered procedures for the production, regulation, distribution of statements.' And he continues: 'Through these procedures "truth" is bound in a circular relation to systems of power which produce and sustain it, and to the effects of power which it induces and which, in turn, redirect it. It is this *dialectical* relation which constitutes what Foucault calls "a regime of truth"' (Tagg 1982: 129, emphasis in original).

Of the numerous items of correspondence addressed to the President, Matabuena Peláez supplies a comprehensive inventory of photographs that were put to use in attempts to influence Díaz to a variety of ends. These include letters in which cartes-de-visite-format portraits of uniformed soldiers testify to services rendered to the 'Patria'; portrait images gifted to the patriarch as a token of respect and admiration; or formal individual and family-group portraits appended to letters detailing all manner of personal requests. Although sent by individuals and groups of different social standing, sex, age and geographical origin, often with the aim of soliciting aid – in the form of grants, loans, gifts, protection or favours – what unites these photographs is that they were deployed to furnish incontrovertible visual evidence that what the sender claims in his or her missive is the truth.

In a letter dated 1907, despatched from the capital, for example, Valentín Sandoval and Hermenegildo Cárdenas explain how they have travelled from their ranch in Jalpa, Zacatecas to request that the President intercede with the state governor on their behalf so that they might retrieve land which has been forcibly taken by a certain Señor Refugio Peña. As they expound in their letter, 'we can barely work any longer as you will note from our physical appearance that you will find in our portrait' (Matabuena Peláez 1991: 78).[6] In their quest for presidential aid, they attach title deeds and a plan of the confiscated property, together with a studio portrait (Figure 3.2) in which the two men pose stiffly in front of the camera, their hands resting on a hip-height, slim wooden table that separates them. The full-body portrait indeed testifies to the age of the claimants and their poverty. Their formal demeanour – Sandoval sports a suit and closed-toe shoes, in contrast to Cárdenas's sandals – and the almost elegant studio setting combine to create an impression of the subjects as the worthy poor. Meanwhile, in May 1909, Señorita Paula Guerrero from Tixtla, Guerrero, wrote to Díaz requesting a pension in virtue of her status as the niece of the illustrious General Don Vicente Guerrero, explaining that as a '*señora* of advanced age who has always supported herself, having never married, my father on marrying for a second time having as good as abandoned me: in the sad situation in which I find myself, unable to work any longer, I am not able to provide for myself'. (Matabuena Peláez 1991: 80)[7] Like Sandoval and Cárdenas before her, *Señorita* Guerrero also provides supporting evidence: namely a list of signatories of 'honourable' people able to testify to her familial relationship with the General Vicente Guerrero and a spartan studio portrait (Figure 3.3), which features a seated, elderly woman with braided hair, clothed in a white dress, her hands resting demurely in her lap.

The inclusion of photographs in such petitions illustrates Tagg's assertion (1982: 117) concerning photography's status as 'a guaranteed witness of the actuality of the events it represents'. Supplementing the textual documentary evidence presented, the photographs declare: 'This really happened. [Or, this is what we look like.] The camera was there. See for yourself.' There are, however, few grounds for belief that Díaz responded in anything but the vaguest terms to such deictic photographic petitions, if at all (Matabuena Peláez 1991: 81). In fact, all the evidence signals that it is unlikely that Díaz responded to down-at-heel Mexicans such as Sandoval and Cárdenas, and Señorita Guerrero, who, for their part, were prepared to invest their last resources in the (albeit thin) hope of economic benefit; on the contrary, these were exactly the kinds of Mexican citizens the President emphatically did not wish to see.

If, on his marriage to Doña Carmen, in contemporary parlance, Díaz had undergone a 'make-over', so too were the popular classes of the capital the target of new city ordinances regulating fashions, 'showing that appearances, especially clothing, made the man' (Beezley 2004: 112).[8] More precisely, introduced in 1893,

003813

Valentín Sandoval - Hermenegildo Cárdenas.
Hotel Seminario

3.2 Valentín Sandoval and Hermenegildo Cárdenas, Hotel Seminario, 1907.

'[t]hese laws, ordered that all males wear trousers and that various groups of employees such as hack drivers and newspaper boys adopt uniforms; moreover, they tried to replace the traditional sombrero with custom-made hats for gentleman and caps for service employees such as porters' (ibid.). In the age of order and progress, which reached its apogee during the celebrations to mark the

3.3 Señorita Paula Guerrero, 1909.

Centenary, increasing efforts were made to erase the presence of Indians and the lower classes from the streets of the capital. In anticipation of the great spectacle of the Centenary, during which all manner of foreign dignitaries would descend upon Mexico City, key areas were cordoned off. So, for example, the Alameda, in the heart of what is now called the *Centro Histórico*, was enclosed by railings, so that the *señoritas* and well-to-do families (las familias bien) did not have to rub shoulders with the hoi polloi ('la plebe') (Martínez Assad 2005: 78). Thus, for all that Sandoval, Cárdenas and Señorita Guerrero had clearly spruced themselves up in order to pose in front of the camera and to present themselves to the gaze of the president, we can surmise that the latter more than likely would have taken a dim view of these Mexican citizens, for they did not conform to the image of modernity and civilisation that his regime was set on promoting at all costs.

FASHIONING THE IMAGE OF NATIONAL PROGRESS AND PROSPERITY

After the post-independence years of political instability, foreign invasions and civil war, the Porfiriato was a period of economic growth, spurred by the influx of foreign capital and concomitant national consolidation. Thanks to the enhanced financial situation, Mexico's nation builders now counted on the funds required to turn their attention to the Republic's image at home, and equally importantly, abroad, to give it material manifestation in the form of all manner of cultural institutions and artefacts. Through participation at the universal exhibitions that were a hallmark of the age, the social and political elite sought to insert Mexico into what Tenorio-Trillo (1996b: 9) terms the 'simulacrum of something that never had concrete existence': the modern world of progress, science and industry. However, whereas European nations and indeed the New World northern neighbour were in a position to build upon pre-existing cultural capital, Mexico and other Latin American countries 'had to produce – industrially, commercially, artistically and scientifically – the image of a modern nation from zero' (ibid.: 19). In an effort to combat Mexico's reputation as a lawless and uncivilised backwater, the 'wizards of progress', as Tenorio-Trillo calls them, who masterminded Mexico's pavilions, emphasised the rapidly expanding modern infrastructure and industrial plants, combined with the abundant natural resources and a selectively interpreted view of the Indian past. In a nutshell: 'constructing a nationalist ideology, the distinctions between form and content vanished. The so-called imagined communities of the late nineteenth century were, as was cultural modernity itself, a matter of form; that is, a question of style' (ibid.: 32).

Participation in overseas exhibitions, such as that hosted by Paris in 1889, in which Mexico's pavilion significantly took the form of an 'Aztec Palace', provided ideal opportunities to confect a national image for consumption overseas. The lessons learnt were subsequently honed, perfected and put into practice on a grand scale for the lavish celebrations to mark the Centenary. Planning started well in advance with the formation of the Comisión Nacional del Centenario in 1907; and, with an estimated total budget of 317,000 pesos (Tenorio-Trillo 1996b: 76), no expense was spared.[9] Although celebrations took place throughout the country, the centrepiece of the Centenary was the balcony of Republic itself, Mexico City, where a host of festivities and ceremonies were scheduled for the month of September 1910. A throng of foreign dignitaries from approximately thirty countries – including representatives from Europe, the Far East and the Americas – was invited to join Mexico's aristocracy in attendance at all manner of receptions, banquets, balls, parades and the inauguration of public works and monuments. Indeed, celebrations got off to a start on 1 September with the inauguration of the *Manicomio General* or General Mental Asylum in Mixcoac, designed to place Mexico up with the most advanced countries in the field of 'alienism' (Martínez Assad 2005: 82). Other important public building works included the remodelling and expansion of Lecumberri prison, which, like the *Manicomio*, demonstrated the Porfiriato's concern with order and discipline, and the inauguration of the Universidad Nacional de México toward the end of the celebrations.

In the symbolic sphere, the architectural *pièce de résistance* was the Column of Independence, located on the topographic textbook of national history, the Paseo de la Reforma, its gleaming golden angel unveiled on 16 September itself. This was followed some two days later by the inauguration of the hastily constructed Hemiciclo a Juárez, situated on the Alameda, in honour of the first liberal president of Mexico, a figure to whom we will return later in this chapter. Meanwhile, other key protagonists in the Porfirian narrative of patriotic history were invoked in the epic parade staged on 15 September. Featuring hundreds of actors, according to its organisers, this was an event which demanded the utmost preparation, 'for it was necessary to choose with care the scenes from history that were to be represented in it' (Lempérière 1995: 331). Three scenarios were duly selected: the encounter between Moctezuma and Cortés; figures from the hierarchical Viceroyalty of New Spain; and from the Independence movement, not Hidalgo and his ragged hordes, but instead, Iturbide and Insurgents loyal to the Plan of Iguala. As Annick Lempérière (1995: 333) observes 'In 1910, the historical memory of Porfirio Díaz's government was the memory of pyramidal and corporative power, embodied in the Caudillo'.[10]

Even as Mexico City was transformed into the mirage of the ideal city, acquiring 'a coherent set of icons that made the idea of the nation discursively, ideologically, and physically real' (Tenorio-Trillo 1996b: 97), arguably the whole dizzy spectacle was oriented around the celebration of the figure of the president himself, who became a spectacle in his own right and at the same time, spectator-in-chief of the achievements of his regime. So, for example, in his survey of the 'Patria' as it was staged on the Paseo de la Reforma, Carlos Martínez Assad (2005: 90) provides a wonderful description of the ball hosted at the National Palace on the evening of 23 September, at which 'Doña Carmelita wanted to look like a queen and . . . had accompanied her husband crowned with a diamond tiara and an emerald necklace made by Cartier'. Not to be outdone, '[o]f course, the President wore all his decorations on his chest, including the medal that Congress had created by decree for the victors of 2 April and 5 May in Puebla'.[11] Significantly, the President was also photographed repeatedly in sites that in different ways placed him in the position of privileged spectator.

PHOTOGRAPHING PRESIDENTIAL POWER

The Centenary celebrations were accordingly the ideal moment for an official portrait of the hero President, such as the half-body image which graced the official programme of the event, in which the octogenarian Díaz sits in full military regalia, his solemn gaze meeting that of his citizen-subjects (see Figure 3.1). As noted earlier, this particular pose bore endless repetition so as to imprint this image of Díaz in the national consciousness, an image of the patriarch that persists to this day. In addition, the Centenary was the perfect setting for a variety of photo opportunities. Of the latter, according to Eduardo Ancira (2005: 340), one image in particular has become one of the most emblematic photographs of Díaz (Figure 3.4). The photograph in question features the President standing erectly below the colossal Aztec Calendar or Sun Stone in the National Museum of History in 1910. Eschewing his military uniform, this time Díaz is dressed in a formal frockcoat, with cravat and cane in right hand. The Calendar itself dominates the photographic frame. The viewer's eye is drawn in the first instance to the face at its centre, taking in the ornate detail in the stonework, before descending to fix on the stiffly posed figure of the President. Below the Calendar, a clearly legible sign informs the viewer in ponderous prose about the archaeological trajectory of the impressive artefact that is the central focus of the image: 'In the month of December of the year 1790, as the work of levelling was being carried out for the new paving for the capital's main square, this monolith was discovered and later placed at the foot of the western tower of the cathedral on the side that looks west, from whence it was transferred to this National Museum in August 1895.'

In accordance with the explanatory sign, the Aztec Calendar was indeed unearthed in 1790, together with the statue of the goddess of war Coatlicue, from what had been the ceremonial centre of Tenochtitlán, where they had remained buried since before the Conquest.[12] As Luis Gerardo Morales Moreno (2001: 40) observes, this finding marked an important moment in the history of New Spain, for rather than ordering their destruction as 'idols', as would have occurred two centuries earlier, the Viceroy ordered that these Pre-Hispanic archaeological artefacts be conserved as items of protonational patrimony. In this way, they came to form part of the indigenous past that the Creoles (or American-born Spaniards) started to embrace as an element of their self-definition, in distinction to Spanish, peninsular-born identity. On achieving independence from Spain, as the nineteenth century advanced Mexico's elite looked increasingly to the pre-Hispanic past – or more precisely to select pristine elements of that past – in the quest to fashion a specifically Mexican identity.[13] At the heart of that identity stood an idealised appropriation of the Aztec empire, which was established as the ancient foundation of the Patria, on a par in its advanced level of knowledge and civilisation with Egypt and Rome. This was nowhere more resonantly symbolised than in the *Mexicas'* sophisticated understanding of time as materialised in the Calendar stone.

CALENDARIO AZTECA O PIEDRA DEL SOL.
EN EL MES DE DICIEMBRE DEL AÑO DE 1790
AL PRACTICARSE LA NIVELACION PARA EL NUEVO
EMPEDRADO DE LA PLAZA MAYOR DE ESTA CAPITAL
FUE DESCUBIERTO ESTE MONOLITO Y COLOCADO
DESPUES AL PIE DE LA TORRE OCCIDENTAL DE LA
CATEDRAL POR EL LADO QUE VE AL PONIENTE
DE CUYO LUGAR SE TRASLADO A ESTE MUSEO
NACIONAL EN AGOSTO DE 1885.

3.4 Don Porfirio Díaz, al lado de la piedra del sol / Don Porfirio Díaz, beside the Sun
Stone, c.1910.

To pose in front of the Aztec Calendar in 1910 was, then, to stand in the 'Hall of Monoliths', the centrepiece of the National Museum, which itself had been remodelled in time for the Centenary. In fact, as the century had progressed, so too the Museum had evolved. From its foundation in 1831 as a 'kind of storeroom of curiosities', it had become a 'powerful instrument of national identity and unity', 'a scientific institution dedicated to the collection and rigorous classification of its holdings, and was transformed into a research and teaching center as well as into a powerful medium of cultural dissemination' (Florescano 1993: 73). To pose in front of the 'Piedra' or 'Stone'– as it was dubbed – which had been converted into an icon of national and nationalist history, was also to pose in front of an obligatory site of civic pilgrimage for any important visitor to Mexico in 1910 (Casanova 2001: 13).[14] But of course, Porfirio Díaz was not just any visitor who had come to see and be seen looking at this icon of national and nationalist history; he personified this abstract entity, the nation. Thus for Díaz to stand in front of this potent monument in national history was to reaffirm his rock-like status in a narrative of national time, in which history was conceptualised linear-fashion as that which moved and developed chronologically in a steady order toward progress.

To be sure, this particular photograph has become one of the most frequently reproduced images of Díaz, continuously disseminated in books devoted to Mexico's photographic and visual cultures. Thus, for example, it appears in Ortiz Monasterio's *Mirada y memoria* (2002), and also in Monsiváis's lavishly illustrated *Imágenes de la tradición viva* (2006), in the latter of which it is attributed to the photographer Antonio Carrillo. There is, furthermore, evidence to suggest that this image circulated widely at the time of its making in 1910. Ancira has located it on the cover of the illustrated magazine *La Semana Ilustrada*, dated 2 September 1910 and attributed to the photographer Samuel Tinoco. It also appeared on the cover of *El Tiempo Ilustrado* dated 4 September, under the headline 'Visita presidencial al museo'/'Presidential Visit to the Museum'. According to Ancira's (2005: 347) meticulous research, Antonio Carrillo was the official, licensed Centenary photographer for both *El Tiempo* and its magazine supplement, *El Tiempo Ilustrado*. With their models in Europe and the United States, newspapers such as *La Semana* and *El Tiempo* emerged in the last quarter of the nineteenth century, acquiring illustrated weekly supplements in the 1890s in line with tech-nological advances in the mass reproduction of photographic images. As Julieta Ortiz Gaitán (2003: 41) observes, during the Porfiriato, the press was subsidised by the regime and predictably was a showcase for the *sueño porfiriano* (Porfirian dream), in the form of articles, editorials, reports and photo-reportage, the latter produced by a new category of reporter, the photojournalist, who went out into the world in search of news and events: events which were now recorded at the very sites in which they occurred. In this way, a relationship between the state and the institution of (photo)journalism developed and with it, the formation of an extended, bourgeois imagined community:

> Print capitalism assisted in informing and connecting the bourgeoisie through a common, 'official' language (Spanish) that was accessible to the educated elite. Compound this print language with a repertory of images that included public events, celebrations of industrial growth, chronicles of the social life of the elite, Mexican customs (social misery replaced by folklore), cultural and entertainment events (mediums for social cohesion and ideological justification), and a newspaper was able to extend its readership to the limits of the educated Porfirian society, while effectively convincing it of the nation's and its own prosperity on the basis of 'objec-tive' visual testimony. (Cuevas Wolf 1996: 202)

When 'El señor don Porfirio Díaz' posed 'at the foot of the Monolith that goes by the name of the "Aztec Calendar"' – as the tagline informs the readers of *El Tiempo Ilustrado* – he did so now as a veteran before the camera's lens and, we can surmise, was captured in exactly the same hieratic pose by a succession of the capital's photographers, representatives of the burgeoning press, keen to reproduce the quintessential spectacle of the Centenary and indeed, the living monument to the nation: the President himself.

PHOTOGRAPHY, POWER AND SOLIPSISM

The Centenary celebrations marked a veritable frenzy of festive events in homage to the Patria and, at the same time, the Patriarch of the Patria, the culminating moment in the age of the simulacrum of progress and modernity. With characteristic humour, sadly somewhat lost in translation, Carlos Monsiváis captures the combination of this climactic moment and the conflation of Díaz with the nation with reference to a joke in circulation at the time:

> In 1910, the dictator Porfirio Díaz, that constellation of medals, years and obsession with power, finds his culminating opportunity in the celebration of the Centenary of Independence. There he is, not the representative of tradition, rather tradition itself, that collection of practices of government, beliefs and customs that are Mexico. In a joke, pointing to his liver, he is attributed with the comment 'Chihuahua it hurts' – [Chihuahua is a state in Northern Mexico and also a euphemism for the ubiquitous expletive 'chingado'; here, the more or less literal translation would be 'this little dog gives me a pain!'] – just one of the many identifications between his person and the nation. (Monsiváis 2006: 176)[15]

As the body of the President came to stand in for the nation, in turn, he carefully promoted identification between his persona and protagonists in recent national history, most notably between himself and the late Benito Juárez. What is more, just as multiple ironies undercut the actions of a man of mixed, Mixtec/Spanish origins, who was said to whiten his features with cosmetic powder, and who posed in front of the Aztec Calendar in tribute to the nation's illustrious, dark-skinned ancestors, Díaz's appropriation of the Juárez myth was no less paradoxical.

Despite Juárez's status as the man who had restored Mexican sovereignty, ordering the execution of Maximilian of Hapsburg, in life he had nevertheless cut a controversial figure. As Charles Weeks states (1987: 17) with the 'spectre of dictatorship, symbolised by Santa Anna' within living memory, Juárez's opponents, among them Díaz, were inclined to take a dim view of the changes made to the Constitution in the interests, Juárez claimed, of establishing some much-needed stability and continuity. No matter that in life the fellow *Oaxaqueños* had been bitter enemies, with Díaz challenging Juárez in the presidential elections in 1867 and again in 1871.[16] This did not prevent Díaz from subsequently steering

3.5 Porfirio Díaz en aniversario luctuoso de Benito Juárez / Porfirio Díaz on the mournful anniversary of Benito Juárez, 1910.

a course of reconciliation with the liberal ghost of Juárez, elevating his retro-spectively claimed political forefather to cult status in the national pantheon. No sooner had Díaz acceded to the presidency for the first time in 1887, than 18 July, the date of Juárez's death in 1872, became officially dedicated to the commemoration of the 'Benemérito de las Américas', an event over which the President presided assiduously (Medina Peña 2004: 86). And no matter either, that the Porfiriato witnessed an erosion of the liberal principles championed by Juárez: 'The touchstone of the system set up by Díaz was to be found in the limits of tolerance and the integration of interests. In the Porfirian political system nearly everything was tolerated, any accommodation of interests was possible as long as a clear limit was not transgressed' (ibid.: 74).[17] In a pragmatic approach to power, Díaz was open to all manner of arrangements with poten-tial opponents – men of the Church, the army, regional caudillos and state governors – so long as they remained loyal to, and respected the limit of his supreme authority.

In another frequently reproduced photograph made on 21 July 1910, we find Díaz presiding at an official ceremony (Figure 3.5). We should note, in passing, the date of the photograph's production: one month after the 21 June election, at which Díaz was re-elected president for a fateful seventh term; some two months before the Centenary celebrations; and a mere four months prior to the official outbreak of the revolution on 20 November. At first sight, the looming presence of the revolution is, it would appear, in no way legible in this emblematic image of Díaz's regime. Closer examination, however, reveals visual clues that point to the unrest that was, in fact, afoot on the margins of Porfirian high society. Like the Aztec Calendar photograph, this image was reproduced in *La Semana Ilustrada*, where it appeared in the issue dated 22 July 1910, accompanied by the caption: 'En honor a Juárez: El señor Presidente de la república presidiendo al acto oficial/In honour of Juárez: the President presiding at the official ceremony'. Dressed in formal, civilian attire, in his left, gloved hand, Díaz holds a stick. Besides him sits another moustachioed man – Mexico's ambassador to the United States and governor of Chihuahua State, Enrique C. Creel – his left hand too is gloved, his right rests in his lap. Both men have solemn, intent looks on their faces. (Did anyone ever smile during the Porfiriato? For that matter, is there such a thing as a photograph of Díaz with anything other than a stern expression on his face?)[18] The President is seated at a table, which is covered by a tasselled and embroidered cloth. (An incidental detail, tucked away beneath it, is the President's top hat.) The chair on which he is seated is ornate, a combination of embroidered velvet upholstery and a (most probably) gilded bas-relief frame. The frame is topped with a circular crest, featuring what we can just make out to be the national symbol, an eagle perched on a cactus, snake in mouth.[19] The regal air that emanates from the photograph is reinforced by the sceptre-like appearance of the stick in Díaz's hand and the heavy, throne-room style drapes that fall behind him.

The connotations of power associated with these material objects are further echoed in the formal organisation of space within the photograph and concomitantly in the dynamics of looking as they play out in this image. Triptych in format, it is obvious, but worth emphasising all the same, that Díaz occupies the central 'panel' and is correspondingly the most important figure in the image. He is proportionately the largest figure within the photographic frame, at once part of the general audience, and at the same time separate from it, insofar as the drapes and the carpet on which the table and presidential chair are positioned create a space for Díaz that is discrete from that occupied by the rest of the audience. Like the President, members of the audience are well dressed and seated in orderly, regimented rows. Mostly comprised of middle- to late middle-aged men, the one exception is the third row from the front on which we find four elegantly-dressed ladies in extravagant, wide-brimmed hats. Playfully, we might wonder, did they impede the view of the men in the row behind? True, this is an incidental detail, one that comes into focus on closer scrutiny of the various elements within the photographic frame; the idea of impeded vision is, nevertheless, emblematic of the broader visual dynamics at stake in this photographic enactment of the power of Porfirio Díaz.

In an essay on the epistemological status of the category 'documentary photography', originally published in 1987, and reproduced in the 1991 *Photography at the Dock*, Abigail Solomon-Godeau places the system of looking-relations built into camera optics in historical context:

Modeled on the classical system of single-point monocular perspective invented in the Renaissance, camera optics were designed to yield an analogous pictorial structure. While natural vision and perception have no vanishing point, are binocular, unbounded, in constant motion, and marked by loss of clarity in the periphery, the camera image, like the Renaissance painting offers a static, uniform field in which orthogonals converge at the single vanishing point. Such a system of pictorial organization, by now so imbued in Western consciousness as to appear altogether natural, has certain ramifications. Chief among these is the position of visual mastery conferred on the spectator whose ideal, all-seeing eye becomes the commanding locus of the pictorial field. (Solomon-Godeau 1991: 180)

Solomon-Godeau was concerned in this essay to examine the connection between ideology and vision, and more specifically the power that is invested in the spectator as master of the gaze, whereby, 'such analyses of the apparatus bring us a good deal closer to understanding why the use of the camera has historically engendered a vocabulary of mastery, possession, appropriation and aggression' (ibid.: 181). Such a vocabulary was, moreover, underpinned by the association between the camera image and the way in which the 'structural congruence of point of view (the eye of the photographer, the eye of the camera, and the spectator's eye) confers on the photograph a quality of pure, but delusory, presentness' (ibid.: 180).

Let's return now to *En honor a Juárez*, to note that at the level of content, this photograph appears to confound Solomon-Godeau's assertion regarding the position of mastery conferred upon the viewer positioned outside the photographic frame. At first sight, *En honor a Juárez* appears to be an image that is all about the visual mastery of the President himself who, placed at the centre of the photograph, at the point at which the orthogonals converge, is at once prime spectacle and spectator-in-chief. That this is the case is further reinforced by the relay of looks that plays out between those located inside and those outside the photographic frame, making of this photograph an intensely self-referential image. Almost all gazes within the photographic frame are trained on a spectacle that exists off-frame and which the external viewer cannot, as a consequence, see. In this way, the photograph sets up a struggle to see between the subject of the photograph (Porfirio Díaz) and the spectator, whereby the spectator's visual mastery is undercut: she cannot see, cannot master a spectacle that ultimately confers power on the central figure who views it: the all-seeing, all-knowing President.

What is it, then, that holds the gaze of all those gathered in these august surroundings that is denied to us, the viewers of this photograph? We can never know the answer to this question with any certainty. And, on one level, it should be clear by now, it does not really matter: what matters is the presence of the President who is captured looking. On another, however, by providing a set of gazes that insistently look upon it, the photograph invites us to speculate on the significance of this absent, off-frame space. Now, as we have seen, according to

Tenorio-Trillo (1996a: 32), in the construction of the modern nation, 'the distinctions between form and content vanished. The so-called imagined communities of the late nineteenth century were, as was cultural modernity itself, a matter of form; that is, a question of style'. How, though, might Tenorio-Trillo's notion of the collapse of form and content into style inflect an understanding of this photographic image and its relationship to that imagined community, the modern nation? The answer lies in the way in which meaning is structured around a series of metonymic displacements – where metonymy, as formulated by Eelco Runia (2006), is a trope of presence in absence – which, when subject to scrutiny, reveal an aporia in the Porfirian visual economy.

If, thanks to the Díaz regime's painstaking efforts in the promotion of civic spectacle, Juárez came to represent the 'Patria' in the popular imagination, then the ceremony to commemorate the death of the ex-President that is signalled by its absence from the photographic frame symbolically invokes the modern Mexican nation. Here, the part, the idea of Juárez, stands in for the whole, the nation. But, of course, the ceremony exists off-frame, its absent presence is instead manifest in the gaze of Díaz who, in turn, through his identification with Juárez, himself stands in for the nation. There is, then, something intensely solipsistic about this photograph: in the final analysis, what we witness is Díaz regarding a reflection of himself, as Virginia Woolf might have said, at twice his natural size. What is more, if meaning is predicated on an understanding of a series of metonymic displacements, then these displacements, in turn, inhere in the very act of photographic representation. That is to say, photographs, by definition, function metonymically, whereby the part, an excision from the profilmic world, comes to stand in for the whole: all that was in front of the camera at the moment of capture, but fell outside the limit-frame.

There is, then, a second element to the self-reflexivity of this image. The photograph not only invites the viewer to reflect upon the act of looking itself by signalling, but denying access to, the off-frame space; in so doing, it brings the limits of the photographic image into focus. What is at stake, though, when we reflect upon the limit-frame in the context of photographic representation in late Porfirian Mexico?

Turning beyond the photographic frame to historical context, there is ample evidence to suggest that as the new century got under way, Porfirian vision, like natural vision itself, was – so to speak – marked by loss of clarity in the periphery. The signs of the times to come were writ large for all those who wished to read them. Popular unrest provoked by pay and labour conditions led to mining and textile strikes in Cananea (Sonora) and Río Blanco (Veracruz), in 1906 and 1907 respectively. Never much minded to attend to social problems, as we saw in relation to the photographic petitions to the president earlier in the chapter, the regime responded with brutal repression. Meanwhile, in 1908, Díaz conceded an interview to the US journalist James Creelman, published in March in *Pearson's Magazine* and subsequently the Mexican daily *El Imparcial*, in which he declared that he would stand down from office before the next election, scheduled for June 1910. 'In retrospect', Paul Garner (2001: 213) notes, 'there is little doubt that the impact of the Creelman interview was devastating. While it was meant to reassure the North American government that Díaz was still firmly in control, its reception in Mexico exposed the political contradictions and the fundamental lack of democratic legitimacy of the Díaz regime. As a result it provided a new stimulus for the revival of anti-re-electionism, which had already gained significant momentum after 1906.'

Political activity increased dramatically, galvanised by the publication of Francisco I. Madero's *The Presidential Succession of 1910*, in which, although finding plenty to praise in the economic and administrative achievements of Díaz's regime, the president-to-be called for constitutional reform under the slogan 'sufragio efectivo y no re-elección'/'Effective suffrage and no re-election'. Finally, Alan Knight offers a telling contemporary description of the encounter between Díaz and US President Taft that took place on the border in October 1909. Ostensibly a meeting to manifest the healthy relations enjoyed by the neighbouring nations, and to assuage concerns about growing unrest in Mexico, it in fact served to reveal Mexico's democratic deficit as visibly embodied in the President: 'Taft [was] soberly dressed, with two gray-uniformed adjutants, Díaz loaded with medals, surrounded by a lavish military escort: "on the one hand, all the simplicity of a true democracy, on the other, the pomp and vainglory of an oriental sultanate"' (Knight 1986, Vol. 1: 70).

PHOTOGRAPHY AND THE LIMITS OF VISION

In the opening paragraph of *In the Shadow of the Mexican Revolution*, historians Héctor Aguilar Camín and Lorenzo Meyer invoke the opinions of contemporary observers, united in their impression that armed insurrection in Mexico was impossible:

> They were not expecting it. The custom of peace was stronger than the evidence of change. *El Imparcial*, the first industrial journal of Mexico and a symbol itself of the enormous transformation that the country had experienced, guaranteed its readers in 1909: "A revolution in Mexico is impossible." Karl Bunz, the German envoy, wrote to his government on September 17 of that same year: "I believe, as does the press and public opinion, that a general revolution is not possible at all." Following his 1910 visit, Andrew Carnegie, the U.S. steel magnate, was left with only the following impression about the country's future: "In all of the corners of the Republic an enviable peace reigns." The Spanish poet Julio Sesto added his own meteorological certainty: "There is no black cloud on the horizon. (Aguilar Camín and Meyer 1993: 1)

That this diverse group of commentators was even speculating about the possibility of revolution, of course, suggests that all was not well, that there was, in fact, a storm brewing. But on reading the signs, foreign and national forecasters alike reached the same tautological conclusion: the unthinkable was unthinkable. The Porfiriato, particularly in its culminating years, as we have seen, was an era of excessive national spectacle. Public opinion therefore formed in response to a combination of textual and, importantly, visual cues. Polite society and its commentators not only read about the Republic's robust health in publications such as those bastions of Porfirian partiality *El Imparcial* and *El Tiempo*. The signs that all was well were writ large around the balcony of the republic, as the nation prepared to celebrate the Centenary. Undesirables – Indians and the lower classes – were banished from sight. Or, when this proved impossible – after all, their presence was inevitably needed, for the Centenary required workers – they were camouflaged (Tenorio-Trillo 1996b: 91).

The signs were also photographic. In addition to the images we have already examined in this chapter, it is worth pausing briefly to note that the Creelman interview in *Pearson's Magazine* not only contained Díaz's declaration of his 'unchangeable intention to retire from power' and his prediction of 'a peaceful future for Mexico under free institutions' (Creelman 1908: 231). Intended as a measure of the stability of the times, it was also lavishly illustrated, for the medium was strongly endowed with the rhetorical power to persuade and convince. Thus, in addition to various views and scenes of contemporary natural, human and architectural landscapes, as might be expected, the interview is accompanied by a significant number of images of Díaz. These range from the kinds of standard portrait we have already encountered – Díaz in full military regalia, Díaz mounted on horseback on the battlefield, and Díaz seated on the presidential throne, captioned 'The master of Mexico in his official chair' (Figure 3.6) – to more informal snapshots. Of the latter a series of three, taken by Díaz's son on a hunting expedition, is particularly striking. For all that they are more candid and therefore unusual images, the captions speak volumes about the desired impact on their viewers. An image of Díaz and two hunting companions (Figure 3.7), for instance, is captioned 'President Díaz hunting in the mountains at the age of seventy five years. Mark the erectness and vigor of the figure, the strength and bearing of the man, compared with his younger companions! This snapshot was made through the camera of his son'. Thus even those images that break with the formality and rigidity of Díaz's visual range, in this case falling loosely into the category of family snapshots, nevertheless serve to reinforce the President's prowess.

What makes of the hunting snapshots such interesting visual documents is precisely their simultaneous status as exceptions to, and confirmation of, the rules of the photography of presidential power during the Porfiriato, which as Monsiváis (1984: 39–40) comments is characterised by a rigid repertoire of poses and forms. In a section of his notes on images from the Casasola archive titled 'The image of the fatherland as an ancient statue: Porfirio Díaz', capturing the severity of the President, he states: 'The aged dictator walks sedately, observes, thanks without gestures, and withdraws amid the orderly throng. He exudes permanence. He

3.6 'The master of Mexico in his official chair'.

has created himself as a revelation in order to die holding fast to Power . . . Don Porfirio is Don Porfirio. Tautology is a privilege of major dictators' (ibid.: 40). What, though, can the photographic record, particularly a monotonous record such as that which documents Porfirio Díaz, tell us about the period, beyond the merely tautological?[20] Or to put this otherwise: can an examination of the President's rigid visual repertoire tell us any more than that Díaz was powerful, therefore he was powerful? To answer this question, we must turn once again to the image *En honor a Juárez* to approach it through the lens of Walter Benjamin's concept of the 'optical unconscious'.

Benjamin wrote about the optical unconscious in his two essays specifically devoted to photography: 'A Short History of Photography' first published in 1931 and the second, 'The Work of Art in the Age of Mechanical Reproduction' in

PRESIDENT DIAZ HUNTING IN THE MOUNTAINS, AT THE AGE OF SEVENTY-FIVE YEARS   MARK THE ERECTNESS AND
VIGOR OF THE FIGURE, THE STRENGTH AND BEARING OF THE MAN, COMPARED WITH HIS YOUNGER COMPANIONS!
THIS SNAP-SHOT WAS MADE THROUGH THE CAMERA OF HIS SON

3.7 'President Díaz hunting in the mountains at the age of seventy-five years. Mark the
erectness and vigor of the figure, the strength and bearing of the man, compared with [that
of] his younger companions. This snapshot was made through the camera of his son'.

1936. In a much-cited passage from the latter essay, he writes of the impact that
photographic representation was to have on human vision:

> Even if one has a general knowledge of the way people walk, one knows nothing
> of a person's posture during the fractional second of a stride. The act of reaching
> for a lighter or a spoon is familiar routine, yet we hardly know what really goes on
> between hand and metal, not to mention how this fluctuates with our moods. Here
> the camera intervenes with the resources of its lowerings and liftings, its interrup-
> tions and isolations, its extensions and accelerations, its enlargements and reduc-
> tions. The camera introduces us to unconscious optics as does psychoanalysis to
> unconscious impulses. (Benjamin 1970: 239)

In other words, in the age of photographic representation, objects and phenomena that had previously been invisible to the naked human eye now came into
the field of vision. To cite the classic example, thanks to work of photographer
Eadweard Muybridge from the 1870s, it was possible to prove that during a
horse's trot, all four hooves were off the ground at the same time. The ramifications of this were two-fold and contradictory. Camera *optics* may have been
'modeled on the classical system of single-point monocular perspective invented
in the Renaissance', offering 'a static, uniform field in which orthogonals converge at the single vanishing point', conferring on the spectator a 'position of
visual mastery'(Solomon-Godeau 1991: 180). At the same time, camera *images*
radically called that position of mastery into question. Thus, on the one hand,

the camera dramatically extended the visual field; on the other, it highlighted the very limits of human vision.[21]

In the current context, Benjamin's notion of the 'optical unconscious', when understood metaphorically, allows us to think about the conjunction of camera images and optics as revealing not only *what* people see at a given time, but also *how* they see. To grasp its utility as a metaphorical hermeneutic tool, we must return finally to *En honor a Juárez* and, in the first instance, recap briefly: I have been arguing three things. First, this is a self-reflexive photograph insofar as it is an image all about looking: the look of the audience at the ceremony echoes our own look outside of the frame. Second, it is also about power and looking: it establishes the spectacle of an all-seeing, all-knowing Presidential gaze in opposition to our own inability to see that which captures the gaze of those within the frame. Third, it is also a profoundly solipsistic image: it is structured through a relay of metonymic displacements – Díaz looking at his own embodiment of the nation through the ceremony dedicated to Juárez. What is at stake, however, to suggest that the photograph introduces us to the 'unconscious optics' of Porfirian vision?

Porfirian photography, we have seen, was focused to the exclusion of nearly all else on the documentation of the authority of the all-seeing Porfirio Díaz in a gesture of 'tautology that is a privilege of major dictators' (Monsiváis 1984: 40). The impoverished, *campesino* masses – such as Sandoval and Cárdenas, and Señorita Guerrero, for instance – belonged to a social class which was imminently to rise up, a class which existed beyond this official frame of vision, and was as good as invisible within such a limited repertoire. And although the aristocratic Madero certainly figured on Díaz's political radar, so convinced was he of his presidential invincibility that he seriously underestimated Madero's sphere of influence. The camera documented a vision of the pomp and power of the President; at the same time, in its monotonous tautology, it registered the very limits of Porfirian vision: a field of vision that was so narrowly focused in on itself that its peripheral vision was severely curtailed. Had Díaz taken the time to look down from the balcony of the republic, he might have seen what was coming. To be sure, in 1911 Díaz accurately predicted that Madero had unleashed a force greater than he anticipated: prescience after the fact is one thing; foresight is another altogether. That the looming presence of the revolution was disavowed until it was too late is clearly manifest in the photographic evidence at the end of the epoch, which reveals a foreshortening of peripheral vision.

NOTES

1 Although, as one historian has it, there is little evidence 'other than that of contemporary photographs' (Garner 2001: 25) that Díaz ever tried to hide his mixed-race heritage. Meanwhile, Mauricio Tenorio-Trillo (1996a: 29) notes that by the 1880s 'Díaz himself, having married Manuel Romero Rubio's aristocratic daughter, resembled a

statesman more than a caudillo. Underscoring this transformation, Díaz, a mestizo from Oaxaca, began to be portrayed as whiter and whiter on the countless canvases that were painted of him at this time.'

2 Significantly, the president, his family, and key government officials were the first spectators of the moving image in Mexico. Prior to the first public screening, the Lumières' representatives arranged a private screening in Chapultepec Castle exclusively for the dictator and his entourage (Noble 2005: 72). Beezley (2004: 57) reminds us that the 'respectable classes' were derisively referred to as the 'frock coat crowd'.

3 Luis Medina Peña (2004: 60) cautions that the term 'dictator', frequently applied to Díaz by conventional historiography, is anachronistic. Díaz's politics were certainly designed to neutralise any possible form of rebellion – whether by the Church, the army, Jacobin liberals, etc. – holding all in thrall to his firm, central rule; but his government always acted within the terms of the Constitution and the law.

4 For Lomnitz (2001), the notion of the balcony represents a metaphor denoting the vantage point from which the intelligentsia surveys the national scene. For some intellectuals of his own generation, Mexico City has been abandoned in preference for another balcony, namely that offered by the US academy. Deploying the balcony as a metaphor for the position of the intelligentsia within cotemporary society, Lomnitz does not, however, tap its full conceptual resonances.

5 Guerra (2007: 140) observes that 'the enormous correspondence that Porfirio Díaz kept with all kinds of people shows his deep knowledge of local political life and the extent of his network of personal connections. The overall cohesiveness of the regime was based on a hierarchical pyramid of personal connections that ascended gradually from nameless hamlets to the president.'

6 'ya casi no podemos trabajar según podrá usted notarlo por el aspecto físico que encontrará en nuestro retrato'.

7 'que soy una mujer avanzada en edad y que siempre me he mantenido de mi personal trabajo pues nunca fui casada y el Señor mi padre al contraer Segundas nupcias me dejó abandonada: que en la triste situación en la que me encuentro ya imposibilitada ya de trabajar, no puedo proveer mi subsistencia.'

8 Wasserman (2000: 164) observes that the make-over was almost, but not quite successful: 'The new Díaz was comfortable in tie, gloves and tuxedo! He had become courtly. No matter how hard she worked, however, Carmen could never erase the Oaxacan accent, nor teach him to write grammatically or spell correctly.'

9 As I write, in 2007, similar advance preparations are afoot for the dual commemoration of the bicentenary of the initiation of the struggle for independence and the centenary of the outbreak of the revolution. Materials related to 'México 2010', including a digital counter to count down the years, days, hours, minutes and seconds to the two anniversaries, are available on a website, including an extensive selection of photographs, which can be consulted at www.bicentenario.gob.mx/.

10 'ya que era necesario escoger cuidadosamente las escenas históricas que en ella habían de representarse.'/'En 1910, la memoria histórica del gobierno de Porfirio Díaz, fue la de un poder piramidal y corporativo, encarnado en el caudillo.'

11 'Doña Carmelita quiso parecer una reina y . . . había acompañado a su marido coronada con su tiara de diamantes y un collar combinado con esmeraldas, realizados por Cartier.'/'Desde luego, el presidente llevó sobre el pecho todas sus condecoraciones

que incluían las que el Congreso había creado por decreto para los vencedores del 2 de abril y del 5 de mayo en Puebla.'

12 See Franco (2004: 207) on the status of the 'much admired' calendar stone, versus the 'horrible simulacrum', Coatlicue.

13 See Widdifield (1996) for a lucid account of how this played out in nineteenth-century history painting. Etherington (1993) provides a comparative analysis of Mexican and US approaches to the Pre-Columbian past in their respective museum cultures.

14 Riley (1997) offers a historical overview of the Calendar Stone in an article that reproduces images of further personages to have posed in front of it, including Venustiano Carranza in 1918, and an image of Cantinflas during the filming of *El signo de la muerte* (Chano Urueta, 1939), in which the famous Mexican comic actor appears to be carrying the Stone on his shoulder. See also Monsiváis (1970: 330) on Díaz posing by the Calendar Stone, of which he states 'La eternidad visita a la eternidad. El Poder en su búsqueda de espejos'/'Eternity visits eternity. Power in its search for mirrors.'

15 'En 1910 el dictador Porfirio Díaz, constelado de medallas, años y obsesiones de poder, halla su oportunidad culminante en la celebración de las Fiestas del Centenario de la Independencia. Allí está él, no el representante de la tradición sino la tradición misma, el conjunto de prácticas de gobierno, creencias, actitudes y costumbres que son México. El chiste que le atribuye al señalar su hígado: "Me duele Chihuahua", es una de tantas identificaciones de su persona con la nación.'

16 See Hamnett (1994) on Juárez, and Garner (2001: 21–4) on the prominence of Oaxaca in national politics in the nineteenth century.

17 'La piedra de toque del sistema que armó Díaz se ubicó en los límites de la tolerancia y de la integración de intereses. En el sistema político porfiriano casi todo era tolerable, cualquier acomodo de intereses es posible siempre y cuando no se trasponga un límite claro.' Although, as Medina Peña notes (2004: 75), Juárez himself had already initiated that process of erosion.

18 Apparently, Díaz did smile, albeit with solemnity. The US journalist James Creelman (1908: 235) reports the President's reaction to his question '"You know that in the United States we are troubled about the question of electing a President for three terms?" He smiled and then looked grave, nodding his head gently and pursing his lips.' A facsimile of the interview as it originally appeared in *Pearson's Magazine* can be consulted at: www.bibliotecas.tv/zapata/bibliografia/indices/entrevista_diaz_creelman01.html. The photographs accompanying the Creelman interview are discussed below in more detail in the concluding section of this chapter.

19 See Florescano (1998) on the origins and development of this symbol on the national flag.

20 In an essay on the social definition of photography, French sociologist Pierre Bourdieu (1990: 77) suggests that as a medium, photography is bound up with such tautological visual statements about the world: 'in conferring upon photography a guarantee of realism, society is merely confirming itself in the tautological certainty that an image of the real which is true to its representation of objectivity is really objective'.

21 See Jay (1995) for a discussion of this phenomenon. See also Hirsch (1997) on the optical unconscious in relation to family photography.

4

The presidential chair

TO JUDGE A BOOK BY ITS COVER

Writing of this iconic photograph (Figure 4.1), Armando Bartra (1997: 79–80) states: 'Villa's and Zapata's encounter with the presidential chair is such an indispensable image-event that, had it not happened, we would have invented it.' Arguably a strong contender for the role of *the* photo opportunity of the revolution, this image – or more accurately, these images, for there are at least four of them in circulation – were made during the brief occupation of Mexico City by Zapatista and Villista troops in December 1914 and capture a smiling Pancho Villa on the presidential chair with an earnest Emiliano Zapata seated beside him. In some, Zapata stares intently at the camera; in others, his gaze is fixed on Villa to his right. A newsworthy occasion that could not have been better stage-managed had it been planned, this festive and impromptu scene stands as a counterpoint to the solemnity and pomp which, as we saw in the preceding chapter, was associated with the presidential chair during the reign of Porfirio Díaz. And, like the heroic statues of revolutionary leaders that sprang up in the aftermath of the conflict, *Villa en la silla presidencial* (henceforth abbreviated to the pleasingly rhythmic *Villa en la silla*) has become something of a (photographic) national monument in its own right.[1]

Testimony to its status as an object of enduring fascination, in December 2000 *Villa en la silla* was the subject of two articles in the cultural supplement of the left-leaning national daily *La Jornada*. The first, 'History and Myth of the Casasola Archive' by photo-historian John Mraz, examines three iconic photographs of the revolution, including this one.[2] And the second, 'Zapata's gaze without chair', is devoted entirely to the image, and constitutes a lyrical meditation on the famous photograph by artist Mauricio Gómez Morin, culminating in a reflection on its on-going significance, in which the intense gaze of Zapata is echoed in the eyes that stare out from behind the ski masks of members of the Ejército Zapatista de Liberación Nacional (Zapatista Army of National Liberation or EZLN), whose uprising on 1 January 1994 was, for many commentators, a watershed in contemporary Mexican history.[3]

4.1 Villa en la silla presidencial/Villa in the presidential chair, 1914.

I will return to the relationship between the EZLN and this revolutionary photo opportunity in Chapter 8. For now, however, we should note that the pervasive presence of versions of this photograph in the Mexican cultural landscape, obsessively reproduced and reinvented across a range of cultural texts, cannot be overestimated. Furthermore, it is an image with a particular affinity with the front cover. A cropped, pointillist-style sketch based on the photograph appears on the cover of Anita Brenner's didactic account of the revolution destined for a North American readership, *The Wind that Swept Mexico: The History of the Revolution of 1910–1942*. This text, originally published in 1943 with an introduction by Brenner chronicling the revolution, is first and foremost a photographic essay, with the photographs selected by George R. Leighton. In addition to the cover image (of the 1984 edition and prior to that), among its 184 images, *The Wind that Swept Mexico* figures a sequence of photographs that contextualise *Villa en la silla* in terms of chronology, location and cultural significance. Each is accompanied by a caption:

> 105. Mexico City was No Man's Land. One day Zapata and his men made a triumphal entry. It was thought that the Attila of the South would butcher the people, but he did not and, after a little while, moved out again.

> 106. Generals swept in and out and no one could be sure at any time who was supposed to be sitting in the presidential chair . . . and most of the time no one was.

> 107. One day Carranza and his staff were photographed standing in front of it.

> 108. Villa had his picture taken lolling in it, with Zapata beside him. (Brenner 1996)[4]

The photograph also graces the cover of Enrique Krauze's 1997 *Biografía del poder: Caudillos de la Revolución mexicana* (1910–1940), where once again it has been cropped and manipulated to bring into golden relief the elaborate plumed chair on which Villa 'lolls'. Significantly, Krauze's text includes biographies of the seven caudillos of the revolution who occupied the historical stage during the conflict and its intense phase of institutionalisation (1920–40), from Madero through to Lázaro Cárdenas. Yet emblematically, it is *Villa en la silla* that is inevitably reproduced on the cover and not, for example, an image of the other, less 'photogenic' caudillos.[5]

And, in 1979, the photograph was reworked and rendered as a mural/painting by the Canadian artist Arnold Belkin (1930–1992) in *La llegada de los generales Zapata y Villa al Palacio Nacional el 6 de diciembre de 1914* (Museo Nacional de Historia, INAH, acrylic on canvas, 230×350cm). A long-term resident in Mexico, Belkin worked from the famous photograph itself, as well as from some fifty additional images to bring in further revolutionary figures, such as Eufemio Zapata and Felipe Ángeles, who stand in the foreground to the right and left (Bartra 1997). As is perhaps fitting for an image that visually dissects the revolutionary leaders, affording the viewer with an x-ray-like vision of their internal organs and skeletal structures, Belkin's painting (see Figure 4.2) appears on the cover of Gilbert Joseph and Daniel Nugent's *Everyday Forms of State Formation: Revolution and the Negotiation of Rule in Modern Mexico* (1994). Belkin's image seems particularly appropriate for the cover of this penetrating edited collection of essays, which functions as a sophisticated corrective to the polarised either/or populist/revisionist approaches that have tended to dominate the historiography of the revolution; instead its concern is 'to fashion an analytical framework "from below" with a more compelling and nuanced "view from above"' (Joseph and Nugent 1994: 12).

Where these three sources of *Villa en la silla* are in many ways diverse, what unites them is their focus on the revolution as a whole event: whether it be as the political and social upheaval in a worryingly close neighbour (Brenner); a more distant product of charismatic human agents in the struggle (Krauze); or a complex historical process (Joseph and Nugent).[6] The point is that via a synecdochal operation this photographic part-object that captures a brief moment in December 1914 has come to stand in for the whole: the revolution. However, if the old adage goes, never judge a book by its cover, a similar principle is applicable to the (iconic) photograph: its very ubiquity hardly encourages us to pause to reflect as we hurry on to get beyond it to something of real 'substance'.

Drawing on Belkin's photograph qua painting as a critical metaphor, this chapter performs a dissection of *Villa en la silla*, in order to explore a series of questions that relate not only to this individual image, but equally to the status and significance of the photographic image within the twin processes of post-revolutionary memorialisation and nation/state formation. Why this photograph? What is it about it that captures the post-revolutionary cultural

4.2 Cover, Gilbert Joseph and Daniel Nugent, *Everyday Forms of State Formation: Revolution and Rule in Modern Mexico*.

imagination? What is its relationship qua photograph to post-revolutionary discourses of memory? If iconic status comes about as a result of repeated exposure, what are the ramifications of this compulsion to repeat? As one of the most salient images of the conflict, what can the iconisation of a photograph like *Villa en la silla* tell us more generally about the relationship between memory, revolution and photographic representation in Mexico?

THE HISTORICAL ENCOUNTER

The first step in the process of anatomisation is, inevitably, to return the immobile bodies traced on the surface of the image back into the flow of history. That is, it is essential to consider the circumstances that brought the caudillos to their encounter with one another in the National Palace: circumstances that, in turn, gave rise to the famous photograph. The second step is to locate the sources of the image's reproduction in the press at the time of the staging of this image-event and then, with more difficulty, to sketch the routes of its dissemination in the aftermath of the revolution prior to its appearance as emblematic cover image. In this way, it becomes possible to start to provide answers to the questions that frame this chapter and that inform the book as a whole.

Villa, Zapata and their troops were propelled into the city at a crucial moment in the revolution shortly after the resignation of the reactionary 'villain' Victoriano Huerta, an event that had given rise to the struggle to define and control the direction that the revolution would take henceforth. This struggle took place between the two official, Constitutionalist factions: Carrancistas and Villistas. Geographically and politically remote from the Constitutionalist north, the southern Zapatista movement was essentially a populist, regional peasant uprising, one which adhered fervently to the 1911 agrarian Plan de Ayala. The months between Huerta's political demise in July 1914 and the October Convention of Aguascalientes, which brought together representatives from the three factions, saw frantic to-ings and fro-ings as both Villistas and Carrancistas attempted to broker a deal with Zapata, who adamantly refused to concede any compromise position on the Plan de Ayala. Finally, the three-way vying for power reached an accord of sorts at Aguascalientes, with the nomination of Eulalio Gutiérrez as provisional president and the forging of an uneasy and short-lived alliance between Villa and Zapata. Carranza, who had been occupying Mexico City, left swiftly for Veracruz at this juncture, vacating the capital for occupation by Villista and Zapatista troops and thereby setting the stage for the legendary meeting of their respective leaders.

Examining the image-event retrospectively, in light of its widespread dissemination, we might expect a photograph with such a distinctive post-revolutionary career to have been splashed prominently across the news media in December 1914. Certainly, it is possible to establish that, in certain instances, the process of iconisation was already under way during the revolutionary process, as is evident, for example, in the case of the famous image of Emiliano Zapata (*c.*1912) (see Figure 8.2), versions of which were reproduced prominently and repeatedly in the national press during the conflict. Where, however, such images of Zapata, as we will see in Chapter 7, subsequently circulated in support of his posthumous status as secular saint, it is important to note that during the struggle they provided visual evidence backing reports sustaining his status as 'public enemy number one'. There is, then, neither a direct correlation between the perception of an image-event at the time of its production and its subsequent passage into post-revolutionary memorial discourse, nor between its contemporary and subsequent circuits and formats of circulation. This is the case of *Villa en la silla*.

On one level, there are prosaic reasons for this. As the foregoing historical sketch reveals, 1914 was a moment of intense political turmoil which, in turn, engendered economic crisis. In her analysis of images reproduced in *La Ilustración Semanal*, Marion Gautreau (2003: 48) notes that rampant inflation of this period led to a paper shortage, with numerous publications either suspending or ceasing production altogether toward the end of 1914 and into 1915. Thus, if it is difficult to locate *Villa en la silla* in the contemporary press, this is due, in part at least, to the fact that this moment marked a partial hiatus in output. A brief glimpse at the places in which the photograph appeared and the formats in which it appeared is nevertheless revealing. A title that continued production through December 1914, *El Monitor: Diario de la Mañana*, reproduced a cropped version centred on the two central caudillos; of the other figures present in the full image, only the comical child's face behind Zapata's left shoulder is visible.[7] Rather than on the front cover, however, the image was reproduced on page three, under the simple caption 'The Generals Villa and Zapata at the Palace'; nor is the making of the image alluded to in the accompanying textual report of Zapata's and Villa's arrival in the capital in the company of more than 50,000 troops.[8]

Locating the photograph in its original contexts of publication at the time of its production is, then, a relatively straightforward task. To trace the subsequent trajectory of the photograph's multiple sources of public dissemination, during the phase of intense post-revolutionary institutionalisation through to its use as cover image on the books cited earlier, is a labyrinthine if not impossible undertaking. It is nevertheless worth pausing briefly to peruse some of the subsequent sites of publication for, although not exhaustive, once again they prove suggestive indices of the photograph's transit into the post-revolutionary imagination. Of particular significance, the image resurfaced in the national press in a report accompanying the news of Zapata's death when it appeared on the front cover of *Excélsior* on 12 April 1919. One of a medley of five images surrounding a map of Morelos, it was published under the headline 'How Colonel Guajardo was able to get to Emiliano Zapata and kill him' (Figure 4.3). Alongside the triumphalist account of the sensational details of Zapata's ambush and assassination, a small but significant caption change takes place: '1. Zapata Muerto. 2. ditto [i.e. Zapata] en la Silla Presidencial'. Although the images receive no editorial comment, the logic of cause and effect that underpins the juxtaposition of an image of the dead Zapata and the live Zapata usurping – via the caption, rather than what is actually depicted – the status of the presidential chair as supreme symbol of sovereign power hardly requires elucidation.

4.3 *Excélsior*, 12 April 1919.

Nonetheless, barely seven years later, in March 1926, *Villa en la silla* materialised again, this time in *Semanario Rotográfico* (Figure 4.4), in which it featured as
the final image in a sequence under the title 'What Mexico has seen in the last 30
years: vicissitudes of the presidential chair'.[9] Based on a selection made especially
for the weekly illustrated magazine from the Casasolas' extensive collection,
the visual layout displays a curious disregard for chronological order. The first
image featured is the chair on its own, with the title 'Silla del Benemérito Juárez';
the next image is *En honor a Juárez* captioned, with wonderful understatement,
'General Porfirio Díaz in the presidential chair he occupied for some years'
('durante varios años'). The images that follow show influential men associated
with the chair – from Madero through Huerta 'in the *primitive* (emphasis added)
chair of Díaz'; Francisco Carvajal; Carranza 'occupying the chair for the first
time after abandoning the title 'first chief'; De la Huerta; Don Eulalio Gutiérrez;
Francisco Lagos Cházaro; and Roque González Garza. The position of *Villa en
la silla* as the final image in this sequence is visually eloquent, for it suggests a
lineage through Juárez (signalled once again via his absence), Díaz (who, as we
have seen, was emphatically present) through to the occupation of the presidential chair by Villa in the company of Zapata. In this way, in the post-revolutionary
period, their *occupation* – rather than *usurpation* – of the presidential chair is
endowed with a degree of teleological inevitability: thanks to the revolution,
radicals rather than reactionaries now occupy the seat of power.

4.4 *Semanario Rotográfico*, 10 March 1926.

While the 1914 report in *El Monitor* that covers the occupation of Mexico City by the troops of Zapata and Villa does not detail the making of the photograph, this is not to say that this image-event is absent from subsequent fictional and factual accounts of the revolution. In *El águila y la serpiente* (The Eagle and the Serpent), written in exile in 1926/27, Luis Martín Guzmán devotes a whole section to 'Los Zapatistas en el Palacio', which, according to Horacio Legrás (2003a: 447) may have been written '*against* the photograph', which at the time of writing, had already become iconic and which, he claims 'condenses all the utopia and innocence of the revolution' (444).[10] The making of the image is also described in Archivo Casasola's 1942 *Historia gráfica de la Revolución. México. 1900–1940*, in which the image is reproduced alongside a textual account detailing how the two leaders spend Sunday 6 December: parading through the capital in a visual display that provokes the fear-tinged delight of the urban onlookers who cannot help but admire 'the capricious attire of this fearsome army'. The parade ends up at the heart of the capital city and also nation, at the National Palace, where the leaders are received by interim President Gutiérrez, before making their way to the presidential balcony to witness the parade and where they are 'applauded at length by the crowd'. Despite the adulation of the crowd, 'as the parade of numerous contingents was so long and tedious, at an opportune moment the Generals Francisco Villa and Emiliano Zapata retire inside, Villa sitting on the presidential chair'.[11] In this instant, the photographs are taken. At Villa's suggestion that it is now his turn to pose on the chair, Zapata apparently refuses, arguing that the 'Silla' as icon of national power is emphatically *not* what he is fighting for. Afterward, of the *silla presidencial*, Zapata is said to assert: 'we ought to burn it to end ambition once and for all'/'deberíamos quemarla para acabar con las ambiciones' (Krauze 1987: 113). Or so the story goes. Made to relieve the tedium of the endless military parades (if we are to believe the anecdotal evidence provided in *Historia gráfica*), at the time of its making, who was ever to guess that this informal and ironic photo opportunity was to echo so resoundingly in the future?

PHOTOGRAPHY AND MEMORY

Returning *Villa en la silla* into the flow of history, and offering a necessarily partial account of its contemporary and post-revolutionary routes of dissemination, are undoubtedly necessary steps in the anatomisation of the photograph. The image demands historical anchorage, without which meaning effectively breaks down. History provides an 'objective' narrative context in which to understand not only how the image came about, but also the historical significance of what it represents: the unprecedented meeting of key revolutionary figures: figures who were of course soon to exit the revolutionary stage as the conservative revolution subsequently triumphed. As discourses of knowledge with a purchase on the past, however, history and photography become bound together in an epistemological hierarchy, whereby the latter occupies a secondary position – as mere illustrative tool – within history's narrative of linear time, linked by cause and effect. To reduce the photograph to its illustrative function to such a linear historical narrative is to overlook the photograph's own narrative potential, which is arguably much more complex than history's linearity will allow. To reinsert the photograph into the flow of history also falls short of the mark when it comes to offering an account of how photographs become iconised and to interrogating what might be at stake in the process whereby a mere 12 years – between the image-event and its 1926 appearance – its valences had apparently shifted dramatically. This is because such photographic images suffer a similar fate to that of the cover images with which I opened this chapter: their meaning is taken as self-evident and is therefore glossed over in the reader's desire for historical substance. In short, historical narrative, while it can furnish answers to 'who', 'where' and 'when', fails to provide the kind of analytical framework that answers the 'how' of *Villa en la silla*'s iconisation and the 'why' of the photograph's enduring fascination.

Even as photographs carry the burden of history, the contemporary turn to memory is arguably an equally productive approach to the historical freight of the iconic photograph. In the introduction to *Memory and Methodology*, Susannah Radstone (2000a: 3) asserts that what she describes as the recent interdisciplinary 'explosion' of interest in memory is due, in part at least, to a '"postmodern" overturning of modernity's (blind) faith in futurity, progress, reason and objectivity'. In the turn to memory, therefore, official history and its associations with objectivity, the public sphere and authoritative master narratives of progress has become a site of contestation. Work on memory, on the other hand, is concerned with subjectivity, and with private and micro narratives. Furthermore, it places an emphasis on the status of memory as representation, where representation is bound up with the structures of narrativisation, and focuses on issues of selection, condensation, repression, displacement and denial. Although the revolutionary photograph as a public, objective and ultimately authoritative document may seem naturally allied with official history, as I have argued, the historical narrative tends to eclipse the photographic image. If we are to achieve an account of the photograph that privileges the productivity of the image, I would argue that it is only to be achieved through a radically different methodology, that of memory. This is not to suggest, however, that photography enjoys a comfortable relationship with memory. Rather, I suggest that this relationship is governed by a paradox that turns on photography's status as ambiguous (counter) memory text. For all that the photography/memory dyad is ambivalent, it is nonetheless a productive one when it comes to analysing iconic photographs.

PHOTOGRAPHY AND MEMORY IN POST-REVOLUTIONARY DISCOURSES

In the aftermath of the revolution in Mexico, discourses of memory came to play an important role in the post-revolutionary drive to institutionalise the armed struggle as a foundational narrative of national identity, where identity was to be forged on a notion of national unity. This was no easy matter, however. As outlined in the historical overview in Chapter 2, the revolution was not a unified event, nor did the triumphant conservatives Carranza and Obregón embody the radical ideals of the struggle. To insert the myth of the revolution into collective memory as a unified, socially radical national event therefore took some astute cultural and social engineering.

The dynamic of post-revolutionary discourses of memory can be understood in the light of theories of collective memory which, as is by now well established, is crucial to the formation of national identities. Drawing on Maurice Halbwachs' (1980) work on collective memory, Nancy Wood provides a helpful definition of this mode of memory: a mode that she sets up in opposition to individual memory:

> What differentiates these two modes of memory [individual and collective] is that while the emanation of individual memory is primarily subject to the laws of the unconscious, public memory – *whatever its unconscious vicissitudes* – testifies to a will or desire on the part of some social group or disposition of power to select and organize representations of the past so that these will be embraced by individuals as their own. If particular representations of the past have permeated the public domain it is because they embody an intentionality – social, political, institutional and so on – that promotes or authorizes their entry. (Wood 1999: 2)[12]

Such a notion of top-down collective memory has informed the work of scholars in the post-revolutionary Mexican context. In *La Revolución: Memory, Myth and History*, Thomas Benjamin explores the way in which in the aftermath of the armed conflict, successive governments turned to remembrances, rites, celebrations, monuments and histories to transform the revolution into tradition within popular memory. In a chapter on monuments, echoing Wood's notion of representations that embody an intentionality, Benjamin asserts:

> Certain monuments are designed to create a setting for ritual performances, for commemorations and celebrations . . . The monument, the setting, the performance and the particular day combine to evoke symbolic reassurance that the state, the regime, or the leader is faithful to those considered the community's founding fathers, and that authority therefore is legitimate. As stages for commemorative performances, monuments encourage people not simply to remember but to remember together, thereby affirming group solidarity and unity. (Benjamin 2000: 117–18)

Although not explicitly articulated within such paradigms, discourses of collective memory are also central to Ilene O'Malley's study of hero cults in the institutionalisation of the Mexican state. O'Malley traces the evolution of the four principle revolutionary leaders in the period 1920–40, examining the transformations that the caudillos as political personages underwent as the state consolidated:

> The propaganda surrounding these four heroes [Madero, Zapata, Villa, Carranza]
> had a number of common traits: the claim that the government was revolutionary;
> the promotion of nationalism; the obfuscation of history; the denigration of politics;
> . . . patriarchal values and the "masculinization" of the heroes' images. These char-
> acteristics form the internal ideology and psychology of the myth of the Mexican
> Revolution. (O'Malley 1986: 113)

Although the object, focus and scope of their studies differ, both Benjamin and
O'Malley concur that, with the rise of the new post-revolutionary elite, the
revolution became a prime site of memory, wherein those representations that
entered the social sphere were harnessed to the project of the revolution as foundational myth of origin.

A curious omission, however, is a detailed discussion of the role of photography in post-revolutionary discourses of memory: an omission that attests further
to the ubiquitous invisibility of the photographic object.[13] That photographic representation occupies an important position within such discourses and therefore
merits discussion is evident on a number of levels. First, taking their cue from
the endlessly photographed Porfirio Díaz, the revolutionary leaders themselves
clearly had an eye to the role of photographic technology in their memorialisation when they hired photographers to follow their campaigns.[14] And furthermore, Olivier Debroise (2001: 177) notes that, by comparison, contemporary
European conflicts (namely, the First World War and the Russian Revolution)
generated relatively few photographic images, unlike the Mexican revolution
which, he claims, 'depended heavily, from its inception, on visual representations
and, in particular, on photographs'. Second, if the photographic representation
of the revolution was endowed with privileged status during the conflict, in the
aftermath visual media, including photography, film and art were central to the
post-revolutionary project of state and forging of nation.[15] Third, of the visual
media involved in this project, none has the kind of special, if equivocal relationship with memory than that which obtains between photography and memory: a
relationship that is at once one of counterparts and antagonists.

Photography and memory are structurally akin insofar as both represent
'windows' on the past. Memory provides access to a mediated representation
of the past that is subject to the processes of selection, repression and revision.
Photography, both despite and because of its privileged purchase on the real
also offers us a vision of the past that is structured according to the same logic of
selection, repression and revision. As a 'cut inside the referent' – to cite Christian
Metz's (1990: 158) definition – the photograph, like memory, is defined as much
by what it does not represent as by what it does. Photographs are, of course,
also material manifestations of memory. As traces of what Barthes famously
describes as the 'this has been' ('ça a été'), photographs permit access to the past
as does no other mode of representation. And yet, even as photographs and
memories represent mediated openings onto the past, and on one level are the
very stuff of memory, they are not, suggests Barthes, commensurate. Indeed,

in *Camera Lucida*, Barthes goes so far as to suggest that they are in a sense antithetical:

> Not only is the Photograph never, in essence, a memory . . . but it actually blocks memory, quickly becomes a counter-memory . . . The photograph is violent: not because it shows violent things, but because on each occasion it fills the sight by force, and because in it nothing can be refused or transformed. (Barthes 1993 [1981]: 91)

Drawing on the one hand on Barthes's insistence on photographic reference as the essential effect of photography, and on the other on his formulation of the photograph as counter-memory, I now focus on the way in which, through its visual rhetoric, *Villa en la silla* plays a role in underwriting a hegemonic conception of post-revolutionary national identity. As an iconic memory-text anchored within the specific processes of post-revolutionary state formation, meaning in *Villa en la silla* hinges on an equivocal relationship between photographic rhetoric and collective memory. That is, as a visual document that entered into circulation in the post-revolutionary cultural landscape, signification in *Villa en la silla* turns on its status as photograph that is structured like memory, that is structuring of memory, and that ultimately constitutes a counter-memory.

VILLA EN LA SILLA AS (COUNTER) MEMORY

What, then, might the post-revolutionary subaltern viewing subject, a subject steeped in the ambient discourses of post-revolutionary Mexico, 'see' on encountering *Villa en la silla?*[16] This subject is overwhelmingly presented with a sea of faces assembled in front of the camera that clamour to get into the frame. As an iconic image – that is to say, as an image reproduced so frequently as to have become familiar to the point of invisibility – *Villa en la silla* contains a series of condensed meanings that would be instantly recognisable to this viewing subject and that combine to make of it a complex memory-text. Of the figures assembled, some look directly at the camera, others look inward at the spectacle of the central leaders, while others still seem to have been caught unawares, their gaze directed at some off-frame space. There is nothing ordered or regimented about this sea of faces and sombreros: this is the revolution as popular struggle. The impromptu scene further bespeaks the legendary meeting of north and south and hence enacts a form of unification that chimes with post-revolutionary discourses of cohesive nationhood. But more than this, this sea of faces with its range of somatic tonalities and associations with the revolution as popular struggle – from the dark-skinned indigenous faces, to the lighter *mestizos* and pale *criollos* – becomes the face of modern *mestizo* Mexico, where discourses of *mestizaje* played a key cementing role in the process of making the Mexican mosaic cohere.[17]

In the foreground sit the caudillos. If hero cults were constructed around the four principal caudillos, nevertheless, as O'Malley (1986) suggests, within a cultural context that valorised virility, Madero and Carranza were by far eclipsed by Villa and Zapata in the masculinity stakes. Both men were charismatic leaders, associated with hypermasculinity in the popular imagination through their legendary, voracious sexual appetites and acts of audacity in battle. Such attributes were consonant with, and therefore co-opted by, the fundamentally patriarchal post-revolutionary state that O'Malley maps in her study. Similarly, both men were associated with a radical political agenda: in the case of Villa, certainly more radical than that of the triumphant conservatives; and Zapata genuinely espoused a radical cause, even if he had no designs on national power. What Villa was lacking in terms of his contradictory political agenda he more than made up for on the nationalistic front: thanks to his famous raid on the American town of Columbus, New Mexico in 1916 he came to represent a supreme symbol of national resistance.

Finally, the photograph also constitutes an act of symbolic iconoclasm, a radical gesture in the context of a nation that was otherwise not given to such displays. As Benjamin (2000: 118) argues, 'The defeat and discrediting of the regime of Porfirio Díaz . . . was not accompanied by any outburst of iconoclasm. This absence of symbolic violence is particularly noteworthy and significant since the Porfiriato was the first great age of commemorative monument building in modern Mexican history.' Just as the Porfiriato gave rise to a proliferation of commemorative monuments, as we saw in Chapter 3, Díaz himself was similarly fond of ceremonial displays of his power, harnessing the visual technology of photography to document that power. Indeed, if the presidential chair was associated with anyone or anything, it was with the power of the deposed president. In this vein, recall Figure 3.6 from *Pearson's Magazine* with its caption, 'The master of Mexico in his official chair'. The revolution may have been lacking in coherent goals and ideals. The one thing it did achieve was, of course, the overthrow of the Díaz dictatorship. Hence the iconoclastic gesture that is enacted within this image lies in its depiction of the desecration of a sacred space with key associations with the *ancien régime*.[18] This gesture points further to the photograph's status as an image in which meaning exceeds its photographic temporality. Rather than representing one, albeit pivotal, moment in the conflict, *Villa en la silla* has come to stand in for the whole event: an event that dis-enthroned the old order to replace it with the 'revolutionary' new order.

Condensed in this single image, therefore, is a series of meanings that are circumscribed by and thereby made consonant with the intentionality of the 'muscular' post-revolutionary state. These meanings, readily legible by its viewing subjects, turn on the image's compressed representation of the revolution as an equation with the following values: Popular + Masculine + Mestizo + Mexican = radical rupture with the past. It is this connotational configuration that on one level accounts for the way in which this photograph has become one of those that, in the words of Monsiváis (1980): 'repeated, commented upon – we could almost say "imprinted on the collective unconscious" – the photos selected demonstrate that the focus of interest is not the examination of popular violence, rather the mythic aestheticisation of the revolutionary process.'[19] As an image 'imprinted' on the collective unconscious, *Villa en la silla* is structured like memory in that within the post-revolutionary context its meaning is constructed via the selective appropriation of elements of the past that correspond to the needs of the present. In its address to the post-revolutionary viewing subject the photograph is also structuring of memory in that through repeated reproduction it reorients popular memory of the conflict. To repeat, after all, is to memorise. Moreover, at the level of address, it must be stressed that this iconic image defies the linear logic of cause and effect that defines historical time. Rather the image is governed by another temporal modality, a modality that belongs to another disciplinary register: namely the psychoanalytic concept *Nachträglichkeit*, or 'belatedness'. Drawing on a definition of *Nachträglichkeit* provided by Laplanche and Pontalis as a 'process of deferred revision', Susannah Radstone formulates the significance of the concept for analytical approaches to memory:

> In place of the quest for the truth of an event, and the history of its causes, *Nachträglichkeit* proposes, rather, that the analysis of memory's tropes can reveal not the truth of the past, but a particular revision prompted by a later event, thus pitting psychical contingency against historical truth. (Radstone 2000: 86)

To the degree that the iconisation of *Villa en la silla* represents a form of (obsessive) 'deferred revision', the photograph indeed does not provide access to 'historical truth'. Rather, to cite Barthes (1993 [1981]: 91) once again, it actually 'blocks memory [and] quickly becomes a counter-memory'. As a memory-text, *Villa en la silla* effectively circulated within a cultural realm that over time became saturated with visual and other discourses – monuments, murals, films, histories, etc. – that coalesced to confirm the state's revolutionary legitimacy. The image's semantic orientation is thereby predetermined by the context of its dissemination that serves to block out or disavow the memory of other, more politically radical meanings.

Such an approach to the image has been outlined by Gareth Williams in an astute critique of an earlier essay of which this chapter is a revision (Noble 2004). In 'Sovereign (In)hospitality', Williams (2005: 98) takes issue with the 'implicit continuum' that underpins my reading of *Villa en la silla*, whereby 'the postrevolutionary state's identitarian cultural nationalism [is projected] back in time, to the photographs taken on December 6, 1914, in order to then project that bourgeois ideal back into a future, in which revolutionary historical experience has already been reterritorialized by the state and its class interests into specific rationalizations and productive biopolitical grids of intelligibility for both the present and the future'. Eschewing such a retrospective reading, the purpose of Williams's essay is to 'return the political content of 1914, along with its *paradoxes and contradictions*, to the image of Villa on the presidential chair' (100, emphasis added).

Drawing on Adolfo Gilly's *The Mexican Revolution* (2005), Williams (101) establishes December 1914 as a crucial interregnum in the revolutionary struggle,
a pivotal moment of institutional vacuum, at which point 'the peasantry was
actually able to capture the social life of the whole nation'.[20] Following Gilly, for
Williams, it was the 1914 occupation of the presidential palace by Zapatista and
Villista troops, and not the 1917 ratification of the Constitution (itself a retrospective statist imposition on historiography), that marks the peak of the revolution's '*social curve*' (103, emphasis in original). This was a profoundly ambiguous
juncture, one at which on the one hand sovereign law was suspended and on the
other it simultaneously continued to hold sway, enacted in the very occupation
of the presidential palace and that supreme symbol of the power, the presidential
chair:

> Just for a few moments and camera flashes, *Villa en la silla* is a singularity in time that,
> while it did not realize another world, certainly created the image and chance of a
> potentially distinct distribution of the relation between that which exists and that
> which does not; between those who speak and those who are forced to remain silent
> or to murmur in the shadows of national social life. No matter how contradictory
> the relation between the figuration of peasant equality and the persistence of the seat
> of sovereign power is in these images, the photographs embody the possibility of a
> reconfiguration of, and a fundamental redistribution of forces in, the field of collec-
> tive perception and political experience. (Williams 2005: 116)

For Williams, in the pursuit of political agency in this image-event within and
beyond sovereign rule, there is in my approach 'a substantial historical unity
grounded in Hegelian supersession: that is, a conceptualization of history in
which later forms are the truth of earlier forms' (119). Although the photograph
animates his argument – is its catalyst – Williams is, however, concerned with
politics, rather than the photographic and much less, the modalities of photo
iconicity. To restore the image to December 1914 is therefore to return it to the
flashes of the moments of its making, before it took on material, photographic
form, and before it acquired iconic status, when it embodies 'the possibility of a
reconfiguration of, and a fundamental redistribution of forces in, the field of collective perception and political experience'. And yet, despite the different empha-
ses, there is much in Williams's analysis that can illuminate our understanding of
the photograph's iconic status.

ICONICITY AND REPETITION

To the degree that *Villa en la silla* captures the post-revolutionary gaze in the
seductive believe in revolutionary unity to guard against the encroachment of
knowledge of other memories of the struggle, our understanding of the photograph's iconic status and its function as counter-memory can, however, acquire
more nuance. Having constructed a strategic working definition of the way in

which the photograph might have interpellated its historically situated viewing subject, I want now to suggest another reading of iconicity and, in so doing, take the concept of the photograph as counter-memory one step further. As a photographic counter-memory, whose meaning turns on disavowal – disavowal not so much of the Barthesian 'what-has-been', as of the what-might-have-been of the interregnum – *Villa en la silla* is also, at the same time, the site of traumatic memory within the parameters of a post-revolutionary hegemonic rhetoric of national identity.

Here it is instructive to align *Villa en la silla* with other key icons of the conflict, some of which we have already encountered and others that will be the subject of later chapters, namely, *Zapatistas en Sanborns* (1914) and *Soldadera en tren* (1912). Within the terms of my argument, it is at once comprehensible and at the same time curious that all three images – probably three of the most widely repro-duced images – invoke the revolution in a similar visual idiom: as a moment of acute rupture and transgression. In short, they hark back to 'the peak of the revo-lution's *"social curve"*' (Williams 2005: 103). Villa and Zapata occupy the sacred space at the heart of the nation; gun-toting indigenous peasants take light refresh-ment at Sanborns; women break out of the sanctity of the domestic sphere and are catapulted into the heart of the conflict. Think by comparison of photographs of the conservative end of the revolution – think, for example, of the diminutive figure of Madero, engulfed by the masses as he enters Cuernavaca on 12 June 1911, or more ominously, pictured in the Zócalo approaching the National Palace on 9 February 1913; or the grandfatherly Carranza or the one-armed Obregón – they simply do not make the same kind of dramatic impact of a world-turned-upside-down. By contrast, insofar as all three of the more 'revolutionary' photographs are put to work in the service of post-revolutionary nation-state formation in a process whereby their meaning hinges on a disavowal of knowledge in favour of belief, their pervasive presence is indeed comprehensible. Nevertheless, to the degree that each of these photographs represents a scene of profound trauma or rupture in the social fabric, on another level it is curious that this emblematic trio should predominate. As (counter) memory texts they represent a vision of the past that paradoxically cannot so easily be integrated into the elitist and conservative realities of the post-revolutionary present. Their affective force is, furthermore, made all the more compelling by their status as photographs. If there is one thing that their evidential force tells us it is that on some level what they portray really did happen.

It is this paradox, however, that may modulate our grasp of the iconic-ity of such photographs. Bearing in mind that iconic status is the product of repeated exposure, the compulsive repetition of *Villa en la silla*, *Soldadera* and *Zapatistas* within the hegemonic post-revolutionary cultural sphere can be seen as attributable to two interrelated and contradictory factors. On the one hand, repeated exposure of an image can be seen, as I have argued, as part of the post-revolutionary state's project to reprogram popular memory of the revolution in order to embed it in the collective (un)consciousness as a socially radical and cohesive event. If the subaltern subjects that are the receptacles of popular memory have eyes, however, so too do those subjects who embody hegemonic power. Viewed through the optic of those subjects who, to cite Wood again, 'promote or authorize' the entry and circulation of images within the cultural sphere, these iconic photographs that document profound rupture are uneasy reminders of a past, they precisely 'embody the possibility of a reconfiguration of, and a fundamental redistribution of forces in, the field of collective perception and political experience' (Williams 2005: 116). Insofar as they enact a view of the revolution 'from below', on one level at least, they are best forgotten.[21] On the other hand, then, the obsessive repetition of these photographs bespeaks a profound sense of anxiety of those with access to hegemonic power in the face of these images as sites of trauma.

In the preface of *Trauma: Explorations in Memory*, Cathy Caruth (1995: viii) suggests that 'traumatic recall or reenactment is defined, in part, by the very way that it pushes memory away'. Bearing this definition in mind, I suggest that we can give the iconicity of these photographs a further psychoanalytic inflection.[22] That is, to the very subjects who authorise and control their circulation, these photographic images, on whose surface are inscribed traumatic traces of the real, represent a past that, ghost-like, haunts the present: in the case of *Soldadera* and *Zapatistas*, the ghost of what was (and, indeed, what still could be); in the case of *Villa en la silla*, of what might have been. Iconicity, in this reading, is a form of compulsive repetition and in the Freudian account, testifies to a psychic need to return to the situation in which the trauma occurred in an endeavour to master the external stimuli retrospectively by reproducing the anxiety.[23] In the psychic domain, the compulsion to repeat, which I am reading as resulting in iconicity, represents an attempt to achieve some degree of mastery over the site/sight of trauma. The iconic status of these three photographic images, therefore, ultimately represents an act of counter-memory insofar as iconicity – as compulsive repetition – works precisely to push the trauma of this memory away. At the same time, however, in this reading, the iconic photograph as counter-memory inevitably tacitly serves as a form of acknowledgement of the potentially subversive charge that is contained within such visual documents.

NOTES

1 'El encuentro de Villa y Zapata con la silla presidencial es una imagen-suceso tan indispensable que, de no haber ocurrido la habríamos inventado.' Four versions of this image are stored in the SINAFO's digital database in Mexico City, with the following inventory numbers: Col. SINAFO-FN-INAH #186381; #335336; #33522; #33863. Thanks to Barbara Tenenbaum for prompting me to investigate this further. As this chapter is not concerned with the slight variations between the images – in some Zapata stares directly at the camera, in others his gaze is trained on Villa – I will refer to the

series henceforth in the singular, signalling my interest in the photographs as iconic 'image-event'.

2   In addition to *Villa en la silla*, Mraz selected the image of Victoriano Huerta, *El Sr. Presidente de la República y su Estado Mayor* (Col. SINAFO-FN-INAH #5764) and *Soldadera en tren* (Col. SINAFO-FN-INAH # 5670). See Escorza (2005) for a discussion of the Huerta image, including information on its original source of publication in *El Independiente*, 5 April 1913; similarly, see Morales (2006) for a discussion of the authorship and original source of publication of Soldadera (or La Adelita, as it is also known). For a brief, impressionistic account of *Villa en la silla*, see also De la Colina (2000).

3   On 'The Eyes of Emiliano Zapata' see Brunk (2006: 124), whose essay concludes: 'In 1989, José Muñoz Cota waxed poetic about a painting by Fernando Alférez that portrayed only Zapata's eyes. "In the sad gaze of Emiliano Zapata," Muñoz Cota wrote, "the tragedy of our history comes to light." Fives years later ski-masked rebels in the state of Chiapas served notice that Zapatismo was somehow an ongoing phenomenon, not a historical relic. It was probably just a coincidence that we saw only their eyes.'

4   The first image that opens Brenner's selection is, significantly, the official photographic portrait of Díaz discussed in the previous chapter, which appears with the following caption: 'In the year 1910 there was a strong Man of the Americas advertised in all the world, and his name was Porfirio Díaz of Mexico.' The images that precede *Villa en la silla* feature the following: (105) A mass of mounted soldiers in an undetermined urban location; (106) The presidential chair with elaborate curtained backdrop; (107) Carranza and others (including Obregón), in military uniform posing in front of the same chair. See Lear 2001 for an analysis of the revolution in Mexico City.

5   Claudio Lomnitz (2005: 351) discusses the origins of 'caudillismo' as a phenomenon that emerged after independence, when 'national unity and political sovereignty needed to be built out of a variety of corporations – cities, villages, haciendas, military and religious orders, guilds, and religious sodalities – that had strong identities and a sense of their traditional rights and prerogatives. In this context, a peculiarly modern political form of sovereignty emerged, a form that came to be known as "caudillismo"'. His point is that caudillismo, far from a traditional phenomenon, is in fact a modern phenomenon, 'inconceivable without competition for the political center, just as it is inconceivable without competitive access to the public sphere' (ibid.: 351–2).

6   Clearly one of the major divergences between the three sources cited is their context of publication and dissemination: Mexico and North America. I would argue that the presence of the photograph *Villa en la silla* across the two contexts attests further to the iconic status of the image, which is not confined to just Mexico. Friedrich Katz (1998: 437) suggests that 'A photographer recorded the scene, and the picture was soon disseminated worldwide, giving additional proof in the eyes of many observers that Villa had become the real strongman and ruler of Mexico.' However, he doesn't provide any evidence for this assertion.

7   Bi100, the website devoted to the Bicentenary of Independence and the Centenary of the Revolution in Mexico City, features a digital clip in which an aged man, Don Antonio Gómez Delgado, claims to have been present during the making of the photograph as a young boy ('yo era chamaco'). From his testimony, it is not clear, however, if he is one of the two children present in the photograph. In an attempt to

engage current-day children with the commemorative events, the website features a visual puzzle in which younger visitors to the site are invited to find the two children featured in the photograph by using the mouse to select them and also to leave comments: www.bi100.df.gob.mx/memorias.html (accessed 15 March 2008).

8 Gautreau (2003: 212) has also located it inside the covers of *La Ilustración Semanal* under the headline 'Generals Urbina, Francisco Villa and Emiliano Zapata on their arrival at the National Palace, el domingo de los corrientes, in a special 'pose for *La Ilustración Semanal*'/'Los generales Urbina, Francisco Villa y Emiliano Zapata a su llegada al Palacio Nacional, el domingo de los corrientes, en "pose" especial para "La Ilustración Semanal"' The caption that appears below the image reads: 'General Francisco Villa, during a moment of rest during the triumphal entry of the "powerful column", sits on the presidential chair, on his right the Generals Zapata and Otilio Montaño, standing is the General Rodolfo Fierro and on his right, Tomás Urbina.'/'El general Francisco Villa, en un momento de reposo durante la entrada triunfal de la "poderosa columna" se sienta en la silla presidencial, teniendo a su izquierda a los generales Emiliano Zapata y Otilio Montaño; de pie se ve al general Rodolfo Fierro y a su derecha al general Tomás Urbina'. I am very grateful to Marion Gautreau for sharing the findings of her meticulous archival research with me.

9 What becomes clear in this sequence, however, is that there is not just one presidential chair, but a number of different chairs, associated with different presidential posteriors. In a short internet article, the historian Víctor Manuel Ruiz of the Museo Nacional de Historia del Castillo de Chapultepec is quoted as stating that the chair's manufacture dates to between 1867 and 1872 and is considered a symbolic rather than utilitarian object. http://mensual.prensa.com/mensual/contenido/2006/03/24/hoy/vivir/542559.html (accessed 15 April 2008).

10 I was reminded of Guzmán's account of this image-event and prompted to read Legrás's reading of *El águila y la serpiente* thanks to the work of Gareth Williams (2005), to which I will return later in this chapter. It is worth noting a small, but not insignificant, slippage that takes place in Legrás's (2003: 444) recollection of the image, when he states: 'Hay una foto, tomada el 6 de diciembre de 1914, que condensa toda la utopía y toda la inocencia de la revolución. En la foto aparecen, sonriendo, Emiliano Zapata y Pancho Villa en el salón presidencial del Palacio Nacional. Zapata está sentado en la silla del presidente.'/'There is a photo, taken on 6 December 1914, that condenses all the utopia and innocence of the revolution. In the photo, Emiliano Zapata and Pancho Villa appear, smiling, in the presidential salon of the National Palace. Zapata is seated in the presidential chair'. Zapata does not smile in any of the versions of this image and neither, of course, is he seated in the presidential chair. This is a telling example of the way in which the image seems to invite us to project our own interpretations onto it, rather than see what is depicted.

11 'la caprichosa indumentaria de este temible ejército'; 'largamente ovacionados por la muchedumbre' 'como el desfile de numerosos contingentes fué tan largo y tedioso, en un momento oportuno se retiran al interior de los salones los generales Francisco Villa y Emiliano Zapata, sentándose Villa en la silla presidencial' (Archivo Casasola 1942: 873–4).

12 The emphasis added is mine: I pick up on the notion of unconscious vicissitudes of collective memory below.

13 It should be clarified that neither scholar is blind to the workings of visual culture. Benjamin incorporates some discussion of muralism and O'Malley includes material on film.

14 Of the caudillos, Villa in particular tapped the propagandistic potential of the visual image to its full; see Aurelio de los Reyes (1985) and Margarita de Orellana (1992).

15 In a working paper on photography and national identity in Mexico, John Mraz (2001: 4) argues that '[T]hough photography was often not as immediately tied to the State as cinema, the only real outlets for photojournalist images were the illustrated magazines such as *Hoy* and *Mañana*, which depended on the government for their existence.'

16 I am aware of the inherent dangers involved in trying to imagine in such a totalising way this putative viewing subject. Not all viewers encountered the image in the way that I map out below, for looking relations are invariably fraught with issues of gender, race and class that do not enter into my analysis here. However, I also believe that some form of construction of an encounter with the photograph is essential and a strategic step in my argument that precisely works toward an understanding of the iconic photograph as the site of resistant memory.

17 See Alan Knight's (1990) important essay, 'Racism, Revolution, and *Indigenismo*: Mexico, 1910–1940', on the deployment of race as a retrospective category in post-revolutionary discourses of identity.

18 In *Death and the Idea of Mexico*, Lomnitz (2005: 484) argues that in the contemporary context, 'Government officials have always tried to avoid violent signs of profanation and insisted on presenting the new order in the frame of natural succession rather than in an iconoclastic idiom.' The example he provides is Carlos Salinas de Gortari's appropriation of Emiliano Zapata when terminating agrarian reform in the 1990s. Meanwhile, he claims 'popular expression has shown no such compunction' (484). Elsewhere, Lomnitz (2006: 344) argues that where official iconoclasm has existed, it has been targeted at the Catholic Church. On anticlerical iconoclasm, see also Bantjes (1994; 2006).

19 'repetidas, comentadas – casi podría decirse "impresas en el inconsciente colectivo" – las fotos seleccionadas muestran que el centro del interés no es el examen de la violencia popular sino la estetización mitológica del proceso revolucionario.'

20 See Ruiz (2007) for a review essay that outlines the trajectory of Gilly's analysis of the revolution.

21 Thanks to John Kraniauskus for prompting me to clarify this point.

22 The deployment of psychoanalytic theories has been frequently attacked as a-historical. In the context of an analysis of the representation of masculinity in French painting, Abigail Solomon-Godeau (1997: 36) makes a convincing case for the usefulness of psychoanalysis as an analytical tool within different historical arenas, without recourse to which the persistent recurrence of certain phenomena and symptoms cannot be explained.

23 The notion of repetition compulsion is at the centre of Freud's 1920 *Beyond the Pleasure Principle*.

5
The firing squad

Sometime toward the end of the twentieth century, French photographer Henri Cartier-Bresson (1908–2004) was asked to name his personal 'photograph of the century'. Perhaps recalling an image he might have encountered during one of his two working visits to Mexico in 1934 and 1964, Cartier-Bresson selected this photograph of Fortino Sámano (Figure 5.1), who stands insouciantly with his back to a wall, hands in pockets, cigar in smiling mouth, facing an off-frame firing squad that will imminently carry out his execution.[1] Or rather, the man often heralded as the 'father' of photojournalism chose an image that is captioned 'Fortuno Sorano. Compagnon de Zapata et Pancho Villa pendant la révolution mexicaine, devant le peloton d'exécution, 1911'. Not only is Sámano misnamed and the year of his execution rather unfortunately brought forward by some six years, but even his status as a 'compagnon' of Villa and Zapata, as if the two represented a united, coherent revolutionary front, is to say the least wide of the mark.

With this perhaps being a part of the 'list-mania' that accompanied the dawn of the new millennium, I would have been unlikely to give Cartier-Bresson's predilection a second thought – it had, after all, come to my attention serendipitously via a Google Image search – had I not come across an anthology of poetry, also in French, with the title *Fortino Sámano (Les débordements du poème)* that could not but pique my curiosity. Collaboratively authored by poet Virginie Lalucq and the philosopher Jean-Luc Nancy, and published in 2004 by Galilée, according to the blurb on the verso, the volume originated in a poem that Lalucq drafted on the back of a photograph, attributed to Agustín Víctor Casasola, of Fortino Sámano. A Lieutenant of Zapata, or so the write-up informs us, Sámano was a counterfeiter of money who, on his execution by federal troops, demanded to keep his hands free and eyes un-blindfolded. The visual impact of this act of bravado was so out of kilter with the reality of the scene that was in fact being played out in this image that: 'on a pu dire qu'il paraissait attendre sa fiancée'.

In one of a number of verbalised references to this photograph of this larger-than-life figure in the revolution, Mexican cultural commentator Carlos

5.1 Fortino Sámano fuma un cigarro antes de ser fusilado/Fortino Sámano smokes a cigarette before being shot, 1917.

Monsiváis imagines the scenario in front of the execution wall in the following terms:

> He who is to be executed poses with grace in front of the camera. He rehearses several times the pose he will repeat for the last time in front of the firing squad. He wants to make sure that the public notices one particular circumstance: being shot affects him only inasmuch as nothing else will affect him any more. For the rest, what will remain after him is his courage. He is a real man, that is, he knows how to leave this world without discomposure. He looks at the photographer with contempt and derision, smokes a cigarette, adopts worldly poses in accordance with this experience, and his smile echoes the sardonic phrase he has just spoken. (Monsiváis 1987: 13)[2]

Be that as it may, standing before the camera's lens, poised between life and death, for Sámano becomes a way of occupying history and culture that is barely conceivable on 2 March 1917, when the shutter was released, and moments later the assembled firing squad pulled the trigger. Indeed, it does not seem too much to claim that, as with those figures who gathered around the presidential chair for the making of *Villa en la silla*, not one of those present at the execution – from visible victim, through invisible photographer, onlookers, and members of the firing squad – can have envisaged just how enduring the scene in which they are participants will prove. For it will traverse time and space, acquiring in the process a resonance not only in the photographic iconography of the Mexican revolution but, curiously, also in the French cultural imagination. While the appropriations of this image-event by both Cartier-Bresson and Lalucq and Nancy, as I shall demonstrate, reveal an – albeit unintentional – catalogue of errors, this chapter takes the 'French connection' as a starting point for an exploration of the relationship between the iconic photograph – both this one and the iconic image as a phenomenon – and conceptualisations of history and time. On the one hand, as we already saw in Chapter 4, iconic photographs acquire their currency retroactively in relation to interpretations of events that are not necessarily available at the time of their making. *Fortino Sámano*, like *Villa en la silla*, chimes with post-revolutionary discourses of cultural nationalism, in this case, with the elevation of the death cult to totemic status in the aftermath of the conflict. On the other, however, tracing another French connection back to another firing squad, namely an image, or more appropriately a series of images related to the French intervention culminating in the execution of puppet emperor Maxmilian in 1867, iconicity must also be conceived as a retrospective category.

THE DEATH OF FORTINO SÁMANO

First things first, then: it is essential to establish some facts, and in this way we will discover that the French are not alone in displaying a rather cavalier attitude to historical accuracy where photographic images are concerned. Fortino Sámano was not a counterfeiter of money; although he is denominated as such by no lesser authorities than Héctor Aguilar Camín and Lorenzo Meyer in *Historia gráfica de México* where, under a reproduction of the image, the Mexican historians note that the execution of counterfeiters was common during the year 1915 (1992: 99). Nor, of course, was he executed in either 1915 or 1911 or indeed on 12 January 1917, as indicated in the exhibition catalogue of *¡Tierra y Libertad! Photographs of Mexico 1900–1935*.[3]

Rather, Captain Carlos Fortino Sámano, as reported on Thursday 1 March 1917 in the Constitutionalist daily *El Demócrata*, was condemned to death for armed robbery. More precisely, on a date unspecified, he had forcibly entered the bedroom of one Luz Guzmán and, threatening the widow with a revolver, had taken jewellery and items of clothing; he was detained several hours later by the police. His execution by firing squad was duly reported in the same newspaper on Saturday 3 March as having taken place the previous day. Under the main headline 'Captain Sámano was executed yesterday in the San Lázaro Air Base', a subheading informs readers that 'He wanted to order his own execution but was not allowed to do so and died with extraordinary sang froid'.[4] The paper goes on to report how Sámano spent the night before his execution 'perfectly calmly' in the company of his wife and mother who did not leave his side for a moment and watched over his sleep. At about 5.00 a.m. he was given the last rights. Some time before 10.00 a.m. a crowd of onlookers gathered outside the National Palace to witness the condemned man 'with a calm appearance' leaving the site of his incarceration under armed guard, and where he also took leave of his friends and companions in arms. He was transported by a special train to San Lázaro, where an even greater number of onlookers were awaiting him. Some minutes before the scheduled time of his execution at 10.00 a.m., Sámano was still conversing with friends. Then, standing before the five soldiers charged to carry out the execution, Sámano placed a neckerchief on his chest and asked the soldiers to fire at that spot.[5] An ambulance brigade then collected his corpse which was taken to the military hospital to be handed over to his relatives for burial if so requested. The report is duly accompanied by two photographic images. The first is circular-formatted and features Sámano striding resolutely, backed by what we assume must be a combination of guards, onlookers and friends and captioned 'Arriving at the gallows'. The second is a rectangular, cropped version of the iconic image of Sámano, is unattributed and simply entitled 'Facing the firing squad'.[6]

Given the facts concerning Sámano's crime and subsequent execution, and notwithstanding the admittedly sensationalist reporting of this event, what are we to make of the multiple misattributions that surround this photographic image? On one level, the gap that opens up between fact and fiction speaks eloquently of the radical decontextualisation that invariably accompanies the process by which photographs become iconic. As modes of what Claude Lévi-Strauss categorises as biographical or anecdotal history – that domain of history that is 'low-powered' and which is 'not intelligible in itself and only becomes so *en bloc* to a form of history of a higher power than itself' (1966: 261) – photographs are readily pressed into the service of the mythologising tendencies that under-pin the official, populist representation of the revolution. That this is the case is evident particularly in Cartier-Bresson's (quite possibly unwitting) denomination of Sámano as a 'compagnon' of Villa and Zapata. This caption erases the prosaic reality behind Sámano's status– he was an armed robber who, after all, attempted to steal from a defenceless lady– and instead imputes to him a heroic status that goes beyond the *sang froid* he evidently displayed as he stood facing the firing squad. Allied with the more radical elements of the revolution – namely Villa and Zapata – whose campaigns are, in turn, erroneously conflated, image and caption supplement one another and Sámano now implicitly faces his death for heroic deeds as a revolutionary. At the same time, as one of a significant number of execution images made during the violent phase of the revolution, this photograph of Sámano acquires renewed semantic force in the context of the distinctively Mexican death cult that emerged in the aftermath of the conflict.

Until recently, it seemed nearly impossible to say anything meaningful about the status and significance of the idea of death in Mexico without lapsing into cliché and tautology regarding the irreverence that surrounds a topic that in other national cultures is treated with greater solemnity and as the ultimate taboo. Beyond restating the obvious – that is, that death seems to permeate life in Mexico to an extraordinary degree, as is refracted in both elite and popular culture – critical reflection seemed to have reached an impasse. But the peculiarly Mexican obsession with death has finally been accorded the proper scholarly scrutiny that it deserves in Claudio Lomnitz's thought-provoking book *Death and the Idea of Mexico* (2005).

Thanks to the work of Benedict Anderson (2006 [1983]), we are now more than familiar with the idea that nationalism is bound up with death, with being prepared to lay down one's life for the imagined community of one's country. But it is one thing to argue that the idea of the nation is founded on the idea of death; it is quite another to assert that death is a national totem. Perhaps Lomnitz's boldest claim, with its risk of essentialism, is that which animates his book: namely 'death is a metonymic sign of Mexicanness itself' (27) and is intrinsically bound up with Mexico's historical experience as a post-colonial and post-imperial nation (30). Yet if the roots of death's totemic status by definition pre-date the twentieth century, for Lomnitz death was consecrated as a pre-eminent national sign in the aftermath of the 'bloodbath' of the 1910 revolution. For artists and intellectuals associated with the modernist cultural renaissance that took place in the first half of the twentieth century, Mexicans' easy acquaintance with death appeared to fuse elements of both pre-Columbian and Hispanic traditions, and thus meshed with the unifying ideal of the mestizo nation that the energetic architects of this entity were busily promoting. The nationalisation of death found its maximum expression in Octavio Paz's *The Labyrinth of Solitude* (1950), an obligatory if problematic touchstone for the study of Mexican culture, in which death became a 'diagnostic feature of the condition called "solitude"' (Lomnitz 2005: 25).[7]

In the later decades of the twentieth century, however, as Lomnitz establishes in an introductory chapter, cultural commentators of a variety of political stripes started to take issue with the notion of the conflation of Mexico with the death totem, condemning it as part of a top-down, reifying myth of *mexicanidad*. For Monsiváis (1987), in particular, the figure of the swaggering Mexican revolutionary who postured stoically in front of the firing squad – and here again, it is not inappropriate to imagine that he has the photograph of Fortino Sámano in mind – was subsequently co-opted and commodified under the rubric of revolutionary nationalism, with particularly pernicious effects. Or as Lomnitz (2005: 55) summarises Monsiváis's position: 'The pride of place given to play with death by postrevolutionary intellectuals is today suspected of legitimating an authoritarian political regime that naturalized its own penchant to trample, mangle, and stamp out life and projected its own tendencies onto "the Mexican's disdain of death".' Viewed in this context, the physiognomic richness of the Fortino Sámano photograph, in which the gravity of the event being represented stands in contradistinction to the relaxed casualness of the condemned man's pose, takes on further connotations. A model of bravado and closed, stoic masculinity (boosted moreover by association with those other hyper-masculine figures, Villa and Zapata) who literally laughs in the face of death, the iconic image of Fortino Sámano fuses potently with the authoritarian, anti-democratic hues of post-revolutionary political culture.

A reading that relies on the construction of a retroactive context in which to account for the enduring status of the Sámano photograph in – to borrow Achille Mbembe's (2003) terminology – the necropolitics of post-revolutionary cultural nationalism is certainly convincing.[8] Beyond the confluence of the semiotic and cultural historical dimensions of such a reading, its temporal logic is also congruent with the medium of representation itself. It is by now a commonplace to note that death is a key trope that haunts photography – or 'thanatography', as Philippe Dubois (1983) terms it. Death inheres in every photograph, but is more poignantly manifest in some than others.[9] It is the overwhelming presence of death, for example, that touches Roland Barthes so profoundly when contemplating the photograph of Lewis Payne in what has become one of the most cited passages from *Camera Lucida*:

> In 1865, young Lewis Payne attempted to assassinate Secretary of State W. H. Seward. Alexander Gardner photographed him in his cell where he was waiting to be hanged. The photograph is handsome, as is the boy: that is the *studium*. But the *punctum* is: he is going to die. I read at the same time: *This will be* and *this has been*; I observe with horror an anterior future of which death is the stake. In front of the photograph of my mother as a child, I tell myself: she is going to die: I shudder like Winnicott's psychotic patient, *over a catastrophe that has already occurred*. Whether or not the subject is already dead, every photograph is this catastrophe. (Barthes 1993 [1981]: 96)

With minimal modification, and strategically glossing over those fraught terms *studium* and *punctum*, this quotation could so easily be made to refer to the photograph of Fortino Sámano: he is dead, he is going to die.[10] What is more, the grammatical tense, the future anterior, not only describes photography's relationship to historical time: this will be and this has been. It is also the tense of photo iconicity. That is to say, if in the modern world – to invoke W.J.T. Mitchell writing in *What do Pictures Want* (2005) – some images accrue a surplus value, appear to have a life of their own in the manner of totems and fetishes in the ancient world, the process by which this occurs, to some degree, can only be understood in the future anterior. The 'what will be' of the iconic image, its affective power, is more often than not invisible at the moment of its production.[11]

A reading of the image that is predicated wholly on the future anterior cannot, however, tell us its full life story. There is, so to speak, life before birth. In this context, Lomnitz's methodological approach to death and the idea of Mexico may provide a further insight into this striking photographic image. This is not to suggest that his argument is particularly attentive to the photographic or indeed the visual more generally. To be sure, Lomnitz's text is illustrated; but the function of the images is merely that: illustrative.[12] Where his approach is illuminating, however, lies in the genealogical thrust of his argument. Lomnitz is emphatically not concerned to affix a 'true' origin or meaning to the potency of the death symbol in modern Mexican culture. His analysis pivots neither on whether its derivation is Spanish or Indigenous, nor on its vulgarisation in the tourist and commercial spheres, nor whether it is in fact an invented tradition that has proved an obstacle to the development of democracy. Instead, taking as a starting point the casual familiarity with death that was adopted as a peculiarly Mexican sign by nation builders in the twentieth century, Lomnitz sets out to trace how by that time, 'a densely layered repertoire of death rituals and death vocabularies had already developed' (Lomnitz 2005: 58).

How then might this genealogical approach illuminate our understanding of the enduring currency of the photographic representation of Fortino Sámano? Here, again, it is instructive to start with Lomnitz's observations concerning killing and deathways during the revolution, in which he notes key consistencies with earlier practices that persisted alongside certain novelties. Of the innovations, the principal was 'the deployment of efficient mechanized killing, with its infrastructure of machine guns, modern artillery, and troop transportation by rail' (ibid.: 383). The emblematic event in this context was the defeat of Villa at the Battle of Celaya in 1915, in which Villa's outmoded cavalry was no match for Álvaro Obregón's use of modern techniques gleaned from the battlefields of Europe, and arms supplied by the United States. The mechanisation of killing, moreover, went hand in hand with the mechanisation of the representation of slaughter: 'Proof of death was now mass-mediated. So was proof of power and military strength' (ibid.: 385). Thus when, for example, Emiliano Zapata was assassinated on 10 April 1919 at the behest of Venustiano Carranza, his corpse was embalmed and photographed, and its image splashed over the front pages of the national press. In turn, so too were those of Carranza himself in 1920 and Villa in 1923.[13]

At the same time, however, certain things remained unchanged:

> The hanging of peasants and ragtag revolutionaries had already been used in earlier campaigns . . . Another staple of revolutionary violence, the firing squad had been deployed to great effect at independence, and much more recently in the wars of the Reforma and during the French invasion. Great figures had faced the firing squad including the liberal Melchor Ocampo and the conservatives Miramón and Mejía, not to mention Maximilian of Hapsburg himself. (ibid.: 383)

Lomnitz is certainly accurate in his assessment of the novelty of the mass mediation of both death and the representation of power and strength. As we have already noted in Chapter 3 on the Porfiriato, by the mid-1890s photography was increasingly put to use in the Mexican press, gradually coming to replace engraved or lithographed illustrations. By 1917, technology had progressed to the degree that the image of Fortino Sámano's execution on the morning of 2 March could be processed and reproduced in the national press the following day. However, when considering the visual representation of that staple of revolutionary violence, the firing squad, it is important to take the long view and to acknowledge its iconographic antecedents in the execution of Maximilian, and his loyal Mexican generals Miguel Miramón and Tomás Mejía. For the death of Maximilian on the Cerro de las Campanas (Hill of Bells), Querétaro on 19 June 1867 not only provides a precursor in terms of the modus operandi, but also in the form of the photographic representation of the firing squad.

THE FRENCH INTERVENTION

In the company of his wife, Princess Charlotte of Belgium (or Carlota as she became known in her new domain), Archduke Ferdinand Maximilian of Habsburg disembarked in the port of Veracruz in May 1864 to lay claim to the restored Mexican throne. Several factors had propelled the European monarchs from the tranquillity of their palace at Miramar near Trieste across the Atlantic Ocean. Post-independent Mexico was in turmoil after the Wars of Reform, as Conservatives and Liberals vied for political dominance. No sooner had the liberal Juárez acceded to the presidency of the virtually bankrupt nation in June 1861, when the British, French and Spanish started to militate in the hope of recuperating the monies Mexico owed in loans totalling over 80 million pesos. Unable to meet the repayments, Juárez had no option but to declare a two-year moratorium on the foreign debt. Under the Tripartite Convention of London of 31 October 1861, the European creditors agreed to exert pressure on Mexico in order to secure repayment, and to this end a force of some 8,000 troops was sent to occupy the Atlantic coast of Mexico. But where the British and Spanish were interested in non-interventionist debt recovery, the French had other designs. Napoleon III, keen to emulate his uncle Napoleon I, was out to enhance his imperial standing with the acquisition of territory in the New World, to use the European nomenclature. The British and Spanish withdrew their troops from Veracruz; France meanwhile supplemented the 2,000 men already on Mexican soil with an additional force of 45,000 and marched on Puebla where, so they had been misinformed, they would be welcomed by the pro-Conservative inhabitants. Undeterred by their historic defeat on 5 May 1862 by a Mexican army under the command of Brigadier General Porfirio Díaz, Napoleon sent further reinforcements and the French finally entered Mexico City unopposed in June 1863.

Encouraged by Napoleon III in collusion with the Mexican Conservatives, Maximilian was persuaded to assume the emperorship on the condition that it had the consent of the people of Mexico. A hasty plebiscite was duly arranged, and Maximilian and Carlota as Emperor and Empress of Mexico entered the capital on 11 June 1864. While, as Erika Pani (2002: 9) notes, not the 'foolish political project' that traditional historiography has asserted, the restored empire was nonetheless doomed from the outset. A liberal at heart, Maximilian did not repeal the Reform Laws as expected and thereby failed to win the support he needed from among the Conservatives. At the same time, if he hoped to win over the

Liberals by incorporating the more moderate among them into his cabinet, he had miscalculated. The French army struggled to hold territory from the Liberals under the leadership of Juárez who had retreated north. To compound matters, at the conclusion of the Civil War, the United States, finally in a position to attend to the blatant infringement of the Monroe Doctrine, started to arm the Juaristas and apply pressure on Napoleon III. The latter, having urgent affairs with which to contend closer to home in the looming Franco-Prussian war with Otto von Bismarck, started the withdrawal of French troops in November 1866. Maximilian was left stranded. In the first instance, he considered abdication, but was dissuaded by Carlota, who returned to Europe to plead, in vain, with Napoleon for assistance. The Juaristas commenced their attack and Maximilian again contemplated abdication, but pride got the better of him and he decided to take one last stand. Forced into retreat in Querétaro, Maxmilian surrendered on 15 May 1867. In the face of pleas for clemency emanating from supporters in Europe and the United States, Juárez was not minded to be lenient and ordered Maximilian's execution forthwith.

The ill-fated reign of Maximilian and Carlota, which ended so dramatically in the former's execution, crystallised important shifts in photographic culture in Mexico that can be traced through the use of photography during the Porfiriato and into the revolution forty years later. As Arturo Aguilar Ochoa (1996: 22) observes, the arrival of the monarchs marked the onset of the commercialisation of the image of the political personality with national standing. In fact, even before they had set foot on Mexican shores, the Emperor and Empress had been preceded by their photographic image in the form of cartes-de-visite. Measuring 11.4 by 6.4 centimetres, cartes-de-visite had been patented by Disdéri in 1854 and functioned much in the same way as calling cards.[14] Unlike in Europe, where, for example, images of Queen Victoria and Napoleon III circulated with great popularity, such a tradition barely existed in Mexico prior to the French intervention, but quickly took off in a country in which the soon-to-be royal subjects – Liberals and Conservatives alike – were avid to know the illustrious and exotic monarchs in advance (ibid.: 33). As the date of their accession to the throne approached, commercial photographs of the royal couple became ever more formal and official, projecting an appropriate image of pomp and majesty (ibid.: 30). But the cartes-de-visite that circulated prior to the arrival of Maximilian and Carlota, creating an unprecedented political cult of celebrity, at once prefigured and were soon overshadowed by the morbid desire to see and know the Emperor at the moment of his death.

Maximilian's private secretary José Luis Blasio, himself incarcerated at the time, recorded the details of the spectacle afforded by his master's execution as told to him by members of the Emperor's retinue. Clad in black, and transported by carriage through the streets of Querétaro, the Emperor was watched by 'men and women in mourning, their handkerchiefs wet with tears, and smothering their sobs, [who] might be seen everywhere' (Blasio 1934: 179). Then, he continues,

Maximilian descended from his carriage and looking at the sky with eyes as clear, blue, and serene as it was, he exclaimed:

'I want to die on a beautiful day like this!'

[. . .]

[A]nd on the hill which constituted the scaffold only three figures remained – Maximilian in the center, Miramón at his right and Mejía at his left.

And facing them, a young officer and a squad of soldiers.

The emperor said a few words, expressing his wishes for the happiness of Mexico. Miramón also spoke. After some brief instants of sepulchral silence the command was heard, uttered by the officer in charge: 'Fire!' The air was rent by a deafening detonation. (Blasio 1934: 179–80)

There is, however, one error in detail regarding the line-up before the firing squad in Blasio's narration; Maximilian apparently did not stand in the centre flanked by his two loyal generals. Rather, on reaching the specially erected adobe wall before which they were to be executed, Maximilian ceded the central position to Miramón. As Blasio's translator and editor Robert Hammond Murray corrects his source in the notes accompanying the memoirs, Maximilian is reported to have said: '"A brave soldier should be honored even in his last hour. Permit me to give you the place of honor", and he made way for him. He then laid his hands on his breast and looked straight before him' (Blasio 1934: 227). And indeed, in the composite photograph (Figure 5.2) that was produced of this event, amalgamating the discrete images made of the various elements of the execution, Maximilian duly stands to the left of his generals.

To twenty-first century eyes, albeit those accustomed to the (it would appear, at the moment, rather more subtle) manipulations enabled by computer programs such as PhotoShop, this composite photograph is a strange-looking document indeed. Photography was banned at the actual scene of the execution; and even if it had been permitted, the speed of the event militated against its capture by the camera's lens. And yet, the very construction of the composite speaks of an intense desire to witness photographically the execution.[15] This collage was composed by cutting out and dividing into two groups a pre-existing image of the firing squad; these figures were then superimposed onto a photograph of the site of execution taken after the event, and pre-existing images of Maximilian, Mejía, Miramón were placed in their requisite positions in the foreground. The whole ensemble was then inscribed with a version of Maximilian's reported last words – 'Mexicans, may my blood be the last to be spilt and may it regenerate this unhappy country' (Aguilar Ochoa 1996: 54) – re-photographed, reproduced and circulated widely, if illicitly in the form of cartes-de-visite on both sides of the Atlantic.[16]

Even in death, however, the visual fascination surrounding Maximilian did not immediately abate. In an appendix to his memoir entitled 'The Disposition of

87

5.2 Adrien Cordiglia. *Commemorative picture of the Execution of the Emperor Maximilian*, 1867.

Maximilian's Body', Blasio (1934: 204) comments: 'Without mentioning details of too unpleasant a nature, the evidence is that the body was handled with a notable lack of elementary respect, or even decency.' In a nutshell, the corpse was to be transported to Mexico City and then, some months later, repatriated to Austria. But first, it was inexpertly embalmed in Querétaro, where 'Glass eyes of the color of Maximilian's could not be obtained. Robbing the face of a portion of its beard and the head of its hair, and changing the color of the eyes, had somewhat disfigured the remains.' (Blasio 1934: 204) Disfigured or not, the corpse, its coffin and the Emperor's last clothes – in short, the full regalia of death – all were photographed by François Aubert and went into circulation alongside the images of the firing squad and site of execution.[17] Furthermore, they were disseminated not only in Mexico, but also in Europe, especially France, where they arrived approximately one month after their production (Wilson-Bareau 1992: 38) and where they were famously and impatiently awaited by Édouard Manet as he refined his *Exécution de Maximilien* series (1867–1869).[18]

In each context, the meanings that accrued to the execution of Maximilian, particularly as they played out in the visual sphere, at once converged in important ways, and at the same time had radically opposed valences. Significantly, in France, while 'written comment was relatively free, the same was not true of visual imagery, where censorship remained very vigilant' (Wilson-Bareau 1992:

37). Manet's work related to the execution was duly banned from exhibition in the Paris Salon, which at the time was the premier venue for large-scale history painting. As John House (1992) has demonstrated, not only was its subject matter controversial; equally, in its portrayal of an impassive Maximilian before the firing squad and the summary brushwork, it was out of kilter with artistic conventions of the time, where history painting was meant to provide an unambiguous inter-pretation of past events through the lens of the present. Not so Manet's series: 'Its detachment and its open-endedness, a distinctively Parisian language of opposi-tion to Napoleon's empire, set up this image of Maximilian's fate, by a rough wall at Querétaro, as an icon of the perils of imperial and dynastic ambitions' (House 1992: 108). In its thoroughly modern representation of the execution, it depicted an event that shattered the international prestige of the nation and hastened the collapse of the Second Empire. In this way, it was a potent visual statement that enshrined subversive republican values. At the same time, however, in France and Europe more generally, the execution of Maximilian 'was greeted with uni-versal horror and condemnation' (Wilson-Bareau 1992: 38). The illicitly-circulated photographic images not only attested to France's incipient republicanism; these images of the event were also a potent visual confirmation of the barbarism of Mexico in the eyes of the 'civilised world'.

Meanwhile, in Mexico the repudiation of the foreign invasion, as in France, signalled the advent of republicanism. It was only after the totemic execution of Maximilian on the Cerro de las Campanas 'that Mexico earned its "right" to exist as a nation. Until that time, no strong central state had existed, and the country's sovereignty was severely limited' (Lomnitz 2001: 87). Thus, if the bullets that ended Maximilian's life induced the birth of the sovereign nation-state, then the necropolitics of sovereignty marked an intensely visual moment reminding us that 'every performance of state violence requires the complicity of onlookers' (Ibsen 2006: 222).[19] The composite photograph freezes a moment in time, or rather in this case, more accurately, photographs (in the plural) freeze several moments in time, condensing them, making them visible and thereby mean-ingful. In short, republican Mexico was symbolically reborn under the (photo-graphic) sign of death.

RELICS AND TEMPLATES

What, though, are we to make of these rather odd photographic relics that docu-ment the execution and how, moreover, might they serve as a form of template for the photographic representation of Fortino Sámano facing the firing squad – and, indeed, for related images of death made during the revolution some forty years later? By adopting a genealogical approach to the display of death, to paraphrase Lomnitz (2005: 58) we might say that by the time of that staple of revolutionary violence, the firing squad, had become an established practice, 'a densely layered [specifically photographic] repertoire of death rituals and death

5.3 François Aubert. *Maximilian's Shirt, 1866–1867.*

vocabularies had already developed'. Thus, on a straightforward level, we can locate the iconographic precursors that will become prevalent during the revolution in the circumstances surrounding the death of Maximilian and its representation. The photographing and display of the Emperor's clothes (Figure 5.3), for example, foreshadow parallel practices that occurred after the assassinations of Francisco I. Madero and Pino Suárez during the Decena Trágica in Mexico City in 1913 (Figure 5.4), or that of Carranza in 1920 (see Figure 7.2). The bullet-ridden

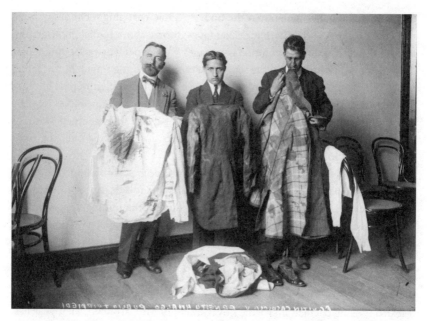

5.4 Agustín Víctor Casasola y otros periodistas sostienen las ropas de Francisco I. Madero y José Ma. Pino Suárez / Agustín Víctor Casasola and other journalists hold up the clothes of Francisco I. Madero and José Ma. Pino Suárez, 3 September 1914.

clothes in which the revolutionary protagonists fell were captured for posterity, where these images have a forensic-cum-trophy status; at the same time, as an indexical trace of the real, they partake of a relic-like quality.

Meanwhile, the composite image of the execution of Maximilian establishes the prototype for a grammar of visual design for the multiple firing-squad images that were made repetitively throughout the revolution. This is not to say that all execution images followed exactly the same format. But on the whole, they combined a varying number of constant elements: the victim, the wall, the firing squad and onlookers. If anything, the Sámano photograph is the exception to the rule, distilling the genre to the bare minimum of victim and wall. Indeed, its correct reading depends upon a familiarity with the existence of other firing-squad images, in which the wall itself is a potent topographic cue, photographically established in the wall erected especially for purpose on the Cerro de las Campanas in 1867. Without this iconographic and contextual knowledge, one could indeed say, following Lalucq and Nancy, that such is the insouciant appearance of Sámano that he could well be a beau awaiting his fiancée.

Some things of course had changed significantly since the execution of Maximilian. Technology, for a start, had moved on, and now it was not unknown for photographers to pay to guarantee a place in the front row of spectators and, at a signal from the head of the firing squad, it was now possible to press the shutter simultaneously with the command to fire and thereby capture the

moment as the bullet penetrated the body.[20] While changing technology facilitated the capture of what Barbie Zelizer (2005) terms 'about to die' photographs,
in both the 1867 and the revolutionary images we can detect overlapping scopic
and economic investments in the representation of the firing squad. In the earlier
image of Maximilian's execution, we can trace an incipient commercial interest,
whereby death circulated as a commodity in the composite cartes-de-visite. By
1917 the full value of the news as entertainment event had emerged, with, as
already noted, the corpses of assassinated leaders now splashed over the front
pages of the national press.

The meanings associated with, and circumstances surrounding the execution of Maximilian also resonate at the time of Sámano's death by firing squad,
even as they are lost in the subsequent iconisation of the photograph, when, as
we have seen, contextual accuracy is erased in successive appropriations. If we
return to the report of Sámano's death as announced in *El Demócrata* – accompanied, it will be recalled, by one of the first reproductions of the image – we
discover that it appeared alongside another news item. Under the headline 'What
the foreign press says', the Constitutionalist daily informed its readers that
'Mexico is being pacified under the government of Mr Carranza'. That year has,
of course, been construed as a turning point in the revolutionary struggle: the
Constitutionalists had almost, but not quite triumphed and the 1917 Constitution
had been approved on 5 February. That this is the case is evinced in the report
which deals with Mexico's image abroad and more specifically in the eyes of its
powerful neighbour to the north. Asserting that anti-Mexican propaganda emanating from the United States is couched in 'alarmist and calumnious' terms, the
report claims that reality is in fact otherwise: 'The truth is that Mexico is being
pacified. The Constitutionalist government exercises its authority in nearly all
the Republic and only in Chihuahua and Morelos are there rebel groups with
little force or prestige.'[21] After detailing the Carranza administration's attempts to
resolve the economic crisis resulting from years of civil war, it refutes in vigorous
terms reports in the Associated North American Press regarding the movements
of Francisco Villa, who together with 'those few men who follow him, have lost
their morale and if they do not yield to the government it is because they know
all too well that the government will not pardon their numerous crimes against
the life and property of supporters of Carranza and neutral people alike. Villa is a
political corpse and in no time at all will be buried'.[22]

Six years would pass before Villa literally became a 'political corpse'.
Assassinated while driving on the outskirts of Parral, Chihuahua, hit by nine
bullets and killed instantly, the photographic image of his semi-naked body,
unceremoniously laid out on a bed in the Hotel Hidalgo, Parral, would then circulate in the form of picture postcards (see Figure 7.3).[23] In the meantime, other
bodies would fulfil the same political function. Indeed, in this context, can it be
a coincidence that the report of Fortino Sámano's execution is juxtaposed with
that detailing the on-going process of pacification that was taking place in 1917?

Amid the chaos of the war years, and in light of Mexico's severe image problem that reverberated beyond the national borders in the United States, it became ever more politically expedient to project a counter-image of order and stability. As had been iconographically established with the photographic dissemination of the execution of Maximilian, what better way to visually mark that restored order than with the image of a firing squad? This scene, with its attendant roles and rituals, represents the ultimate political spectacle in the necropolitics of sovereignty. In short, the execution of Fortino Sámano on 2 March 1917, during which this armed robber was subordinated to the rule of law, reverberates beyond the circumstances of the crime itself in the wider visual political sphere. The execution by firing squad makes legible the guilty man's crime, the instants before his death are captured by the touch of the finger on the shutter, the camera endowing the moment with posthumous power in that strange iconic photographic tense, the future anterior.

TIME, HISTORY AND ICONICITY

It is to time, photography and additionally, materiality that I want to turn to work toward some summarising and concluding remarks, realigning once again the two execution photographs that have been at the centre of this chapter, in the process, revisiting one final instance of the 'French connection' that has been the thread woven throughout. To recap, I have been arguing two things regarding photo iconicity. On the one hand, iconicity is a retroactive phenomenon. Ideologies that are latent or do not exist at the time of the photograph's production determine which images become iconic and help us to shed light on why this might be. In the case of Fortino Sámano, his hypermasculine posturing before the camera lens meshes with post-revolutionary ideologies of Mexicanness, which in turn converge with the peculiarly Mexican privileging of death as national totem in this period.

Time and history, it should be added, as they inhere in the combination of this photograph's narrative and visual grammars are to be conceptualised in terms of an irreversible linearity. Fortino Sámano has committed a crime in the immediate past for which he will be executed moments after the making of the image. The camera's shutter is released and the firing squad's bullets will be discharged. He is dead and he is going to die. This, as Mary Ann Doane (2002: 30) has noted, is also the temporality of the photographic apparatus itself: 'linear, irreversible, "mechanical"'. Linearity, we should note, albeit in shorthand form here, also characterises the time of the modernising post-revolutionary nation. There is, as Lomnitz (2005: 35) observes, more than a little irony to the fact that death became a national totem at this historical juncture. This is because '[n]ation-states as cultural constructs are supposed to be forward-looking, a promised land in which collective dreams can be achieved. The nation is always a project, always in the process of becoming'. In this respect, Mexico was no exception. As we saw in the introduction, the groups that emerged triumphant post-1917 seized the levers of power and set Mexico on a course toward economic, social and cultural modernisation. The coordinates were fixed on progress and the future to the degree that Lomnitz (2005: 35) muses: 'How could any nation choose Death itself for its sign? The very idea seems bizarre.'

On the other hand, taking my cue from Lomnitz's genealogical approach to death and the idea of Mexico, I have also argued that we must take the long view and understand iconicity as a retrospective category. Images not only accrue surplus value in relation to ideologies that post-date them, but also in relation to ideologies and, importantly, iconographies that precede them. In terms of specifically photographic precursors, the French invasion and execution of Maximilian represent a particularly rich interpretive seam for a variety of reasons that bear reiteration and extension here. During the revolution, the caudillos had a keen eye to their photographic representation, hiring photographers to follow their campaigns, taking their cue from the example set by Porfirio Díaz. In turn, the antecedents of his larger-than-life image are to be located in the cartes-de-visite images of Maximilian and Carlota that circulated even prior to their arrival in the New World. And it was in the execution of Maximilian and more specifically the reconstruction of this momentous event in the form of the composite that the visual grammar for the multiple firing-squad images of the revolution was established.

The transition from cartes-de-visite of Maximilian and Carlota, as initiating a photographic cult of celebrity, to those of the execution of the emperor marks an important moment in the development of the medium, particularly with regard to the uses to which it was put and the demands made upon it at this historical juncture. In a fascinating essay on photography, narrative and the Paris Commune of 1871, Jeannene Przyblyski (1995: 257–8) states: 'In general these photographs speak to the growing tendency throughout the 1860s and 1870s to turn the camera upon contemporary events, as well as to the popular desire that the camera, cumbersome and slow as it was, be there as significant happenings were occurring.' And be there it was: in the Crimean War in 1854–1855; during Garibaldi's campaign for Italian unification in 1860; and the American Civil War in 1861–1865 (ibid.: 274). In fact, taking the Mexican case into consideration, we can extend this temporal window to note that the camera had already made the transition from studio to the streets, and was present as historical witness to record the Mexican-American war of 1848. Przyblyski's essay, with, in the current context, its resonant French focus, not only provides insights into this important transitional moment in the history of the medium. Significantly, it also discusses a number of images by Eugène Appert that went by the title of *Crimes de la Commune* and appeared in a variety of formats – portfolios, cartes-de-visite and postcards. Significantly, the series included a firing-squad image *Execution of Generals Clément-Thomas and Lecomte*. This was not, moreover, just any photograph; it was also a composite.[24]

Writing of images in this series, which were used as visual evidence for consumption by the middle classes, keen to justify the brutal suppression of the Commune, Przyblyski (ibid.: 261) argues: 'Combinations of the fake and the real, the prop-like and the relic-like, the layered accumulation of fairy-tale illusion and the tissue-thin veneer of documentary truth . . ., Appert's composites were . . . hybridized objects complex in their assembling of photographic cues and contrary in the way they complicated the legibility of a photographic point of view.' To note their fictional, fragmentary status is not, however, synonymous with calling into question their evidential power. Rather, as Przyblyski persuasively establishes, to nineteenth-century viewers such photomontages, with their blend of reality and artifice, combined to produce a 'true-to-life' representation of historical events that were consonant with visual registers of the time. In short, enmeshed in wider socio-historical systems of representation, they drew on codes and conventions that were readily legible to their contemporary viewers and which coalesced discursively to constitute documents perceived as bearing the mark of authenticity to those viewers. They might look unreal or 'fake' to twenty-first-century eyes, but in the historical context of mid-nineteenth-century photographic discourses, such categories are anachronistic.

Przyblyski's analysis of nineteenth-century reality effects provides useful insights for this discussion of Mexican-produced firing-squad images for a number of reasons and at the same time, requires further elaboration. Let us imaginatively place the two images – of Fortino Sámano and the Execution of Maximilian – together side-by-side and read the former through the latter, rehearsing Przyblyski's (271) statement that 'the technique of the composite fairly does away with a fixed point of view, vacating the monocular authority of photographic vision for a potentially contradictory montage of fragments and cuts that disperses points of view across the surface of the photograph'. To put this otherwise, the composite image of Maximilian's execution reminds us of the materiality of this individual photograph and indeed of *all* photographs.[25] To read the materiality of the composite photographic image is also, so to speak, to see its different temporal layers, and in so doing, to perceive time as splintered, fractured, blown-apart. By contrast with the composite of Maximilian, the image of Fortino Sámano conforms more closely to contemporary notions of the integrity of the photographic surface and, in turn, complies with current notions of the reality effect. Taken at face value, photographs such as this one become easily aligned with, indeed supporting documents within, teleological narratives of national progress. To read it through the Maximilian composite, however, is to recognise that it is a no less fragmentary or relic-like entity. Approached in this way, this iconic photograph and by extension photographs more generally, far from being low-powered, anecdotal history – to return to Lévi-Strauss – become intelligible in their own right. Understood as material artefacts that are bound up with questions of temporality – where time is fractured, splintered – photographs have the power to tell another kind of history that is at odds with the commemorative practices of the state and its linear, forward march.

NOTES

1 See Cartier-Bresson's *Mexican Notebooks* (1995) for a selection of photographs made while he was in Mexico on these two visits. Significantly, the introduction by Mexican novelist Carlos Fuentes opens with a clear reference to the Fortino Sámano photograph: 'Wounds scar the whole landscape of Mexico . . . But in front of the wall, a man with a cigar between his teeth, hat firmly on his head, collarless shirt, hands tucked into his belt, stares at the firing squad and grins from ear to ear. Go fuck your mother.' (Cartier-Bresson 1995: 5) Equally noteworthy, the collection features a photograph, made in 1934, of an execution wall in front of which it would appear are posed life-size model soldiers, while the figure of a man, his back to us, looks on. Cartier-Bresson's 'image of the century' can be found on the Portfolios website dedicated to popular photography, alongside selections by Helmut Newton, Sebastião Salgado, among others: www.photo.fr/portfolios/siecle/index.html (accessed 20 April 2007).

2 Monsiváis (1980) must also be referring to the image of Sámano when he describes 'a man facing the firing squad with a look of premeditated contempt or refined irony'.

3 The exhibition ran between 16 June and 28 July 1985 at the Museum of Modern Art, Oxford. The exhibition catalogue featured the full image and a cropped version, focusing on Sámano's insouciant facial expression as a frontispiece.

4 'Fue Fusilado, Ayer, el Capitán Sámano en el Campo de Aviación de S. Lázaro'/'Aunque quiso Ordenar su Ejecución, no se le Permitió que lo hiciera, y Murió con Extraordinaria Sangre Fría'. *El Demócrata*, 3 March 1917, p. 7. The description of the execution that follows is based on a loose translation of the same report.

5 Juan Manuel Casasola's *Pueblo en armas* (1977) reproduces two images of the Sámano execution. The first, a cropped version of the photograph that is the subject of this chapter, appears in a two-page spread alongside another of two dead peasants who have been hanged from a tree. The two images share the same caption 'Así mueren los machos'/'this is how machos die'. A fuller execution scene, captioned 'Ejecución del Cap. Fortino Sámano' is then reproduced across the following two pages. It features Sámano at the wall to the left, his hat in hand and a neckerchief at his chest, and to the right, the firing squad with rifles poised, the head of the firing squad with his sword raised, about to give the order to fire; behind them we find a crowd of spectators. Symptomatically, the images are not dated. Monsiváis (1977) provides an introductory essay to the volume.

6 As noted above, on the verso of the Lalucq and Nancy volume the photograph is attributed to Víctor Agustín Casasola. While the photograph belongs to the Casasola Archive, as we have seen, this provenance in no way guarantees its author as Casasola himself.

7 In an allusion to *The Labyrinth of Solitude*, Alan Knight (1992: 99) neatly captures the problematic status of Paz's text in the opening lines of his essay 'The Peculiarities of Mexican History' when he states: 'This is a piece of comparative history, not an exercise in folkloric whimsy. It does not attempt to probe the secrets of *lo mexicano*, *la mexicanidad*, or any of the other quasi metaphysical concepts which litter the field of Mexican cultural history.' For historicised, textual analysis of Paz's essay, see Bell (1992) and Stanton (2001 and 2008).

8 Mbembe's (2003: 11) term 'necropolitics' turns on the notion that 'the ultimate expression of sovereignty resides, to a large degree, in the power and the capacity to dictate who may live and who must die. Hence to kill or to allow to live constitute the limits of sovereignty, its fundamental attributes'. Thanks to Gillian Rose for bringing Mbembe's work to my attention in a stimulating seminar presentation to Durham's Centre for Advanced Photography Studies in February 2007.

9 For analysis of the relationship between photography and death, see also Cadava (1997) and Mulvey (2006).

10 James Elkins (2005: 938) observes that the *punctum* has 'arguably been one of the two most often misused terms in recent photography theory'. I am inclined to agree and certainly see no point in working with the concept here. The notion of future anteriority is, however, another matter.

11 Hariman and Lucaites (2002: 384) discuss a possible exception to this in the case of the photograph of the three firefighters raising the US flag captured amid the rubble of the World Trade Center in the aftermath of the attacks of 9/11, with its echoes of the 'Iwo Jima' image made in 1945. 'What we find noteworthy is that this is the first instance of an iconic photograph being created out of the template of a predecessor.' They then cite its photographer, Thomas E. Franklin, who states: 'As soon as I shot it, I realized the similarity to the famous image of Marines raising the flag at Iwo Jima.'

12 For example, in his analysis of Monsiváis's critique of the death cult that has been an obstacle to the proper development of democracy in Mexico, Lomnitz correctly picks up on his references to *corridos* – it is a *corrido*, incidentally, that is the source of the wonderful Spanish title of Monsiváis's essay 'Mira muerte no seas inhumana'/'Look death don't be so inhumane'. He does not, however, spot the reference to the photographic representation of the revolutionary facing the firing squad (Monsiváis 1987: 13), which is striking given that photography is an important strand in Monsiváis's work on popular culture.

13 See for example *Excelsior*, 12 April 1919 and *El Universal*, 25 May 1920 for graphically illustrated reports of the assassinations of Zapata, Carranza and Villa respectively.

14 For a useful glossary of photographic terms see Baldwin (1991); Marien (2002: 84–5) provides a useful brief description; see McCauley (1985) for a detailed account.

15 The image is discussed by Wilson-Bareau (1992); Aguilar Ochoa (1996); and Lerner (2001/02).

16 'Mexicanos, que mi sangre sea la última que se derrame y que ella regenere este desgraciado pays [*sic*]'. Aguilar Ochoa (1996: 54) notes that those words inscribed on the composite photograph are more likely apocryphal and that the emperor's servant Tüdös's version is probably more accurate: 'Perdono a todos y pido a todos que me perdonen. Ruego que mi sangre, que tanto será derramada, se derrame por el bien de este país. ¡Viva México! ¡Viva la independencia!'/'I pardon everyone and ask everyone to forgive me. I pray that my blood that is to be spilt, is spilt for the good of this country. Long live Mexico! Long live independence!'

17 François Aubert (1829–1906) was a French photographer resident in Mexico between 1864 and 1867 who set up as a studio photographer and documented the imperial society established by his compatriots. He was present at Querétaro during the siege and execution. For more on Aubert in Mexico, see the special issue of *Alquimia*, guest-edited by Aguilar Ochoa (2004).

18 Manet produced three large paintings, an oil sketch and a lithograph of the execution. The three completed paintings of the execution are typically identified in art historical texts by their current locations: Boston Museum of Fine Arts; Ny Carlsberg Glypotek, Copenhagen; Städtische Kunsthalle, Mannheim. The National Gallery, London holds the fragmented oil sketch. For a discussion of this series, see Wilson-Bareau (1992) and Ibsen (2006); on the relationship between the photographs and paintings see Scharf (1968). For an excellent digital resource related to the exhibition 'Manet and the Execution of Maximilian', hosted by the Museum of Modern Art (5 November 2006–29 January 2007), see the website listed in the Bibliography under 'Internet Resources'. Although it is beyond the scope of this chapter, it would be interesting to follow through the ramifications of the parallel trajectories of Manet's *Exécution* series in France, where its politically risqué subject matter meant that it was debarred from appearing in the Salon, and the composite image of Maximilian in Mexico, who is similarly occluded from the sphere of visual representation to be replaced by a more 'Mexican' line-up of national heroes in the domain of history painting. On nineteenth-century Mexican painting, see Widdifield (1996); for a fascinating discussion of a lost history painting by Manuel Ocaranza relating to the pleas for clemency on behalf of Maximilian, see Acevedo (2001).

19 On the relationship between the body, power and punishment, see Foucault (1977).

20 Olivier Debroise (2001: 181) cites the case of Walter Horne who 'photographed the executions of Francisco Rojas, Juan Aguilar, and José Moreno by Mexican forces in Chihuahua on January 15, 1915. To capture these images . . . Horne had to give a substantial bribe to guarantee his place in the first row: at a signal from the head of the firing squad, Horne took his own shot'.

21 'La verdad es que México está pacificándose. El gobierno constitucionalista ejerce su autoridad en casi toda la República, y apenas sí en Chihuahua y en Morelos hay partidas rebeldes, con poca fuerza y mucho desprestigio'. *El Demócrata*, 3 March 1917, p. 7.

22 'los pocos que lo acompañan, han perdido la moral y si no se someten al Gobierno, es que saben demasiado que éste no los perdonará los numerosos delitos que han consumado contra la vida y la propiedad de carrancistas y neutrales. Villa es un cadáver político, y poco falta para que se le dé sepultura.' *El Demócrata*, 3 March 1917, p. 7.

23 See Katz (1998) on the 'life and times' of Pancho Villa. See the on-line collection of postcards held by the Universidad Autónoma de Ciudad Juárez, URL listed under Internet Resources.

24 A selection of images of the Commune, including those by Appert, can be accessed at 'Luminous-Lint: for collectors and connoisseurs of photography', where they are denominated 'fake' photographs: www.luminous-lint.com/__sw.php?action=ACT_SING_TH&pi=237. See Wilson (2007) on Paris and the Commune.

25 See the essays in Edwards and Hart (2004) on the materiality of photographic images.

6

Seeing women

On 28 April 1912, *El Diario* devoted a full-page spread to a poem by Julio Sesto, dedicated to the female participants in the revolutionary struggle, known as the *soldaderas*:

Por los caminos de la campaña;	Along the paths of the campaign;
por la llanura, por la montaña,	Across the plains, across the mountains
por los desiertos secos y ariscos,	Through the dry and arid deserts,
por las arenas y por los riscos	Through the sands and across the crags
que ardiendo al fuego del sol están;	Burning in the heat of the sun;
marchan constantes, marchan ligeras,	They march constantly, they march lightly,
marchan jadeando las soldaderas	The *soldaderas* march gasping
como una sombra, tras de su "Juan".	Like a shadow, behind their 'Juan'. . . . .

Running to fifteen florid verses, Sesto's poem invokes the *soldaderas*' motivation for joining the fray that is political and personal in equal measure – 'They go to war for patriotism and love'. The poet details their activities while on the move, providing a snapshot of the wide-ranging roles and functions that are encapsulated in the capacious term *soldadera*, which by the time of the 1910 revolution had come to designate a variety of roles played by women, ranging from camp followers to front-line combatants. In Sesto's poem, these include traditionally feminine, caring tasks – 'those children will be brave, because they have suckled breasts hot through contact with a gun cartridge'; tending to the wounded and dying – 'they see those who fall in battle, they staunch blood, heal wounds and console them in their moans'; to active service: 'they load guns, they roll canons'.[1] Finally, in the penultimate verse, the poet declares:

¡Oh soldaderas tan desdeñadas,	Oh, *soldaderas*, so scorned,
tan escondidas, tan olvidadas. . . .;	So hidden, so forgotten. . . .;
tan solas mueren en sus afanes	So alone they die in their eagerness
por ir siguiendo los pobres "Juanes". . . .;	To follow the poor 'Juans'. . .

For all that it is laboured, Sesto's 1912 homage, with its recognition that the *soldaderas* were being erased from the narrative of the revolution even before

6.1 Soldaderas en el estribo de un vagón en Buenavista/Soldaderas at the door of a train in Buenavista station, 1912.

it had been written, while certainly not penned in the name of a proto-feminist project, nevertheless proves prescient. Writing in the introduction to the co-edited volume *Sex in Revolution*, Mary Kay Vaughan (2006: 23) states 'Skeptics (until recently the majority of Mexican historians) derided the act of exploring Mexican women's history as one of feminine romantic wilfulness: the search for small groups of insignificant actors in obscure places.'[2]

Dominant historiography notwithstanding, women did not hide out in obscure places during the revolution, a fact that is amply demonstrated in the photographic record of the conflict. Indeed, by coincidence, barely three weeks prior to the publication of Sesto's poem, on 8 April 1912, the pro-Madero newspaper *Nueva Era* published what was to become one of the most reproduced images in the photographic iconography of the revolution (Figure 6.1). Under the tagline 'Defenderé a mi Juan' (I will defend my Juan), it precisely featured those scorned, hidden and forgotten figures: the *soldaderas*. Showing eight women poised in the open carriage of a train, this image – alongside *Villa en la silla presidencial* – has to be a strong contender for the role of *the* most famous photograph of those produced during the revolution. Frequently cropped to focus on the *soldadera* in the left-hand side of the frame, like *Villa en la silla*, this image too has arguably come to stand for the struggle as a whole event in the contemporary imagination, as evinced, for example, by its appearance on the cover of the Spanish translations of Jean Meyer's *La Révolution mexicaine* (2004) and Thomas Benjamin's *La Revolución: Mexico's Great Revolution as Memory, Myth, and History* (2003).[3] Yet, as Miguel Ángel Morales (2006: 68) points out: 'Amongst the many decontextualised press photographs, none is as famous and so erroneously attributed as that which, towards 1960 was first denominated *La Soldadera* and, later, in 1987, *La Adelita*.'[4]

In a fine piece of detective work, Morales traces some of the steps in the iconic photograph's travels and the attendant definitional dilemmas that these throw up: from its first publication in *Nueva Era*, through its reappearance in 1960 in the second volume of the Casasolas' *Historia gráfica de la revolución mexicana*, to its 1987 publication in *Historia gráfica de México siglo XX*, compiled by Enrique Florescano. He notes how, at each stage, seemingly inconsequential caption changes, often amounting to no more than a few words, contribute to the process of mythification and obfuscation to which the photograph has been subjected.[5] Thus, in the 1960 Casasola volume, the cropped image appears under the caption 'All Mexico saw that *soldadera* cross from border to border'; while in Florescano's text, the central female subject and, with her, the image itself, acquire a new sobriquet – 'Soldadera Adelita', and the photograph is described as having been 'taken by Agustín V. Casasola in 1910, it quickly became one of the emblems of the revolution, like the famous, almost homonymous song, 'La Adelita' (Morales 2006: 72).[6] Meanwhile, observes Morales (ibid.), in 2000 the photograph came under the scrutiny of John Mraz, who not only contested its authorship – it could, the graphic historian asserted, have been taken by any one of a number of photographers who happened to have been present at the scene – but also suggested that, travelling inside the train and not on its roof, La Adelita was unlikely to have been a combatant; rather, she was most probably a prostitute.

Morales, however, puts paid to the speculation. Locating the image within the pages of *Nueva Era* allows the Mexican researcher to establish that it was taken during the brief presidency of Francisco I. Madero and depicts the departure of a military advance, en route to Chihuahua, where the unit would do battle with General Pascual Orozco, who had risen up against the President some weeks earlier (Morales 2006: 72). Furthermore, the woman represented in the image was one of the cooks on the train: 'It's not for nothing', he points out, 'that her companions are carrying baskets, surely containing foodstuffs.' (ibid.)[7]

Although mitigated by the rise of women's and gender studies over the last three decades of the twentieth century, illuminating and accounting for female agency in the revolution remains a methodologically challenging task. This is thrown into sharp relief when we attempt to explore the place of women in the photographic record of the conflict. True, this record features a significant repertoire of images that depict women engaged in a range of activities – from supportive roles to active service – where women are certainly there to be seen. But on closer scrutiny, for all that photographic images possess a powerful combination of deictic and indexical qualities – 'look: women were there; they were even active participants; and these photographs prove that they were present!'— *really*

101

seeing women in the photographic record of the revolution is far from straight-forward. Indeed Morales's investigation – while articulated from within a socio-historical and photographic, rather than feminist, framework – exemplifies one dimension of the problematic associated with seeing women in the revolution. Locating the original source of publication certainly allows him to construct a more historically accurate narrative for the image and also attribute authorship to the photograph; but it does not necessarily solve the problem of inserting women as agents into that narrative. For as Morales (2006: 72) puts it: 'On Saturday 6 April two lives crossed in Buenavista train station: that of the presumed cook for the Huertista troops and the photographer of *Nueva Era*. Neither the name nor the military trajectory of that humble woman are known. The photographer's name [Jerónimo Hernández] is.'[8] To name the photographer further allows Morales to offer a sketch of Hernández's professional activities, which become the main focus of his essay, with male agency eclipsing female agency.

The problems associated with the insertion of women into a historical narra-tive anchored in the photographic image are further underlined in the collection of images of women combatants and camp-followers in the revolution compiled by Elena Poniatowska, one of Mexico's foremost literary figures and champions of women's rights. Well known, particularly for the testimonial novel *Hasta no verte Jésus mío* (1969), based on the experiences of Josefina Bórquez in the revolution and its aftermath, in 1999 Poniatowska collaborated on the project *Las soldaderas*, which comprises a selection of photographs related to women partici-pants in the revolution, preceded by an introduction. In it, Poniatowska (1999: 14) celebrates the female participants in the struggle, claiming that without the *soldaderas*, 'there is no Mexican Revolution: they kept it alive and fecund, like the earth. They were sent on ahead to collect firewood and to start the fires, and they fed the revolution throughout the war years. Without the *soldaderas*, the men taken by levy would have deserted.[9]

On one level, Poniatowska is undoubtedly right in her assertion that without these women, who have been excluded from the masculinist historiography of the revolution, there can be no revolution as we know it. And, to be sure, the fifty-two images of feisty women warriors that follow her celebratory introduc-tion attest precisely to the role of the *soldaderas* as protagonists of history. With the iconic Soldadera/Adelita photograph on the front cover, the images that comprise the volume appear to proclaim, 'Look! Women were there', and not only in domestic, sexual, and supportive roles. 'Look!' they cry, 'these women also carried guns and even knew how to use them'. There are, however, prob-lems associated with reading such images as evidence of women's participation in the revolution: problems which turn, in part, precisely on their status as pho-tographic images. In a nutshell, put to work in the name of a quasi-feminist effort to celebrate the woman warrior, the 'pure deictic language' (Barthes 1983: 5) of the photographic image ultimately does this feminist project a disservice. This is because the antiphonic 'look, see, here women are' ends up producing nothing more than the well-worn 'power of women' topos. Viewed from a celebratory feminist optic as a form of reversal – 'look, women are powerful too!' – these photographic images of feisty women, 'inevitably signify the mechanism of reversal itself, constituting themselves as aberrations whose acknowledgement simply reinforces the dominant system of aligning sexual difference with a subject/ object dichotomy' (Doane 1982: 77).

Simply to reinsert women into the thrust of the historiography of the Mexican revolution as it has been conventionally configured, however, is to neglect to tackle the conflicts and tensions that relate to issues of sexual difference that inhere within it. Or as art historian Griselda Pollock puts it:

> Never simply a matter of shifting existing methods and theories to other subjects: women, feminist cultural studies and histories disturb the very frameworks that have been established for cultural analysis. Sexual difference, what it means, how it is produced, lived, negotiated, how it shapes and is shaped by cultural practices, is . . . the compelling perplexity for an academic adventure that demands realignments of both the forms and the contents of knowledge. (Pollock 1999: 75)

Morales's photo-historical work and Poniatowska's celebratory approach ultimately bring us only so far in our quest to see to women participants in the revolution because, to different degrees, they are blind to the workings of sexual difference in the production, dissemination and reception of photographic images. If we are to embark on the adventure of disturbing the established frameworks for cultural analysis, we must find a more sophisticated way of reading the relationship between sexual difference and its attendant historical and photographic narratives.

In the opening to *Family Frames*, Marianne Hirsch (1997: 1) argues that 'multiple looks circulate in the photograph's production, reading, and description'. Later, she states that 'between the viewer and the recorded object, the viewer encounters, and/or projects, a screen made up of dominant mythologies and preconceptions that shapes the representation' (ibid.: 7). Although Hirsch is concerned with private, family photographs, her account is nevertheless suggestive in the present context – namely, an examination of the work of sexual difference at play in public, historical documents – for it alerts us to photography's status as a highly mediated cultural product, whose meanings are framed by the complex discourses that operate in the production and reception of photographic images. In what remains of this chapter, I pursue two case studies of well-known revolutionary photographs, in which I focus precisely on the multiple looks that circulate in the photographs' production, dissemination and reception. The first explores the series of images that tend to go by the common title *Zapatistas en Sanborns* (Figure 6.2) and returns us to the moment in December 1914, when Zapatista troops briefly entered Mexico City, when the capital became the stage for the historic encounter between Emiliano Zapata and Pancho Villa. The second is a lesser known photograph of María Zavala (Figure 6.5) Made during the De la Huerta uprising of 1923/24, it takes us beyond the conventional 'end-date' of the revolution, and back to the idea of death that we have already started to explore in relation to the image of Fortino Sámano. This time, however, the focus of analysis is death as it is associated with femininity. The photographs under discussion here foreground female subjects in ways in which attention to the drama of looking provides us with clues to help us see – not more clearly or transparently, but certainly more critically – women in the photographic record of the revolution.

ZAPATISTAS EN SANBORNS

During the occupation of Mexico City in December 1914 by the troops of Villa and Zapata, the capital became a backdrop for a number of photo opportunities that endured beyond the troops' retreat to their home territories in the Republic's northern and southern provinces. The most famous photograph of these, as we saw in chapter four, is arguably *Villa en la silla presidencial*. But the brief encounter marking the peak of the 'social curve' of the conflict, that moment 'when the peasantry was actually able to capture the social life of the whole nation' (Williams 2005: 101), produced a number of images that have persisted in the national imagination. Indeed, similar in iconic impact to *Villa en la silla presidencial* are those photographs taken during the visit by Zapatista troops to the establishment known as Sanborns, at the time a North-American owned soda fountain cum drugstore, then (and now) a site of bourgeois sociability par excellence.[10]

There are a number of different shots of this event, all of which tend to go by the title *Zapatistas en Sanborns*; two in particular have continued to circulate widely. In the first (Figure 6.2), two seated male figures appear in half-body close up, their elbows resting on a bar containing delicate-looking cups and plates containing pastries. With cartridge belts slung across his chest, the Zapatista to the right of the frame is about to sip from a cup that is poised just below his lips. Meanwhile, his companion-in-arms sports a large, wide-brimmed sombrero, below which his narrow, slit-like eyes directly confront the camera lens, giving him a sinister, challenging air. Has he been blinded by the brightness of a magnesium flash, or is there something more at stake in this man's threatening regard? At this stage in the argument, we should simply note the apparently confrontational burden of this gaze; its implications will become clearer later in this section. Meanwhile, in the second version (Figure 6.3), the photographer is positioned further from the bar at an oblique angle, affording the viewer sight of its length, along which are lined more troops, their guns propped against it. On the other side of the bar are two waitresses, who occupy the central foreground of the image, captured in the act of serving their incongruous new clients, whose very incongruity in this hub of bourgeois sociability renders them photogenic.[11]

We will return below in greater detail to the bar and its role in determining the gendered dynamics of looking in both photographs. First, however, we should

6.2 Jefes zapatistas toman sus alimentos en el restaurante Sanborns/Zapatista leaders eat in Sanborns restaurant, 1914.

6.3 Meseras de Sanborns atendiendo a zapatistas/Sanborns waitresses serving Zapatistas, 1914.

observe that these images, depicting Zapatistas partaking of light refreshment in Sanborns, have not passed without comment in the historical literature devoted to the revolution. In his political biography of Zapata, Samuel Brunk (1995: 135), in an implicit reference to the photographs, notes that, despite fears to the contrary: 'All over the city people were soon commenting about how much better behaved the Zapatistas were than their Carrancista counterparts – rather than simply taking food, they politely begged it. The Zapatistas had much to learn. They became acquainted with the Mexican institution known as Sanborn's, a restaurant where they paid their tabs, at least at first.' Meanwhile, more explicitly, in an essay on photography in Mexico that focuses on the meanings the images acquired in the aftermath of the conflict, Carlos Monsiváis states:

> Subsequent readings of these photographs were based, never explicitly, on the fascination with the unknown and the domestication of radical impulses. *Los zapatistas en Sanborns*: primitivism turns up in a neuralgic site of Porfirian values, affording protective comparisons with the elegant 'científicos' of the fallen regime. Is it not true that any contrast leads to moving paradoxes? These soldiers enter a sacred zone in order to commit a profanation and then disappear without recourse. (Monsiváis 1981, unnumbered pages)[12]

Monsiváis does not clarify which of the images in the series he is alluding to – whether that including the waitresses, or the Zapatistas alone; nor does he specify who the 'reading subject' invoked might be. Nevertheless, his remarks are worthy of further comment, where the referential ambiguity will become a productive element in the process of laying bare the gendered ideological formations that are played out in the reception of the Sanborns photographs in the post-revolutionary period.

The sanctioned reading of all versions of *Zapatistas en Sanborns* evoked by Monsiváis suggests that the images document the transgressive, but temporary, irruption of a racial and social Other into the 'civilised' and sacred space of the bourgeois legitimate order, represented by Sanborns and its regular clientele, the *científicos*. In the post-revolutionary period, the meanings associated with such a scene of the world-turned-upside-down are profoundly ambivalent, and parallels can again be drawn with those associated with *Villa en la silla*. On the one hand, insofar as these photographs project an image of the revolution as a moment of rupture to the established social and racial order, they are consonant with and lend legitimacy to the hegemonic project of revolutionary nationalism. On the other, as we saw in Chapter 4, they are an anxiety-arousing reminder of what might have been, had the conservative revolutionaries not won out. At the end of a decade of upheaval, in a country that was 'left relatively unchanged with respect to basic socioeconomic structures, but politically revolutionized' (Knight 2007: 154), the sight of Zapatistas in Sanborns would have looked more or less the same to eyes of the post-revolutionary elite as it would have to their Porfirian predecessors: an alarming sight, not least because the dark-skinned 'barbarous hordes' (Brunk 1995: 135) now occupy their place as consumers on the other side of the bar.

The full implications of the sanctioned reading of the Sanborns series invoked by Monsiváis can, however, only be understood when questions of sexual difference are brought into play. In Figure 6.3, the caption clearly signals that the Zapatistas are the centre of interest in the image; it is, however, the first waitress with the notepad tied to her apron who occupies the centre of the image and who sets the tone for the viewer of the photograph. Her solemn gaze structures the viewer's, directing that gaze off toward the right of centre, where the Zapatistas are seated along the other side of the bar. In this way, the image establishes an off-centre centre. Indeed, the two men who meet our gaze in the right-hand corner are argu-ably the real centre of the photograph; they are the focus of the photographer's interest, as is corroborated in Figure 6.2, in addition to the caption itself. The technique of the off-centre centre is an effective means of conveying a sense of the marginalisation, or out-of-place status of the Zapatistas in this site of elite urban power, and also the heart of the nation.[13] However, this decentring effect functions not only at the level of content; it is also played out in the looking relations that are set up within the photographic frame and, significantly, beyond it. This is because the logic of the bar is structured according to gendered looking relations.

To explore these issues further, it is instructive to bring the *Zapatistas en Sanborns* series into dialogue with another image with a bar its centre, namely the classic painting by Édouard Manet, *A Bar at the Folies-Bergère* (1881–82) (Figure 6.4). Manet's painting, an icon in its own right, has become a critical trope in con-temporary art-historical debates related to modernity and attendant questions of class, gender, power and vision, particularly in Griselda Pollock's pioneering feminist work produced in the late 1980s and 1990s (Pollock 1988; 1995). In a playful essay, partly written in an epistolary style, the feminist art historian asks one of her addressees, 'a famous [male] professor':

> Given all that has been said about this painting, all the significance it has acquired, what can I say about it? As I stand in front of The Bar and the discursive field to which it is central, where can I be? What I am asking about are the possibilities for a female spectator, and further for a **feminist** relation to this work and the art historical practices which have defined its significance in all the existing histories of modernism? (Pollock 1995: 3, formatting in the original)

In brief, Manet's *The Bar* poses a dilemma for the female spectator who wishes to establish a feminist relation to the painting – and the art-historical practices and discourses that traverse it – because it unequivocally establishes a confluence between the male client who is reflected in the mirror behind the bar (figured in his top hat in the extreme right-hand corner of the painting) and the viewer of this painting. This position and concomitantly that of the viewer is encoded as the overlapping site of social and sexual power and implicitly as masculine. In this reading, narratives of class and gender coincide in the body of the barmaid who is the

6.4 Édouard Manet, *A Bar at the Folies-Bergère*, 1882.

monumental figurative centre of the painting. She provides the invitation to the presumed or, what should be called, the preferred spectator. A narrative reading of the
painting defines her as a barmaid attending to a customer. 'What do you want?', she
asks, which read metaphorically, clearly means 'What do you desire?' (Pollock 1995: 6)

Occupying the centre of the image, the barmaid's subjectivity remains an
enigma; she is simply a commodity and cipher for masculine desire. By bringing feminist scholarship to bear on *The Bar*, Pollock starts to elaborate a 'view
from elsewhere' in relation to the gendered subject positions that are central to
this seminal painting, where feminism provides *'a language in which to critique the
image and to insist upon the sexual differentiation of spectatorship'* (1995: 10, italics in
original). How, though, might Pollock's reflections on Manet's painting inflect
our understanding of the gender and class dynamics of the bar of Sanborns in the
two photographs taken in Mexico City in 1914?

If we return, in the first instance, to the version that includes the waitresses, we
discover that meaning in the image is condensed in the bodies of the two women
at its centre, who are nevertheless rendered invisible by the photograph's caption.
By occupying the space on the other side of the bar, the Zapatistas have usurped
the place of the male, bourgeois client and, at the same time, the conventional

locus of the male gaze. What is more, through the oblique camera angle, the photograph stages a charged and contestatory encounter between the 'rightful' but
temporarily ousted occupant of the other side of the bar – who is now positioned
with the photographer, alongside the waitresses – and the transgressive usurpers
of that space, the Zapatistas. The third parties in this encounter are, of course,
the waitresses. A narrative reading of the photograph defines the waitresses
as attending to their new, subaltern customers: '¿Qué desean ustedes?' In this
exchange, the social hierarchy conventionally in operation between waitress and
bourgeois client has been temporarily reconfigured, replaced by an encounter
between social, if not necessarily racial, equals. Indeed, the body language and
facial expressions of both waitresses and Zapatista clients suggest unease in this
socially incongruous situation. At the same time, however, the other side of the
bar now occupied by the Zapatistas remains the site of sexual power.

On a symbolic level, by bringing questions of sexual difference and spectatorship into play, it becomes clear that what is being contested in this image is the
right to gaze at the women behind the bar. The waitresses, in turn, embody a
series of distilled meanings: the female body stands for Sanborns, and by association, for the capital city. In the photograph, women provide the grounds or
conceptual space for an exchange of looks, while they are effectively displaced
from the occupation of space and history. The more frequently-used caption
of the image is, after all, *Zapatistas en Sanborns* and not, for example, 'waitresses
serving Zapatistas in Sanborns'; their everyday labour is rendered invisible in the
presence of their exceptional new clients. Elizabeth Grosz (1989: 147), in a reading
of the work of French feminist philosopher Luce Iragaray, explicates the ambivalent role that women have traditionally been assigned within culture that bears
citation here, for it encapsulates the dynamic at play in the gendered viewing
relations established in *Zapatistas en Sanborns*:

> [I]t is the silent bodies of women . . . which provide the supports for . . . various
> exchange relations. This implies that while women are the conditions of symbolic
> exchange and thus of culture, they function as objects of exchange and are prevented
> from being participants or active agents within exchange. This means that the
> exchange relations which guarantee it are *hommosexual* (sic) relations between men
> alone. Women are merely the 'excuses', the 'goods' and mediating objects linking
> men to each other. (Grosz 1989: 147)

In short, it is not simply the caption that renders the waitresses invisible. An
analysis that is attentive to the gendered dimensions of spectatorship as it is structured around the bar demonstrates that while they may stand at the centre of
the photograph, the women are nonetheless merely ciphers or mediating objects
between two categories of male subjects: the Zapatistas and the temporarily
ousted bourgeois client.

Not only do issues of sexual difference in Manet's *A Bar at the Folies-Bergère*
enhance our understanding of the bar in *Zapatistas en Sanborns* in which the

waitresses are present; Manet's famous painting also provides insights into the photograph of Zapatistas alone, helping us to grasp the nuances associated with the ominous demeanour of the sombrero-wearing soldier on the left, where the threat enshrined in the photograph does not derive from his demeanour alone. Rather, it is equally associated with the viewing position in which the photographer/spectator is placed. Following the gendered logic of the bar, as we have seen, the waitresses focalise the gaze and in the process become the cipher for the bourgeois male subject's anxieties to reassert his position in the face of the occupation of the capital by the primitive *campesino* hordes. By the same logic, in the absence of the waitresses in the other version of *Zapatistas en Sanborns*, that same viewer is made to occupy the feminine space of the subservient side of the bar. That is to say, the viewer is made to confront the dark-skinned hordes full-on, from a symbolic site that is socially and sexually encoded as belonging to the disempowered, to those whose subjectivity and right to historical agency have conventionally been disallowed. To meet the inscrutable yet compelling gaze of the other from this site of alterity does not make for comfortable viewing.

MARÍA ZAVALA

The waitresses serving at the bar of Sanborns in December 1914 will, more than likely, remain nameless and their everyday labour, unless foregrounded, unremarked upon.[14] As the caption that accompanies the photograph that is the second case study of this chapter indicates (Figure 6.5), the woman depicted was

6.5 María Zavala arrodillada sobre vías del ferrocarril/María Zavala kneeling on the train track.

called María Zavala, also known as 'La destroyer', who 'was famous for helping the fallen to die well' (Ortiz Monasterio 2002: 73). Although apparently well known to her contemporaries, the question remains, however, who was María Zavala and what was her role in the conflict? Was she, to return to Julio Sesto's verse, one of those *soldaderas* who tended to the wounded and dying – those who 'see those who fall in battle, . . . staunch blood, heal wounds and console them in their moans'? Is this the meaning of her fame for 'helping the fallen to die well'? What is the significance of her anglicised *nom-de-guerre* – 'La destroyer' – which seems sinisterly at odds with her nurse-like qualities? What, moreover, of the objects that she proffers for display in the image? Are these the tools of her trade? And what should we make of her male garb, and masculine physique? Is it possible to determine with any accuracy when this image was made? Finally, beyond these prosaic questions of fact, on a more affective level, there is something captivating about María Zavala's gaze: what is it that makes her gaze so compelling?

The combination of Zavala's intense stare, her serenity and the mystery surrounding the status of her labour have ensured that this frequently reproduced, rather than iconic, image has continued to prove a source of fascination. On discovering the photograph, for example, the Mexican photographer and critic Pablo Ortiz Monasterio (2000: 24–5) attests that its subject instantly captivated him. It is worth pausing for a brief digression to consider Ortiz Monasterio's fascination with this image: on the one hand, his account of how he came across the photograph exemplifies the serendipitous and ultimately subjective routes that can lead to the public dissemination of certain images over others of the revolutionary struggle; and on the other, his curatorial role in bringing *María Zavala* to light and publishing it in a range of contexts that subsequently have come to frame its meanings will also inform the analysis of *María Zavala* in the pages to follow.

In the 2000 issue of *Alquimia*, titled 'Figuraciones y signos', Ortiz Monasterio provides an anecdotal yet revealing account of his discovery of the photograph which, he recalls, fell into his hands thanks to a donation of photographic materials by the Culhuacán Archive to the Fototeca Nacional in Pachuca. Or, as he reminisces: 'At that time [unspecified, but presumably 1979], a series of cardboard boxes had been sent in, containing "diverse" photographic materials, one of which had the word "Revolution" written on one side. We opened the box and examined its contents carefully. It held a series of notebooks or albums of small format photographs, stuck on pages with brief allusive captions that the noted collector Felipe Teixidor had put together' (Ortiz Monasterio 2000: 24). And there, by chance, María Zavala was discovered in the context of an album documenting the devastation left in the wake of the uprising against Álvaro Obregón, led by Adolfo de la Huerta in 1923. In the process of selecting images for inclusion in *Jefes, héroes y caudillos* (1986), Ortiz Monasterio and his collaborators were immediately fascinated to the degree that this 'assured [the image] a relevant place in our book'.[15]

To be sure, Ortiz Monasterio's account of happening upon the photograph of María Zavala is anything but scholarly; it is nevertheless revealing, for it illustrates the haphazard processes that can lie behind archival and curatorial practices and, in the final analysis, shape broader collective memories of the revolution as they are mediated by photographic images. At the same time, in the face of the challenges posed by photographs as ephemeral objects that defy attempts at accurate dating and labelling, this anecdote furnishes fairly conclusive evidence to pinpoint the making of *María Zavala* to some time between December 1923 and March of the following year, locating it historically within the context of the De la Huerta rebellion.[16] In short, made some years after the official end of the violent phase of the revolution, the image dates from the period in which the protagonists of the Constitutionalist triumphant faction – the so-called *familia revolucionaria* (revolutionary family) comprising De la Huerta, Obregón, and Calles – jockeyed for power. Led, as its name suggests, by De la Huerta, the uprising was triggered in part by Obregón's backing of Calles as his presidential successor in 1923. How, though, might we find out more about the role of the mysterious María Zavala in this short-lived insurrection?

In a slim volume, *La rebelión delahuertista*, in the illustrated Secretaría de Educación Pública series, significantly titled 'Memoria y olvido: imágenes de México' ('Memory and Forgetting: Images of Mexico'), Enrique Arriola situates the De la Huerta uprising as:

> A significant moment in the process of consolidation of the new State and the insti-
> tutionalization of the armed forces . . . The rebellion can be considered as a decisive
> moment in the formation of the army as defender of that abstract entity, above
> and beyond class, that is the nation, and as the safeguard of the interests of all the
> members of or interests of this latter. (Arriola 1983: 7)[17]

The De la Huerta rebellion was, then, a turning point in the revolutionary trajectory, a moment at which the struggle was purged of dissident voices and retrospectively constructed as a coherent project of social and political progress. The stage was set for the election of Calles to the presidency on 6 July 1924, and with him a new phase of greater political centralisation that, by 1929, led to the formation of a new political party, the Partido Nacional Revolucionario (PNR). Although it was to undergo further name changes –finally to the Partido Revolucionario Institucional (PRI) in 1946 – it hardly requires stating here that the party's control over Mexican political life in the name of the revolution would remain intact until its defeat in July 2000.

However, among the many images in Arriola's book, replete with photo-graphs of railways, locomotives and military men, the reader is hard-pressed to find many women, let alone a reproduction of *María Zavala*. Indeed, beyond a brief mention in the essay 'Beyond Decoration: Towards a Graphic History of Women in Mexico', in which John Mraz alludes to, but does not reproduce the photograph, María Zavala has proven elusive. Mraz, however, provides further insights into María Zavala's 'professional' status:

> It could be argued that the questions that photographs [of women in Mexico] suggest are as important as what they show. There are one or two of those published that serve to open up the panorama of the different roles played by women in the revolution. For example, that of María Zavala, 'The Destroyer', whom we find sitting on a rail track. The foot of the photo makes us think that she must have blown up trains during the De la Huerta rebellion. (Mraz 1992: 160)[18]

In different ways, Ortiz Monasterio, Arriola, and Mraz provide us with clues that allow us to piece together an – albeit sketchy – historical framework in which to insert the photograph of María Zavala. But as we saw in the case of Morales's painstaking scholarship, in which he managed to track down *Soldadera/Adelita* to its original source of publication and thereby re-anchor it in its historical context of production, context does not necessarily provide answers to the kinds of question that we might want to ask of images of women in wartime. What arguably gets left out of the equation in such approaches is attention to the status of photographs as visual documents embedded in broader historical and ideological structures. Once again feminist scholarship in visual studies may provide a useful heuristic tool, for it urges us to examine the multiple looks that circulate around a given photographic image and the ideologically inscribed screen that exists between viewer and image and which I now pursue further in my analysis of *María Zavala*.

We can identify (at least) four different, yet interconnected, looks in circulation around this particular photograph, which I propose to set up here as a chain of looking that will serve as a defining nexus in my exploration of the relationship between photograph, historical narrative and sexual difference. The first is a contextualising look and takes us back to Ortiz Monasterio, this time in his role as editor of the volume of images from the Casasola Archive – *Jefes, héroes y caudillos* – to which he alludes in his brief intervention in *Alquimia*. Originally published in 1986 by the Fondo de Cultura Económica, Ortiz Monasterio's role in the volume was to select and edit the images. Hence, he was responsible for, among other things, the order in which the photographs appear in the collection. With the first image of the volume dating from 1903, and depicting Porfirio Díaz in the twilight years of his rule, *Jefes, héroes y caudillos* takes the viewer through a more or less chronological photographic narrative: through the rise of Madero; his assassination at the culmination of the Decena Trágica; the interim presidency of Huerta; the caudillos, Villa and Zapata; the triumphant constitutionalist *jefes*, Obregón and Carranza; to the De la Huerta rebellion, where *María Zavala* is the final image to appear in the selection. In this sense, *María Zavala* is literally the ultimate image in Ortiz Monasterio's collection.

The second look to identify in this chain of looking is that of the subject of the photograph, María Zavala, who holds our gaze so insistently. This look,

113

in turn, takes us to the third and fourth looks engaged by the photograph: the look of the viewer, and the gaze that mirrors it in the photograph, the gaze of the row of male onlookers who stand on the other side of the rail-track and for whom María Zavala is also clearly the object of scrutiny. Or is she? If the notion of a chain of looks implies continuity, then here the constitutive optical relations that link viewing subject to viewed object break down. A fascinating element regarding this row of onlookers is that, without exception, their gaze is occluded from the viewer outside the frame through cropping, the shadows cast by the onlookers' hats or the lighting effects produced in the image that serve to render their eyes invisible. What, then, are the implications of this occluded look? Or, to rephrase the question, what is it that this row of male onlookers gazes upon that – according to the logic of looking set up in and around the image – is signalled to the viewer as that which cannot be looked at?

Let us move back to the look of the editor whose task it was to collate and organise the photographs of *Jefes, héroes y caudillos*, and who placed alongside *María Zavala* another image: *Jefe revolucionario muerto en los combates de Palo Verde. Jalisco, 1924* (Revolutionary chief dead in the battle of Palo Verde. Jalisco, 1924) (Figure 6.6).[19] When we take into consideration the position of this pair of images, it is important to note the wide format of *Jefes, héroes y caudillos*: a format that obliges its reader to take in the two photographs side by side. Beyond the book format that positions these photographs contiguously, there are further formal

6.6 Revolucionario muerto/Dead revolutionary, *c.*1923.

and thematic correspondences between *María Zavala* and *Jefe revolucionario* which merit attention. If the central focus of *María Zavala* is (of course) María Zavala herself, as both caption and image inform us, then there is also a thematic relationship with the adjacent image. That is, if one of Zavala's roles in the armed conflict – a role that, allied with her 'nurse-like' quality – was to 'help soldiers die well', then the viewer cannot help but speculate that the *Jefe revolucionario* may well have been one of Zavala's 'victims'. In other words, read in tandem with *María Zavala*, *Jefe revolucionario* performs an illustrative function. There is, however, another correspondence between the two photographs. The row of onlookers in the first image is echoed in the second by a similarly face-less group of federal soldiers whose posture suggests to us that they are looking at the dead man, but whose gaze again is uncannily occluded. Here, once more, the viewer is presented with, indeed implicated in, the double drama of looking and not looking.

Before moving to conclude this case study, there is one final correspondence between the two photographs that requires elucidation. This third parallel functions at the level of the trope, and again engages the viewer's gaze. As we look at these contiguously located images, our gaze slips from *María Zavala* to the unnamed *Jefe revolucion*ario. Or, to put it another way, our gaze slides between femininity and death: between figures which, as Elisabeth Bronfen (1992: xii) has argued in her study *Over Her Dead Body*, are linked as 'superlative sites of alterity'. The focus of Bronfen's analysis is the ubiquity, within Western culture, of images of the death of women. The pair of images that are the focus of this case study would appear to fall outside the remit of the insights offered by Bronfen, on two counts. First, on the grounds that they derive from a non-Western context with, as we saw in Chapter 5, its own unique death cult that developed particularly in the aftermath of the revolution. And second, the death they depict – or in the case of *María Zavala*, signal as taking place off-frame – is male death. Bronfen's analysis is, nevertheless, relevant to the present discussion precisely because death and femininity are conflated in the two images, via their alignment. Positioned alongside *Jefe revolucionario* and linked to it via caption and formal elements within the frame, the photographic subject María Zavala comes to embody death. As feminine death embodied, following Bronfen's analysis, María Zavala is burdened with further connotations: 'Femininity and death cause a disorder to stability, mark moments of ambivalence, disruption or duplicity and their eradication produces a recuperation of order, a return to stability' (Bronfen 1992: xxii). What then is at stake in the position of these two photographic images, placed side-by-side *and* located as the final images in a photo-story of the Mexican revolution? There are two points to signal about their tropic interrelationship.

The first is concerned with the chronological photo-narrative that *Jefes, héroes y caudillos* constructs. The collection provides, primarily, a linear narrative of progress centred on the revolution and its protagonists, both well-known and anonymous. The De la Huerta uprising of 1923/24, scenes from which are depicted in the final section of the collection, marks a significant moment in the consolidation of power that was to give birth to the modern Mexican (party of) state, the PRI. Further, and as we saw in Chapter 5, the revolution and its association with narratives of progress were to play an important role in the legitimisation of post-revolutionary political regimes, at the same time as a peculiarly Mexican valorisation of a posture of stoic fortitude in the face of imminent death, as outlined by Lomnitz (2005), emerged as a national totem in the post-revolutionary period. A mode of representation loaded with the power of objective transcription, the photographic representation of death – particularly in those images that exemplified an attitude of disdain in the face of annihilation – came to play a role in embedding the revolution and its ideological underpinnings within cultural memory.

Located within the context of the photo-narrative of *Jefes, héroes y caudillos*, however, and drawing on Bronfen's observations regarding death and femininity (rather than Lomnitz's regarding death and masculinity), *María Zavala* becomes charged with meanings that resonate on quite another scale. That is, following Bronfen, if the sight of death and femininity 'cause a disorder to stability', if they are the scene of disruption and ambivalence, then *María Zavala* and *Jefe revolucionario*, as the ultimate images in *Jefes, héroes y caudillos* – images, moreover, that appear to proscribe the act of looking at death –signal not a teleological narrative of order and progress. Rather, their alignment and collocation at the end of the collection, combined it should be added with María Zavala's ambiguous gender status, point instead to a much more ambivalent reading of death, not so much as national totem, but rather as the ultimate site of alterity. Or to put this otherwise, and to address a key issue at the heart of this book, photographs are frequently mobilised to illustrate broader historical narratives. But to pay attention to photographs in and of themselves – where and how they are positioned, what they depict and the broader ideological and iconographic codes and conventions on which they draw – can reveal so much more than an understanding of them as mere supplement, or illustration. In short, to assay the construction of historical narratives of progress through the optic of photographic artefacts – as we saw in relation to questions of photographic materiality in the closing section of Chapter 5 on Fortino Sámano – opens onto the fragmenting, fracturing possibilities that are enshrined in all photographic images.

CAVEAT

But herein lies a problem that has been woven throughout this chapter. To return to Hirsch's notion of the encountered or projected screen between viewer and photographic image, one of the dominant mythologies writ large on that screen is 'Woman' as site of alterity: as that which, like the racial Other that confronts the viewer from across the bar of Sanborns, is the site of fear and anxiety. And, as long as 'Woman' is reduced to a telos of alterity, it will be impossible to offer an account of her agency. This agency is, I believe, visualised in photographic artefacts such as the images that appear in Poniatowska's collection *Las soldad-eras*: it is there in the indexical 'look' I have pointed to in the photographs that comprise this parade of woman warriors. However, as Philippe Dubois (1983: 80–1) asserted in the neglected *L'Acte photographique* (The Photographic Act), we must not allow the index – a term that has accrued much critical currency within theories of photography – to become photography's 'new epistemologi-cal obstacle'. We cannot take the evidential force of such photographs of female subjects of the revolution at face value: as images that simply document female participation and therefore affirm female agency. To do so is to overlook pre-cisely the screen of representation that determines looking. Photographic images are much more complex than their apparent transparency would have us believe. If we bring to the fore questions of race and gender in relation to photographs, are we not invited to look differently at the historical narratives in which they are embedded? And, by learning to look differently, do we not begin to disturb the frameworks of cultural analysis that have long clouded our vision of Others?

NOTES

1   'van a la guerra por patriotismo y por amor'/'aquellos niños serán valientes, porque han mamado pechos calientes por los cartuchos de algún fusil'/'ven los que caen en la batalla, restañan sangre, curan heridos y los consuelan en sus gemidos'/'cargan fusiles, ruedan cañones'. Elizabeth Salas (1990: xii) traces the etymology of the word 'soldadera' back to the time of the conquest: 'Both domestic and foreign troops after the Spanish Conquest in 1519 used women as servants (*soldaderas*). Soldiers used their pay (*soldada*) to employ women as paid servants (*soldaderas*).' See also Linhard (2005) on the role of women in the revolution.

2   There is now a burgeoning literature devoted to the analysis of what the revolution meant to women. See, for example, Olcott (2005) and Mitchell and Schell (2006).

3   The English edition of Benjamin's text features the photograph of a statue of an anony-mous revolutionary on horseback, while the front cover of the Spanish edition is split in half by the title, with the famous photograph of Zapata above and the Soldadera below.

4   'Entre las muchas fotografías de prensa descontextualizadas, ninguna tan célebre y erróneamente atribuida como la que primero se denominó, hacia 1960, *La Soldadera* y después de 1987 como *La Adelita*.'

5   Lest evidence of the iconic status of the image were required, we might note that Morales's discovery of the original source of the photograph and with it his resolution of a mystery merited an article in the cultural section of *La Jornada* on 16 February 2007. See www.jornada.unam.mx/2007/02/16/index.php?section=cultura&article=a 04n1cul (accessed 19 November 2007).

6   'A esa soldadera la vio todo México cruzar de frontera a frontera. . .'/'Adelita sol-dadera, *una foto tomada por Agustín V. Casasola en 1910, muy pronto se convirtió en uno de los emblemas de la revolución, al igual que la famosa canción casi homónima*: La Adelita' (emphasis in the original). Morales does not address the question regarding which version of the image is included in either of the volumes mentioned. In my 1942 edition of *Historia gráfica de la revolución*, the cropped version appears, under the

capitalised banner LA SOLDADERA, and is captioned 'Esa soldadera la ha visto México todo, cruzar de frontera a frontera . . .' (664).

7 'No en balde sus compañeras llevan canastos seguramente con alimentos.'

8 'El sábado 6 de abril confluyeron dos vidas en la estación ferrocarrilera de Buenavista: la de esa aparentemente cocinera de las tropas huertistas y el fotógrafo de *Nueva Era*. No se concoce ni el nombre ni la trayectoria militar de esa mujer humilde. Se sabe el nombre del fotógrafo.'

9 'no hay Revolución Mexicana: ellas la mantuvieron viva y fecunda, como a la tierra. Las enviaban por delante a recoger leña y a prender la lumbre, y la alimentaron a lo largo de los años de guerra. Sin las soldaderas, los hombres llevados de leva hubieran desertado.'

10 Sanborns was founded in 1903 by the North American brothers Frank and Walter Sanborn. Originally located in Calle Betlemitas (now Filomeno Mata), Sanborns moved in 1918 to its current location in the Casa de los Azulejos on Calle Madero. Other frequently reproduced images made during the occupation of the capital include those documenting Villa and Zapata at a banquet, seated alongside interim President Eulalio Gutiérrez and José Vanconcelos (e.g. Col. SINAFO-FN-INAH #5706); and that featuring Zapata and the American Consul, Mr Carothers, as they await Villa in Xochimilco (Col. SINAFO-FN-INAH #687563).

11 A third, rarely published version of the same scenario (Col. SINAFO-FN-INAH # 6011) appears to feature the same group of men, where again the photographer is positioned further from the bar at an oblique angle, but this time, the angle is narrower and the space occupied by the waitresses is empty. It is worth noting that the waitresses in the second version of the photograph bear a striking resemblance in dress to their modern-day counterparts working in the Sanborns restaurants, now an extensive chain of department stores, in which Mexican magnate Carlos Slim Helú – purportedly a rival to Bill Gates for the rank of richest man in the world – owns a controlling share.

12 'La lectura posterior de estas fotos se basó, sin jamás explicitarlo, en la fascinación ante lo desconocido, y en la domesticación de los impulsos radicales. *Los zapatistas en Sanborns*: el primitivismo se asoma a un sitio neurálgico del porfirismo, para permitir las comparaciones protectoras con los atildados "científicos" del régimen caído. ¿No es cierto que todo contraste remite a paradojas conmovedoras? Estos soldados acuden a una zona sagrada para incurrir en profanación y, luego, desaparecer sin remedio.'

13 I pick up this theme again in Chapter 8, in relation to the performance in 1999 by the Neo-Zapatistas of this photograph.

14 To my knowledge, the waitresses have not come forward to identify themselves, nor have they been tracked down subsequently. Identifying the anonymous subjects of iconic photographs has been a common approach to this cultural phenomenon, particularly in journalistic accounts, but also in scholarly work. Notable cases include Dorothea Lange's Depression-era *Migrant Mother* (1936); Nick Ut's Vietnam War *Accidental Napalm* (1972); Steve McCurry's *Afghan Girl* (1985); and most recently Luis Sinco's *Marlboro Marine* (2004) from the second Iraq war. For scholarly approaches to some of these photographs, see Stein (2003); Hariman and Lucaites (2007); Edwards (2007); Sinco tracked down Lance Corporal James Blake Miller, the subject of his photograph, to tell his post-conflict story: www.guardian.co.uk/theobserver/2007/nov/18/featuresreview.review1 (accessed 30 May 2010).

15 'Por esos días habían enviado . . . una serie de cajas de cartón con materiales fotográ-
ficos "diversos", una tenía escrita la palabra "Revolución" en un costado. Abrimos la
caja y la revisamos minuciosamente. Contenía una serie de cuadernos o álbumes de
fotos más bien pequeñas, pegadas a unos folios con breves leyendas alusivas, que había
armado el notable coleccionista Felipe Teixidor' (24); 'aseguró un sitio relevante en
nuestro libro' (25). Ortiz Monasterio omits to mention the year in which the Teixidor
Collection was entrusted to the Fototeca. In their rather more rigorous study,
Casanova and Konsevik (2006: 134) date this to January 1979. Again, reading between
the lines, the book in question is likely to have been *Jefes, héroes y caudillos*, the first
edition of which was eventually published in 1986.

16 This assertion is not without its own attendant irony. *María Zavala* is reproduced in
Alquimia, dated 1913. But in all probability, given the content of the article it accompanies, this is a typographical error and should read 1923. This still does not explain its,
albeit inexact, dating *c.*1915 in the later *Mirada y memoria* (2002), also researched and
compiled by Ortiz Monasterio.

17 'un momento significativo en el proceso de consolidación del nuevo Estado y de
institucionalización de las fuerzas armadas . . . La rebelión puede plantearse como
un momento decisivo en la formación del ejército como defensor de esa entidad
abstracta, por encima de las clases, que es la nación, y como salvaguarda de los intereses de todos los miembros o intereses de la misma.'

18 'Ahora bien, se podría argumentar que las preguntas que las fotos [de las mujeres en
México] sugieren son tan importantes como lo que muestran. Hay una que otra de las
publicadas que sirve para abrir el panorama de los diferentes papeles de la mujer en
la Revolución. Por ejemplo, la de María Zavala, "La destroyer", a quien encontramos
sentada en una vía ferroviaria. El pie de la foto nos hace pensar que debe haber sido
una dinamitera de trenes durante la rebelión delahuertista.'

19 In Casanova and Konzevik (2006: 44) this image is captioned *Revolucionario agonizando*,
or *Dying Revolutionary*.

7

The photographic morgue

It is the evening of Thursday 10 April, 1919. The corpse of Emiliano Zapata has been slung unceremoniously over the back of a mule and transported the 31 kilometres from the site of death – at the Hacienda de Chinameca – to the town of Cuautla, both in Zapatista heartland in the state of Morelos. There, it is anxiously awaited by the intellectual author of Zapata's assassination, the Constitutionalist general, Pablo González. At 9.10 p.m. the corpse arrives. The dead man is officially identified; an autopsy is carried out that confirms that the body presents seven bullet wounds; the corpse is injected with an embalming agent; it undergoes a change of clothing and is placed on display. There it remains for some twenty-four hours, during which onlookers flock to Cuautla from the surrounding *pueblos* to take in the sight of the legendary revolutionary leader in death. At some point, both before and after the post-mortem processes are performed, the corpse is photographically documented by, among others, local photographer J. Mora (Figure 7.1). And then Emiliano Zapata is given a high-profile burial on the evening of Saturday 12 April, an event that is also recorded on celluloid.

According to one demographer, 'the human cost of the Mexican revolution was exceeded only by the devastation of the Christian conquest, colonization and accompanying epidemics, nearly four centuries earlier' (McCaa 2003: 397). The combat zones of the Mexican revolution were strewn with corpses; consequently death, as we have already seen, looms large in the photographic representation of the conflict. In addition to the images of firing squads, or the 'nurse of death', María Zavala, explored in Chapters 5 and 6, the 'photographic morgue' houses the material remnants and corporeal remains of the more celebrated figures in the struggle. Dating, as we have seen, at least as far back as the execution of Maximilian, a range of relics and famous bodies belong to this macabre photographic tradition, including an image by Carlos Muñana of three journalists, Publio Treppiedi, Ernesto Hidalgo and Agustín Víctor Casasola himself, holding up the blood-spattered clothes of Pino Suárez and Francisco I. Madero (see Figure 5.4); the group portrait of the doctors who carried out Venustiano Carranza's autopsy, gathered around the assassinated president's corpse in Villa de Juárez, Puebla, in May 1920 (Figure 7.2); and images made in the aftermath

7.1 Cadáver de Emiliano Zapata exhibido en Cuautla/Corpse of Emiliano Zapata displayed in Cuautla, 10 April 1919.

of the assassination of Pancho Villa in Parral, Chihuahua, including shots of his naked and bullet-lacerated body, laid out on a bed at the Hotel Hidalgo, a white sheet the only concession to his modesty (Figure 7.3). In fact, of the revolution's protagonists, only the 'villains' – the deposed dictator Díaz himself and the 'reactionary usurper' Victoriano Huerta – were to die of natural causes in exile.[1] The rest met with violent ends at the hands, or more accurately, on the orders of one

121

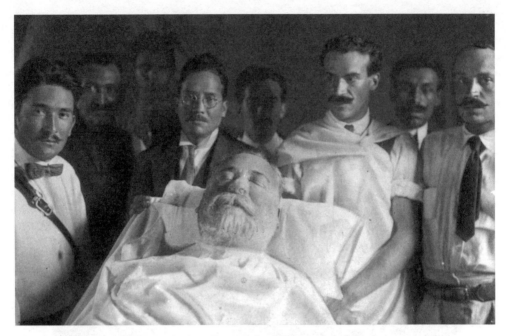

7.2 Cadáver de don Venustiano Carranza y médicos que le hicieron la autopsia / The corpse of Don Venustiano Carranza with the doctors who carried out his autopsy, May 1920.

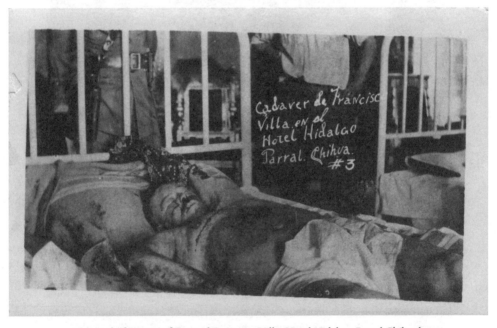

7.3 Postcard of Corpse of General Francisco Villa, Hotel Hidalgo, Parral Chihuahua.

another. Zapata's corpse is, then, one of many, and the photographic images made in Cuautla on 10 April 1919 form part of a vast photographic archive documenting both celebrity and anonymous death.

Some photographed corpses, however, have proved a more persistent presence than others. To be sure, the images of the corpses of Carranza and Villa have certainly enjoyed a degree of longevity. Carranza's death portrait, for instance, was originally published on an inside page of *El Universal* on 25 May 1920, before going on to feature in a number of photographic anthologies documenting the revolution, including *Jefes, héroes y caudillos* (Lara Klahr 1986). Meanwhile, various takes on Villa's corpse were similarly splashed over the front covers at the time of his assassination in 1923, as well as circulating as picture postcards, such as those that form part of the collection held at the Universidad Autónoma de Ciudad Juárez.[2] Most recently, the photograph of Villa's guard Miguel Trillo was reproduced in *Mirada y memoria* (Ortiz Monasterio 2002: 60), his lifeless body hanging out of the passenger-side of the car in which they were ambushed and which Villa had been driving, a handful of onlookers visible on the other side of the open vehicle. On the same page are two smaller images: one of a hand holding bullets discharged at the scene; and another of a bullet-perforated coin that was apparently in the revolutionary's pocket at the time of his assassination.[3] These corpses and other material remains do not, however, boast the kind of afterlife such as that experienced by the photographic corpse of Zapata. For instance, the leader's photographic death mask notably resurfaced in the 1970s, when Héctor García (b. 1923) produced a photomontage, titled *La Verónica* (1972), using Zapata's head extracted from Mora's famous image, imprinted on a piece of cloth proffered to the camera's lens by an elderly indigenous woman (see Figure 7.5); or fragments of the same image were used by the artist Alberto Gironella (1929–1999) in his mixed media *La muerte de Zapata No. 2* (1974) (see Figure 7.6).

It should not surprise us then that Zapata's death-mask photograph has already attracted critical attention. Most pertinent in the current chapter is the work of Samuel Brunk, and particularly his 2004 essay 'The Mortal Remains of Emiliano Zapata', which offers a fascinating account of the value and place of Zapata's body in commemorative discourses in the post-revolutionary period. Nevertheless, while Brunk is attentive to issues of the display and photographing of the corpse, his focus is firmly historical rather than visually oriented. That is to say, the display and photographing of the corpse form part of the wider historical narrative he traces, concerned to explore the way in which 'the body played a critical role in the launching of the cult, helping to make Zapata a point of discussion, a subject of interest, and a symbol that local, regional, and national identities could eventually form around' (Brunk 2004: 154). Brunk's emphasis is, however, on the meanings associated with the body itself rather than on those that pertain to its photographic representation. While it is essential to attend to the broader historical picture, and the pages that follow are indebted to the work of Brunk, to privilege historical narrative over image runs the risk of eliding a key feature of Mora's photograph, namely its considerable visual eloquence. Taking visual cues from within the photographic frame as my point of departure, I explore this visually striking image of Zapata in death, paraphrasing and extending questions posed by Ariella Azoulay (2001: 4) in the introduction to her analysis of the display of death in contemporary culture, *Death's Showcase*: what are the conditions that make the display of death permissible, even desirable? What is the visual work of death in the age of mechanical reproduction? How do we frame these questions with due respect to the historical and cultural circumstances of the photograph's context of production? What relation exists, moreover, between the display of death in the age of mechanical reproduction and its exhibition in other, pre-photographic visual traditions?

CLAMOURING TO GET INTO THE FRAME

What is it about Mora's photograph (Figure 7.1) that makes of it such a richly eloquent image of Zapata in death? We might begin to answer this question by offering a simple description of what the viewer encounters when looking at this image in order to build a platform on which to base analysis. The corpse of Zapata occupies some two-thirds of the lower section of the image. The revolutionary leader's head, located in the very centre, is the point of sharpest focus. The eyes that have attracted such scrutiny are closed – recall José Muñoz Cota's declaration that 'In the sad gaze of Emiliano Zapata the tragedy of our history comes to light' (cited in Brunk 2006: 124), and return to the caudillo's intense stare as he sits beside Villa on the presidential chair – and his trade-mark moustache glistens above a blood-stained white shirt. It hardly requires stating that Zapata's corpse is the central focus of this photograph; it is clearly being propped up and proffered for display to the camera's lens. Nevertheless, what fascinates equally are the unnamed male figures in the upper section of the image, who support the corpse and who appear to jostle to get into the photographic framing of this instant in national history. Imagine for a moment that they were not there and, I suggest, the dramatic impact of the photograph is significantly attenuated.

Arguably, it is through their presence as participants in this scene that death as spectacle is constituted. Unlike the unseeing Zapata, their gazes shoot out of the photographic frame across space and time, mirroring (to some degree) our own look outside the frame. And yet, look again, and the dynamics of this spectacle are neither straightforward nor conventional. This is because convention dictates that their looks would either be directed toward the camera – meeting our gaze as spectators outside the frame – or else at the corpse itself. It is instructive here to compare this photograph with that of the corpse of Carranza (Figure 7.2), in which, with one exception (the figure second from the left) the gaze of all the doctors present converge with ours at a point outside the frame. Similarly, in the image of Trillo's corpse hanging out of Villa's car, the bloody scene has clearly attracted a flock of onlookers who, although blurry figures in the background, have evidently come to gawp at the victims of this political ambush. Not so in Mora's photograph of Zapata's corpse. With the exception of the man to the extreme left, whose body is bisected by the frame and whose stare meets that of the viewer, the other three central figures look anywhere but at us or at the corpse. Their gaze is caught by something or somewhere off-frame that is invisible to the viewer of the photograph. It is in the relationship between our own look and that of these participants in the scene, one might say, that the drama of the image resides.

There is, most likely, a pragmatic explanation for these disparate looks that shoot off in different directions that can be backed up by circumstantial evidence. Testimony related to the display and burial of Zapata's corpse in the form of both written accounts and moving image footage suggests that Cuautla was flooded with onlookers, curious to catch a glimpse of the leader's mortal remains. This was, however, not a spontaneous gathering; rather, as we shall see in greater detail later on, it was an orchestrated, albeit chaotic, media event designed to garner the maximum publicity possible. As a locally-based photographer, Mora had the good fortune to be on hand to capture the scenes in his home town for posterity; he was joined, however, by photographers and film crews from the capital, including the pioneer cinematographer Salvador Toscano.[4] If the anonymous male subjects look off in different directions, it is likely because, in the clamour to see the corpse of Zapata, to put it with colloquial simplicity, there was a lot going on around them. Indeed, most probably a number of different photographers and cameramen were present at the scene, all vying to capture the men's attention. Nevertheless, in the absence of a self-reflexive image documenting this photo opportunity *as* photo opportunity, we cannot know with any certainty what exactly was the scene facing these anonymous figures, for we are left with visual fragments, of which the Mora image is but one shard that will never again coalesce into a coherent whole.

Having already followed the corpse's journey on the back of a mule to Cuautla on 10 April 1919, and having started to tune in to the hubbub taking place in the space outside the photographic frame, let us now plot the photograph back into the micro history that led up to its making. What relationship did the young men who clamoured to get into the photographic frame have to the corpse, how and why did the photograph come to be made, for whom and to what ends? What forms of knowledge and affect, moreover, did the photograph communicate to its viewers in 1919?

THE ROUTE TO CHINAMECA

After the 1914 'social curve' of the revolution, when Zapata and Villa had occupied the capital and, backed by widespread agrarian mobilisation, had come as close as they ever would to controlling most of Mexico, Zapata and his troops had retreated in the first instance to Puebla. By January of 1915 his alliance with and trust in Villa were placed under severe strain. A combination of intelligence that reached him regarding Villa's perfidy, the latter's delay in supplying promised arms and the murder, by Villa's men, of Paulino Martínez, Zapata's chief delegate in the capital, led the southern leader to withdraw to Morelos 'in evident confusion and disgust' (Womack 1968: 222). As the Villa-Zapata association waned, so that of the Sonorans, comprising Álvaro Obregón, Plutarco Elías Calles, Adolfo de la Huerta and Benjamín Hill, was on the rise. They manoeuvred themselves into key positions in Carranza's movement and worked tirelessly to push back the more radical forces associated with Villa and Zapata. Thus, Villa was militarily defeated by the superior tactics of Obregón in the two battles of Celaya on 6 and 7 April and 13 April 1915. At this point, the División del Norte 'had ceased to be a major military force' (Katz 1998: 497) and beat a retreat northward toward Torreón and Chihuahua.

Although the Sonorans also succeeded in pushing the Zapatistas back into Morelos, they still had a tenacious hold over the rural communities of Morelos and continued to represent a nuisance to the nearly, but not quite, triumphant Constitutionalists. It remained therefore for the Constitutionalists to assert their authority in Morelos. Hence the plot was hatched between General Pablo González and Colonel Jesús Guajardo for the latter to lure the notoriously cautious Zapata to the Hacienda de Chinameca.

In 1919, rumours started to reach Zapata that Guajardo had fallen out with González, an ambitious man with designs on the presidency, which would come up for grabs in 1920. The rumours were not without foundation. Womack (1968: 322) recounts: 'In mid-March González had ordered Guajardo to operate against the Zapatistas in the mountains around Huautla. Hours later he had caught the handsome young officer carousing in a local cantina; Guajardo tried to duck out the back door, but González had had him tracked and arrested.' Believing Guajardo to be harbouring a grudge against González, and finding himself in a militarily precarious position in need of troops and arms, on 21 March Zapata wrote to Guajardo, inviting the Constitutionalist colonel to defect and join him. González spotted his opportunity. First, however, Zapata required Guajardo to demonstrate his loyalty, demanding that he detain a defector from the Zapatista movement, Victoriano Bárcenas. Guajardo duly complied, attacking the Carrancista garrison at Jonacatepec on 9 April, 'feigning the battle so well that several people died' (Brunk 1995: 223). With Zapata satisfied with this proof of Guajardo's integrity, the two men met at the station of Jonacatepec, where Zapata congratulated Guajardo; for his part, in a further display of loyalty and integrity, Guajardo presented the revolutionary leader with a horse as a gift. Later that night the two men and their followers set off for the hacienda at Chinameca, Guajardo reaching his destination, Zapata stopping en route to sleep. The following day, in the company of about 150 men, Zapata proceeded to Chinameca, where Guajardo was awaiting him in the interior of the hacienda. With ten men in tow, Zapata entered the gates; a bugle sounded three times, in honour of the caudillo's arrival. Shots then rang out, fired at point-blank range. The rest, so to speak, is history.

As soon as the news of Zapata's death was confirmed, word was relayed to Carranza in Mexico City, who received it with pleasure and gave the order to pass the intelligence on for dissemination in the national press. At this point, Zapata's corpse was put on display in Cuautla. Brunk (1995: 227) reports that it was also 'suggested that the body be taken to Mexico City too, to calm metropolitan fears, but apparently it seemed too morbid, for González sent photographs to the press instead. In one, excited young soldiers propped up the bloated head of the corpse so the camera might leave no doubt'.[5] This was not, however, the first time that such sensational news about the death of the revolutionary had been splashed across the front pages of the national press.

Some five years earlier, on 30 March 1914, the headlines of El Diario announced 'Zapata has died: The corpse of the feared ringleader is collected from the village of Ayoxoxtla in the state of Puebla'. The report goes on to characterise Zapata and the movement to which he gave rise: 'Emiliano Zapata, who took up arms in February 1911, under the cover of the Maderista revolution, embodied destruction, cruelty and banditry in the south of the Republic. His feats introduced a terrible word into our vocabulary: Zapatismo'.[6] What is more, as the report makes clear, this was not the first time since Zapata's entry into the armed struggle that he had been declared dead in the national press. Mindful of past apocryphal reports, in the March 1914 announcement, it was asserted that the news was beyond doubt, having been certified by the authorities of Puebla.[7] This news item was not, however, accompanied by an image of the corpse of Zapata; instead it featured a sketch of a larger-than-life Zapata in wide sombrero, mounted on horseback.

In view of the fact, perhaps, that those who followed news of the conflict might have grown weary of false reports of his demise, when Zapata was indeed assassinated in April 1919 – albeit falling short of taking the corpse itself to the capital so they could even see with their own eyes – these same readers were left in no doubt regarding the veracity of events. According to the front-page report in El Demócrata on 11 April 1919, it was in fact Carranza himself who opposed the transportation of Zapata's corpse to the capital on the grounds that the tactic might backfire, running the risk of 'honouring his sorry ('triste') memory' (Figure 7.4).[8] The editorial voice of constitutionalist daily, for its part, favoured such a move for it would 'counteract the pessimism of the public in the face of news of this nature, which is maximal in this concrete case, in which as on many other occasions, some may doubt the death of the southern "chief", even if it has been totally confirmed today.'[9] So, although the actual corpse was pointedly not put on display in the capital, nevertheless its image was widely disseminated, for as

7.4 *El Demócrata*, 11 April 1919.

we have already seen by the time of the revolution, 'Proof of death was now mass mediated. So was proof of military power and strength' (Lomnitz 2005: 385). To this end, the national and capital city dailies offered detailed written reportage spanning several pages, accompanied by copious graphic illustrations that attested to 'Como fue la muerte del "Atila del sur"' (How the "Attila of the South" died), as the headline of *El Demócrata* put it in its edition of Saturday 12 April. Indeed, it is worth pausing to consider the ways in which text and image combine in *El Demócrata* to provide a rich and detailed forensic portrait.

Below the bold, capitalised headline 'HOW THE "ATILLA OF THE SOUTH"

DIED', a second-level subheading reads: 'Intelligence and cunning, in the service of men of resolve, overcame the armed suspicion of the southern rebels'. Finally, a third sub-heading serves as a caption for what can only be described as the photographic collage featuring different shots of Zapata's head and upper body: 'Three photographs showing the famous Emiliano Zapata, now a corpse, which are full proof of his annihilation'. Below the collage, made up of images which, it is indicated, had been obtained thanks to the generosity ('bondad') of Pablo González, the report outlines how Zapata had died alongside men from his escort: 'We are illustrating this information with the photographs taken the same night of the tenth, five hours after the death of the "chief" of the southern rebellion, when his corpse was already in the police station of the city of Cuautla, on public view.'[10] The cropped photographs themselves that feature in the collage are readily recognisable from the selection of images in circulation of the corpse. In the lower section, two images in circular frames comprise, on the left, a detail from the Mora image, captioned 'Emiliano Zapata on public display'; and on the right, a detail from the same scene, this time of the corpse positioned on its side. Significantly, this detail is captioned 'The Attila of the south, surrounded by his executioners', thereby confirming the identity of the men who surround the corpse, to whom we will return below.[11] In the centre, an enlarged cut-out of Zapata's head alone, again extracted from Mora's photograph, intersects with the two lower images in a style reminiscent of a Venn diagram. A set of five fingerprints protrudes crown-like from behind the corpse's head, as if it were resting in the palm of this handprint. What though are we to make of this, to contemporary eyes at least, rather curious collage?

Grounded in the truth value associated with photography as an indexical medium of representation, two discursive registers intersect in the layout and design of this collage. First and foremost, it carries forensic weight, derived from the visual analogy between the fingerprint and the photograph. Tom Gunning (1995: 24) traces the dual emergence of photography and the fingerprint into new state discourses of power and control, stating: 'While the clearest and ultimately most successful example of new systems of criminal identification was the gradual adoption of the fingerprint, throughout the latter part of the nineteenth century (and into the twentieth) photography was used both as a means of identification and as a means of gathering evidence of a crime'. Let us leave to one side the notion of crime scene evidence, to return to it later on.[12] For now, we should observe that the combination of the trio of images and the fingerprints testify to the death of Zapata as a unique individual. Alongside the legal documents that were drawn up certifying the identity of the corpse and the results of the autopsy, to paraphrase Gunning (1995: 20) through its indexicality, iconic accuracy, and mobility of circulation, this collage 'provides the ultimate means of tying identity to a specific and unique body'. It is significant to note, however, that the editor of El Demócrata felt the need to deploy the combined testimonial force of both photographs and fingerprints on the front cover.

129

If the editorial staff of El Demócrata appear to insist on the forensic status of its photographic collage, it had just grounds to do so that go beyond combating the 'false alarms' that had previously heralded Zapata's death. Many simply refused to accept that it was in fact Zapata who had been ambushed and annihilated at Chinameca on 10 April 1919. To be sure, in the presence of a notary, the corpse was formally identified by an imprisoned Zapatista, Eusebio Jáuregui, who had known Zapata well. But, from the moment the corpse was formally identified, rumours began to circulate that Zapata had not died, that he could still be seen riding through the sierra of Morelos.[13] The body that had been brought to Cuautla, it was alleged, did not display the wart, the scar, the missing finger, in sum, all manner of minor, but telling, idiosyncratic features that confirmed that the corpse was not that of Zapata. For his part, having served his purpose, the witness Jáuregui was executed on 14 April on the orders of González.

At the same time, however, the palm of the hand in which the caudillo's head appears to rest invokes the second discursive register at play in this image, namely, its status as a trophy photograph. In the style of François Aubert's photograph of Maximilian's corpse made just over half a century earlier, a visual totem that declared the Mexican republic's right to exist as a sovereign state, this collage is a visual statement of Constitutionalist power. In presenting the actors in the ambush and assassination holding up their victim, it inscribes the power of the living over the dead and victors over the vanquished. At the same time, it also proclaims the triumph of middle-class metropolitan values over traditional peasant values and, by extension, mestizo Mexico over indigenous Mexico. In the context of such a strident visual statement, the editorial design decisions made by the staff of El Demócrata are worthy of further comment.

Not content to display a single image of Zapata's corpse, through the trope of repetition, the design and layout bespeak an overdetermined insistence on Zapata's annihilation. This is nowhere more evident than in the form of visual decapitation that is graphically enacted, whereby Zapata's head, trophy-like, rests as if in the palm of a hand. And here, it is possible to give the hand another inflection, namely as bloody palm print, where to have 'blood on one's hands' is an allusion to the blood of the enemy and therefore has positive connotations. Indeed, this form of trophy-like visual display harks back to the origins of the struggle for independence, to the execution in 1811 of the four insurgent leaders Miguel Hidalgo, Juan Aldama, Mariano Jiménez and Ignacio Allende, whose corpses were decapitated, their heads placed on display on the four corners of the Alhóndiga de Granaditas in Guanajuato. There they remained as a potent warning against future rebellion until independence was finally won in 1821. It also anticipates the fate of Villa's corpse, which, even after it had been laid to rest in its grave, was not exempt from post-mortem attention. 'On February 6, 1926, the administrator of the cemetery [of Parral rather than Ciudad Chihuahua where Villa had hoped to be buried in an ostentatious crypt he had prepared during his life] found that Villa's grave had been opened, and that his head had disappeared' (Katz 1998: 789).[14]

In this way, the photographic collage spread across top fold of the front cover of *El Demócrata* did more than simply serve as a guarantor of the identity of the corpse; it was also a form of visual enactment of the historical practice of the decapitation of those political agents cast as public enemies. Like the heads of the insurgent leaders of the 1810 insurrection, like Maxmiliano and, on a micro scale, like Fortino Sámano in 1917, the visual display of Zapata's corpse enacted the violent imposition of power and sovereignty. The photographic image of Zapata's body, combining forensic evidence with trophy status, was thus freighted with narrative burden, warning those who might defy the Constitutionalist regime of the consequences that would befall any such seditious action in the future.

FORGETTING FORENSIC EVIDENCE

The photographic reproduction and mass mediation of Zapata's corpse not only functioned simultaneously as evidence and a warning; one of the purposes governing its widespread display was also to promote forgetting, reminding us once again of photography's complex relationship with discourses of memory. In this regard, it bears underlining that after the corpse was photographed, it was subsequently buried in a simple, but deep grave, so that '"Zapatista fanatics" would not try to move it' (Brunk 2004: 149). And with it, so the Constitutionalists hoped, the revolutionary ideology of Zapatismo would also be buried. In the words of González: 'Zapata having disappeared, Zapatismo has died' (Knight 1986, Vol. 2: 366). In the slow process of pacifying the country after nearly ten years of warfare, in 1919 the last thing that the Carranza regime wanted was a martyr.

Zapata's post-mortem image was indeed bound up in the dynamics of forgetting; just not quite in the fashion envisaged by the Constitutionalists, however. As we have already seen, with the triumph and consolidation of that oxymoron the conservative revolution, Zapata – 'the most vilified of the revolutionary leaders' and the figure who most embodied 'middle-class fears of an imagined dark, rural, unruly, Indian Mexico' (Gilbert 2003: 127) – did not simply disappear from the cultural imaginary, to be replaced by visual celebrations of the Constitutionalist caudillos. Rather, his stature continued to grow in both popular and official commemorative discourses, albeit at different rhythms and paces and with distinct ideological connotations. It was neither Zapata nor Zapatismo that were erased from memory. Instead, what had to be forgotten were the 'sordid details' (ibid.: 133) of the assassination plot, of which Mora's photograph provided graphic evidence.

Given Zapata's post-revolutionary status, it would indeed be legitimate to imagine that his photographic death mask would conveniently disappear from circulation. As the official mythology associated with Zapata developed in the post-revolutionary period, there are, however, no grounds to suggest that this image, as evidence of Constitutionalist responsibility for the murder of a figure who went on to become a national hero, was assigned to the inner recesses of the nation's archives. On the contrary, as Brunk (2004: 150) establishes in relation to the display of Zapata's corpse, 'In the decades that followed, the lasting significance of the viewing of the body periodically reached print. In 1938 a newspaper article written for the anniversary of Zapata's death described an exchange in Yautepec, Morelos, during which a local doctor averred that some who had examined the corpse claimed it was missing the wart Zapata had on his left cheek.'

Making a martyr of Zapata would have been inconvenient to the Constitutionalist cause in 1919; nevertheless, before long, such a figure became indispensable. As Anderson (2006: 206) puts it in the concluding lines of his classic study of nationalism, 'the nation's biography snatches, against the going mortality rate, exemplary suicides, poignant martyrdoms, assassinations, executions, wars and holocausts. But, to serve the narrative purpose, these violent deaths must be remembered/forgotten as "our own"'. Zapata's death is emblematic of one such assassination that, as is commonly accepted, became a 'poignant martyrdom' within the sedimenting processes of remembrance and forgetting that structure the biography of the Mexican nation: a national biography in which, as we have already seen, the dead and the about-to-die were endowed with special status.

As early as 1924, historical amnesia regarding the facts surrounding his demise set in under the astute political leadership of Obregón, and Zapata rapidly made the transition into the official post-revolutionary pantheon, his memory readily harnessed to state projects of consensus-building. Or as Brunk (1998: 464) puts it: 'Once cleansed of certain troublesome realities – like the fact that Zapata had fought for years against the Constitutionalist faction to which Obregón belonged – the memory of the Martyr of Chinameca promised to be helpful in retaining the support of the peasantry.'[15] To grasp the specifically visual factors that might have facilitated this process of cleansing, we must once more return briefly to Mora's image and reconsider its particular visual eloquence, this time in the light of broader iconographic traditions in the context of a profoundly Catholic country.

As we saw in relation to the about-to-die photograph of Fortino Sámano in Chapter 5, photographs can linger in the public domain because they chime with discourses that are not visible at the time of their making. Such, without doubt, is the case of Mora's photograph. Once again, it is worth rehearsing an idea that has become a thread running throughout the present study: namely, that the assassins assembled in the frame cannot for one moment have imagined the afterlife that the dead Zapata, and his photographic image in which they are participants, would go on to enjoy in the post-revolutionary imagination. This, as we have already seen, is the 'future anterior' of photographic iconicity. At the same time, and as we also saw in relation to the photograph of Fortino Sámano, images get lodged in a given cultural imagination because they echo those that precede them. In short, the future anterior of photographic iconicity is invariably anchored in past templates that antedate the photographic event. If Zapata's death was readily recuperated into an official narrative of martyrdom, ironically, the composition of Mora's trophy photograph itself promotes such recuperation, where key elements mesh with the visual repertoire associated with the passion of Christ, in particular, in the way in which it combines elements of the iconography of the Man of Sorrows and the entombment.[16]

The Man of Sorrows, as Martin O'Kane (2005: 69) notes, 'became one of the most popular of all devotional images throughout medieval and early renaissance Europe'. Part of the Christian iconographic traditions, it travelled to the so-called New World, participating in the process of evangelisation of the Contact period.[17] The wounded body of Christ – sometimes featured alone, sometimes held up by angels – is generally depicted in half length; his hands, displaying their stigmata, are often crossed in front of his body. Designed to draw the viewer/worshipper into an affective relationship with Christ in his suffering, one of the defining features of the Man of Sorrows is the way in which it 'depicts Christ wounded, bleeding and dead in the tomb, yet paradoxically alive, upright and suffering, animated by a mysterious life-force' (ibid.). As should be clear, the disposition of the body of Zapata in Mora's photograph mirrors many of the iconographic features of the Man of Sorrows, including the half-length, wounded body, the crossed hands and perhaps most strikingly, the sense of being alive while dead. In fact, the body appears to be in a position of repose; it is almost as if Zapata were asleep.

At the same time, the assembly of human figures holding up Zapata's body also invokes the tradition of religious imagery in which Christ's body is displayed as it is being transported to the tomb, usually featuring Mary and St John, among other dramatis personae. Writing of one such image, namely Michelangelo's *Christ Carried to the Tomb* (undated, National Gallery, London), Alexander Nagel (2000: 29) states the following:

> The figure of the dead Christ is a calm center surrounded by effort and struggle. Those around him strain upward, but his figure describes a relaxed curve against their strict isocephaly. They pull and hoist, evidently struggling under great weight, and yet Christ's figure seems to rise by itself . . . His limbs are passive, pushed and turned amidst the jostling, and yet a hint of torsion gives the sense of a body controlled from within. Christ's body is held up to view, almost inadvertently, in the midst of the carrying, and yet it presides, ambiguously enthroned, in the center of the composition. Christ assumes an unwitting majesty in death. (Nagel 2000: 29)

To be sure, Nagel's analysis is devoted to a painting produced in quattrocento Italy. Nevertheless, with some minor modifications, it would not be too fanciful to replace the name of Christ with that of Zapata, and Nagel could almost be describing Mora's image. In Mora's photograph, a calm centre that is offset against the effort and struggle of those who jostle to get into the frame, Zapata 'assumes an unwitting majesty in death'.

To see the process of the sanctification of Emiliano Zapata at work in the broader sphere of post-revolutionary visual culture, it is instructive to turn briefly to the state-sponsored mural project, and particularly the work of Diego Rivera, where the revolutionary's death was painted into a narrative of sacrifice and martyrdom, with all the paradoxes that this entailed. In Rivera's mural cycle, executed between 1923 and 1927 in the newly established public university for agronomy and agriculture at Chapingo, 'the revolutionary ideal of agrarian land reform in conjunction with that of free, secular education for all . . . [found] their most commanding pictorial representation' (Craven 2002: 51). Formerly a hacienda, owned by a powerful landlord during the Porfiriato, the university was itself a key example of revolutionary reform, having been subject to land-redistribution policies instituted during Obregón's regime. Rivera's cycle, painted in the seventeenth-century ex-chapel at Chapingo, was inspired by a popular saying associated with Zapata's political cause: '"Enseñar la explotación a la tierra y no la del hombre". (Here one teaches to exploit the land not other people)' (Craven 2002: 52). Not only did the spirit of Zapatismo animate the images at Chapingo; an allusion to the revolutionary leader in death also features in a panel on the southern wall of the chapel. *La sangre de los mártires revolucionarios fertilizando la tierra* (Blood of the revolutionary martyrs fertilising the earth, 2.44m × 4.91m, 1926) offers the viewer a cross-section of the ground in which the horizontal bodies of Zapata and author of the 1911 Plan de Ayala, Otilio Montaño (1877–1917), lay foot to foot. Wrapped in red shrouds, Zapata and Montaño lay buried below *milpas* – maize fields with their connection to Mesoamerican culture – which spring up in the fertile earth above them. In a country with deep-rooted Catholic beliefs, such an image of human sacrifice for the common good cannot but have resonated deeply. The fecundity of the land vindicates the deaths of Zapata and Montaño, which have not been in vain.

It is important to underline that this is not to assert that Rivera worked directly from photographic images of Zapata's corpse for his frescoes on the south wall of Chapingo. Rather, it is to suggest a confluence: Rivera produced *La sangre de los mártires revolucionarios fertilizando la tierra* at a time when the 'sordid details' of Zapata's assassination – of which Mora's image furnished graphic evidence – were still lodged in living memory. That Rivera invoked Zapata in death, melding Pre-Columbian and Marxist elements with Christian motifs, on the one hand, chimes with the resonances already present in the trophy photograph; on the other, it points to the processes of disavowal at work that were playing out in the sphere of state-sponsored visual culture.

In this way, it is possible to trace the paradoxes of an iconographic thread that twines a deep-seated religious visual tradition associated with the suffering of Christ, through Mora's trophy photograph, with its uncanny echoes of that pre-photographic religious precursor, to the post-revolutionary visual culture. In the post-revolutionary sphere, as Adrian Bantjes (2006: 138) argues, defanaticisation campaigns 'were linked to national politics and followed a coherent cultural script aimed at establishing a revolutionary, nationalist civil religion'. Insofar as Zapata was central to the establishment of that civil religion, to home in on and tease out the meanings that traverse the photographic representation of the revolutionary leader's corpse is to come face to face with an array of paradoxes. In this reading, the photograph of Zapata's corpse is put into the service of the official project of reprogramming popular memory. The circumstances of the production of the photograph are disavowed. Instead the photograph as bearer of knowledge – Zapata was assassinated by the conservative faction of the revolution, his memory co-opted by it – is disavowed and becomes a site of production of belief – in Zapata's status as a secular Christ figure – where belief, ironically, is supported from within the very frame of the forensic photograph itself.

AFTER IMAGES

In the early 1970s Mora's photograph of Zapata resurfaced: in Héctor García's *La Verónica* (1972) (Figure 7.5), and Alberto Gironella's *La muerte de Zapata No. 2* (1974) (Figure 7.6). In *La Verónica*, picking up on the religious inflections at play in the photograph on the one hand, and echoing the uses to which the photograph was put in *El Demócrata* on the other, the head of Zapata appears on an embroidered cloth, proffered to the camera's lens by an indigenous peasant woman. Or as García describes it in an interview with Cristina Pacheco (2005: 286): 'I took the photo of a peasant woman who is displaying a napkin to sell it, its corners embroidered onto a sugar sack from the 'Emiliano Zapata' refinery. Gironella mounted the face of the murdered Zapata onto this photo, converting the napkin into another veil of Veronica'.[18] *La Verónica* invokes the legend of Saint Veronica who, moved by Jesus's suffering on his way to Mount Calvary, wiped his face with a veil or napkin to then find a true likeness of it imprinted on the cloth. In a self-referential gesture, the image draws a parallel between the imprint of Christ's face onto Veronica's veil and the photograph as indexical trace of that which was before the camera's lens, which in the words of García is 'una especie de magia, de milagro no resuelto racionalmente en el prodigio de la fotografía' / 'a kind of magic that is not resolved rationally through the marvel of photography' (Pacheco 2005: 285).

If *La Verónica* invites its viewers to reflect on the quasi-magical power of photographic representation, it does so in precise terms and at a specific historical moment. Extracting the head of Zapata in Mora's photograph from its contextual base in the hands of his assassins, his true likeness is now to be found imprinted on an embroidered cloth in the hands of an elderly indigenous woman, flanked by a young boy. Both woman and child, unlike the assassins in the original full version, stare insistently into the camera's lens, meeting the gaze of the viewer. Set against a non-descript, rural backdrop, the deep furrows that mark the woman's leathery skin and her unkempt hair, combined with the frayed neckline of the child's serape, speak of hardship and poverty. García's image conflates two temporalities within the space of the photographic frame – namely 1919 and 1974 – in this way commenting on the continuing marginalisation of indigenous peoples and the

7.5 Héctor García, *La Verónica*, Estado de México, 1972.

7.6 Alberto Gironella. *La muerte de Zapata No. 2*, 1974.

lack of social justice in the fifty-five years since the death of Zapata; and this despite his sacralisation in official discourse. The material manifestation of Zapata's death mask in 1974 also acts as a ghostly premonition of what was to come. As we shall see in the next chapter, the posthumous career of (the photographic image) of Zapata and his cause was to take on new life, especially in the aftermath of the 1982 debt crisis, this time in the hands of the consummately media-savvy EZLN.

NOTES

1 Díaz died in 1915 at the age of 84 in Paris. Huerta's route through exile took him initially to England and Spain via Jamaica, before returning to the US in 1915. There he died of cirrhosis of the liver that same year, incarcerated in Fort Bliss (Texas), not managing to return to Mexico as planned.

2 Significantly, in addition to those featuring Villa's corpse, of the 364 postcards categorised under the heading 'revolution' held by the Universidad Autónoma de Ciudad Juárez, 46 are related to scenes of death, from the incineration of corpses through executions by firing squad, to so-called necktie parties, according to the English caption denominating a scene of multiple hangings. See http://bivir.uacj.mx/postales/ (accessed 14 May 2007).

3 Col. SINAFO-FN-INAH # 6818/68189.

4 Moving images captured at Zapata's burial are included in *Memorias de un mexicano* (Carmen Toscano, 1950), based on footage compiled by her father, Salvador Toscano, and edited after his death by his daughter. Further details regarding this film can be consulted at: www.fundaciontoscano.org/esp/memorias_mex.asp. At the time of writing it was possible to consult scenes of Zapata's funeral on YouTube at: www.youtube.com/watch?v=XFxSy2ZzvXw&NR=1 (accessed 10 August 2007).

5 In the context of a discussion of the way in which the artist Felipe Ehrenberg (1943–) has taken up the figure of Zapata in his work, Victor Sorell (1987: 23) claims that 'the face appearing immediately above Zapata's in Mora's photograph is that of Sánchez Paboada [*sic*], the political godfather (padrino) of Luis Echeverría'. This appears to be a typographic error and is a reference to Rodolfo Sánchez Taboada (1895–1955), president of the PRI under whom Echeverría served as personal secretary.

6 'Zapata ha muerto. Es recogido el cadáver del temible cabecilla en el pueblo de Ayoxoxtla, del E. de Puebla. Emiliano Zapata, levantado en armas en febrero de 1911, al amparo de la revolución maderista, encarnó en el Sur de la República la destrucción, la crueldad y bandidaje. Sus hazañas introdujeron en el idioma un vocablo terrible: Zapatismo.'

7 'Como algunas veces se ha propagado la igual noticia y a los pocos días ha sido rectificado, en esta vez el público no se impresionó, y la especie fue acogida con indiferencia.'/'As the same news has been spread on other occasions and then corrected some days later, this time the public was not impressed and the news received with indifference.' *El Diario*, 30 March, 1914.

8 Based on textual accounts, Brunk (2004: 147) comments 'The bloodstained clothing Zapata had been wearing also apparently made its way to the city, where it was placed for a time in the showcase in front of a newspaper building facing the Alameda Central, a downtown park.' The Casasola Archive holds a photograph (Col. SINAFO-FN-INAH # 64355) of the showcase and its blood-spattered remains, which is reproduced in Casanova and Konzevik (2006: 42), where a sign in the lower right-hand corner of the case states, 'Pistola, espuelas, sombrero y prendas de vestir que llevaba Emiliano Zapata cuando fué muerto. Estos objetos fueron enviados por el Gral. Pablo González a *El Pueblo*'/'Pistol, spurs, hat and clothing that Emiliano Zapata was wearing when he was killed. These objects were sent by Gen. Pablo González to *El Pueblo*'.

9 'hacerle honor a su triste memoria'; 'contrarrestar el pesimismo del público cuando de semejantes noticias se trata, máximo en este caso concreto en que como en tantas otras veces pueden dudar algunos de la muerte del "jefe" suriano, aunque ella está hoy perfectamente confirmada'.

10 'COMO FUE LA MUERTE DEL "ATILA DEL SUR"'; 'La Inteligencia y la Astucia, al Servicio de Hombres Resueltos, Vencieron la Desconfianza Armada de los Rebeldes

Surianos'; 'Tres Fotografías que Muestran al Famoso Emiliano Zapata, ya Cadáver, y que son la Prueba Plena de su Aniquilamiento'; 'Ilustramos esta información, con las fotografías tomadas la misma noche del día diez, cinco horas después de muerto el "jefe" de la rebelión suriana, cuando su cadáver se encontraba ya en la inspección de policía de la ciudad de Cuautla, a la expectación pública.'

11 'Emiliano Zapata expuesto al público'; 'El Atila del sur rodeado de sus ejecutores'.

12 For an excellent discussion of crime photography in Mexico City, see Lerner (2007).

13 The myths surrounding the circumstances of Zapata's death continue to circulate. For example, Francesco Taboada Tabone's documentary *Los últimos Zapatistas: Héroes olvidados* (2002) features the testimony of surviving Zapatistas, in which veterans deny the leader's death, alleging that he went to 'Arabia'. See Brunk (2008) on the 'posthumous career' of Emiliano Zapata.

14 See Braddy (1960), on the possible perpetrators of the decapitation of Villa, whose ghost, so popular folklore has it, appears either headless or carrying its own head. Sergio González Rodríguez (2009: 27), invokes Miguel Hidalgo y Costilla and Villa in his literary essay *El hombre sin cabeza*, a discussion of the terrifying escalation of drugs-related violence in Mexico since 2006 and associated decapitations as a favoured modus operandi of the cartels.

15 By contrast, while the figure of Villa has equally gripped popular memory, his official consecration occurred rather later, namely in 1976, when 'President Luis Echeverría decided that the proper place for Villa's remains was the monument of revolutionary heroes in Mexico City, and on November 18, his remains were solemnly dug up in Parral to be brought to the Monument of the Revolution' (Katz 1998: 790). Meanwhile, Carranza's remains were transferred from their original place of burial in a pauper's grave to the Monument of the Revolution in 1942, where they rest uneasily in what has become an ideologically fraught site of commemoration, with erstwhile mortal enemies making strange bedfellows in death. See Benjamin (2000) on the Monument to the Revolution.

16 I would like to thank my colleague Stefano Cracolici for drawing my attention to these iconographic traditions and to the work of Alexander Nagel.

17 On the role of the visual in the Contact period, see for example Gruzinski (2001); Lara (2008).

18 'Tomé la foto de una campesina que está mostrando, para venderla, una servilleta bordada en las esquinas sobre una manta de costal de azúcar del ingenio "Emiliano Zapata". Sobre esa foto Gironella engastó el rostro masacrado de Zapata con lo cual la servilleta se convirtió en otro manto de la Verónica.' See Segre (2005) on this photograph within the context of the hermeneutics of the veil in Mexican photography.

8

Zapatistas in the city

In August 1994, erecting a make-shift 'convention centre', or 'Aguascalientes', named after the revolutionary Convention of 1914, the EZLN hosted the first of a number of extraordinary gatherings, deep in the jungle of Chiapas. The first Convención Nacional Democrática (CND) was attended by some 7,000 Mexican and foreign delegates, who converged on the *ejido* Guadalupe Tepeyac in the heart of rebel-held territory. There they engaged in debate on democracy, justice, the rights of indigenous peoples and civil rights in Mexico more generally. *Cronista* Carlos Monsiváis, one of the delegates to make the arduous journey into the jungle, charts the moment when Subcomandante Marcos took to the stage in the playfully titled 'Crónica de una convención (que no lo fue tanto) y de un acontecimiento muy significativo' (Chronicle of a convention (that wasn't really one) and of a very significant event).[1] In a vignette that highlights both the historical trajectory that has led to the CND and the theatricality of the occasion, Monsiváis observes: 'It is Marcos's turn at the podium. The moment is electric, or the shining faces proclaim it to be so on seeing that, at least in this supreme allegory, what has been awaited since 1914, or some other legendary date, has come to pass' (1994: 320).[2] Later, at a press conference held on the final day, Marcos invites audience participation in the spectacle. Offering to take off his mask, he receives an unequivocal negative response: '*Marcos sin pasamontañas no es admisible, no es fotografiable, no es la leyenda visible*' / 'Marcos without the mask is not acceptable, not photographable, he is not the visible legend he is' (Monsiváis 1994a: 323, italics in the original).

The historical and symbolic resonances of 'this very significant event' and others like it hosted by the EZLN cannot be overestimated. As established in the burgeoning literature devoted to the formation and uprising of the EZLN, 'The group's name, methods, and message clearly invoked the spirit of the Mexican Revolution, advancing a simple platform of work, land, housing, food, health, education, independence, liberty, democracy, justice, and peace in the names of Emiliano Zapata and Pancho Villa' (Stephen 2002: 144). But the spirit of the

8.1 'De la selva de concreto a la selva Lacandona' / 'From the concrete jungle to the Lacandon jungle'. Convención Nacional Democrática, Chiapas, August 1994.

revolution is not confined to the group's name alone, or to its invocation of historic events such as the 1914 Convention of Aguascalientes. It is also established in the EZLN's relationship to the photographic image, which exceeds the fundamentally photogenic status of the mask – '*Marcos sin pasamontañas no es admisible, no es fotografiable*' – and involves a performative appropriation of photographic icons produced during the 1910 revolution.

In fact the preparations for the 1994 CND provide a significant instance of such an appropriation. According to sociologist Sergio Sarmiento, 'the CND symbolizes, for the first time [in Mexican history], the Indians summoning the rest of the nation, summoning us, the *ladinos*, to the project of remaking the nation, to form a new constituency together' (cited in Saldaña-Portillo 2003: 332). The 'rest of the nation' called to Chiapas for this momentous occasion was hailed, in part, by a poster appropriation of *Villa en la silla presidencial* (Figure 8.1). Pasted up in locations across Mexico City, in the place of Zapata, the poster featured 'the EZLN's most prominent spokesman, Subcomandante Marcos, wearing his signature ski mask, but also with the sombrero. Beside him, supplanting Villa, was social activist and professional wrestler Superbarrio Gómez, in his customary wrestling garb' (Brunk 1998: 459).[3] Drawing on and reworking an instantly recognisable photographic icon which, as we saw in Chapter 4, has come to stand in for the revolution as a unifying myth in the cultural imagination, the neo-Zapatistas at once projected a virtual presence in the heart of the nation; at the same time, they invited their urbanite compatriots to join them at the margins of the nation – 'Todos a la Convención Nacional Democrática' – to reflect on the state of the nation and particularly the place of indigenous subjects within it.

141

A complex temporal and spatial dynamic underpins the EZLN's appropriation of *Villa en la silla*-as-poster that will form the organising principle of this chapter. In 1914, the troops of Villa and Zapata came in from the provinces to occupy Mexico City at the peak of the revolution's 'social curve', the culminating – post factum – visual event being the photo opportunity on the presidential chair. In 1994, under the slogan 'De la selva de concreto a la selva Lacandona'/'From the concrete jungle to the Lacandon Jungle', Villa and Zapata have morphed into Superbarrio and Subcomandante Marcos, and now point Mexican citizens back to the margins, to Chiapas, a state that largely remained unaffected by the revolution. Shuttling between urban centre and rural margin, this chapter explores the ways in which iconic photographs have been transformed and performed in Zapatista activism. Through their mobilisation by the EZLN, iconic photographs have acquired strategic performative force in the movement's engagement with civil society in the struggle for what anthropologist Guillermo de la Peña (1999) has termed 'ethnic citizenship': an understanding of citizenship that encompasses both the right to equality before the law and the right to cultural specificity.

CONTEXTS

The antecedents and trajectory of the Zapatista uprising are by now well documented in an abundant critical literature that includes the extensive writings produced by the EZLN itself, analyses by journalists, *cronistas* such as Monsiváis, political activists and academics of varied disciplinary stripes, and internationally disseminated across a range of different media: from the printed word to documentary films to the Internet. A few, albeit schematic, pointers are nevertheless expedient in order to signpost the analysis that follows of the Zapatistas' performative engagements with photographic icons of the revolution.[4] As is well known, the Chiapas uprising took place on 1 January 1994, when armed, masked rebels, in their majority comprising indigenous peasants, occupied seven towns in eastern and central Chiapas, declaring war on the Mexican government. With its historical roots in the ethnic divisions established as a result of Spanish colonisation on the one hand and, more recently, in the Mexican government's relentless pursuit of neo-liberal reform on the other, the rebellion occurred in one of Mexico's poorest states, home to a diverse Mayan population of Tzetzales, Tzotziles, Ch'oles and Tojolabales, to name but the largest groups.

The classification 'Indian', as Alan Knight (1990: 76) argued in an influential essay, was born with the conquest and 'remained part of Spanish rather than Indian usage. It defined those who were not Spanish or *mestizo* and it lumped together the wide range of Indian groups, languages, and communities'. As a homogenising category, it has also been mobilised at various points in the historical trajectory of the entity that we now know as Mexico in attempts to fashion successive Creole, post-independence and post-revolutionary identities. The events in Chiapas, populated as it is by myriad ethnic groups, must be framed within the broader context of such hegemonic projects to appropriate elements of indigenous identity, and most particularly *indigenista* discourses that emerged in the aftermath of the 1910 revolution. The post-revolutionary period ushered in a programme of intense social reform, spearheaded by influential anthropologists-cum-missionaries of the Mexican state such as Manuel Gamio and Moíses Saénz, who called for the assimilation of the Indian into the nation. Through educational, social and cultural projects, their aim was to foster a national community in which 'the old Indian/European thesis/antithesis [would give] rise to a higher synthesis, the *mestizo*, who was neither Indian nor European, but quintessentially Mexican' (Knight 1990: 85). This was to be achieved by promoting and thereby installing select, folkloric elements of indigenous culture as foundational in the myth of national origin. In the final analysis, then, *indigenismo* was in no sense about incorporating a complex, pluralistic notion of the multiple indigenous ethnicities within national culture. Rather, as David Brading (1988: 85) puts it in powerfully blunt terms: 'The ultimate and paradoxical aim of official *indigenismo* in Mexico was thus to liberate the country from the deadweight of its native past or, to put the case more clearly, finally to destroy the native culture that had emerged during the colonial period. *Indigenismo* was therefore a means to an end. That end was cultural *mestizaje*.'[5]

If the post-revolutionary project of cultural *mestizaje* provides the broader framework in which to situate the Zapatista uprising, this must also be understood in relation to specific socio-economic factors at work in Chiapas over two crucial periods: on the one hand, the economic boom related to the oil industry (1970–1982), and on the other, the 1982 crash and its aftermath. The increased revenues associated with the expansion of the oil industry brought significant changes to the indigenous peasant communities of Chiapas. Support for traditional, small-scale agricultural production by the governments of Luis Echeverría (1970–1976), and José López Portillo (1976–1982) went hand in hand with programmes that encouraged the diversification of the peasant economy, thereby integrating small land-holders into the wider pattern of national and international market forces. The diversification of small-scale agricultural production – to include coffee, meat and speciality fruit and vegetables, in addition to the more traditional beans and corn – brought with it the migration of significant numbers of indigenous peasants from the Chiapanecan highlands to the state's lowland Lacandon jungle. As a result, and of consequence in the formation of the EZLN, the jungle was colonised by newly formed, pluri-ethnic communities, in which Tojolabales, Tzotziles, Ch'oles, etc. lived alongside one another.

Based precariously on borrowing set against future income, the boom inevitably led to bust when, in 1982, international oil prices fell precipitously. In response to the crisis, President Miguel de la Madrid (1982–1988), implemented the structural adjustments counselled by the World Bank and International Monetary Fund. These dramatically reversed the populist and protectionist government policies that were put in place after the revolution, privatising state-owned industry and eliminating agricultural subsidies, making way for foreign investment and free enterprise. In the process, the strongly corporativist relationship that had existed between the PRI and the peasantry, which had held firm since the 1930s, was abandoned overnight. Nowhere was the withdrawal of the social contract between state and peasantry more keenly felt than among the colonists of the Lacandon jungle, who were even more severely affected by the intensification of neo-liberal reform during the presidency of Carlos Salinas de Gortari (1988–1994). Fixed on a course to insert Mexico into the global economy through the North American Free Trade Agreement (NAFTA), Salinas made dramatic changes to Article 27 of the Constitution, allowing the privatisation of communally held peasant holdings (or *ejidos*). In the eyes of the modernising technocrats who now governed Mexico, small-scale production, which the state had hitherto supported, was 'backward', inefficient and no longer economically viable. They therefore set out to eliminate the peasantry as an economic formation that was out of place in, and more to the point, outside the timeframe of the modern nation. Even as neo-liberal reform constituted an attack on the peasantry, as an economic category, it nevertheless coincided with a revitalised *indigenismo*, or what De la Peña (2006: 281) terms a 'peculiar (neo-liberal) defense of cultural diversity which emphasises the need for governments to "transfer functions" to ethnic organisations and accept certain minority rights (such as bilingual education), yet to do all this without touching the political structure of the nation'.

While the government forged ahead with neo-liberal reform, over the ten-year period between 1984 and 1994, far from the centre of power, in Chiapas the EZLN took shape as a movement propelled by serious social grievances, with membership rising sharply during the Salinas *sexenio*. During the economic boom, with the influx of colonists, the demographic make-up of the Lacandón jungle had changed irrevocably. Left destitute by the onset of economic crisis, these colonists came to assert a reconfigured, overarching identity as *indígenas* (rather than as members of specific indigenous groups): an identity grounded in a sense of shared poverty. In other words if, in Knight's formulation, Indians had traditionally been the objects rather than subjects of *indigenismo*, the formation of the EZLN involved a radical reappropriation of indigenous difference. The assertion of a shared indigenous identity now became an avatar for political protest and agency, a vehicle via which to establish these ethnic subjects' legitimacy and rights in the national public sphere. A complex phenomenon, the EZLN's demands as articulated in the first *Declaración de la Selva Lacandona* in January 1994 were, as noted, straightforward. The rebels called for work, land, housing, food, health, education, independence, liberty, democracy, justice and peace. In so doing, and as the movement gathered momentum, aided and abetted by extensive national and international media attention, their demands came to reflect and refract concerns that were simultaneously local and national and, indeed, international.

TRANSFORMING ICONS

In her excellent study *¡Zapata Lives!*, anthropologist Lynn Stephen offers an account of the imbrication of the local in the national and vice versa in the emergence of the mythical figure Votán Zapata. The product of a hybrid fusion of Tzeltal deities Ik'al and Votán with the historical personage Emiliano Zapata, Votán Zapata was fashioned by Marcos in conjunction with indigenous founders of the EZLN as they mobilised in south-eastern Chiapas through the 1980s, forming 'a local icon embodying the spirit of the new indigenous Zapatismo there' (Stephen 2002: 158). In time, after the 1994 uprising, Votán Zapata was projected back into the wider national sphere, where he was invoked in, for example, EZLN communiqués, such as that issued on 10 April 1995, addressed to 'all the peoples and governments of the world':

> United with Votán, Zapata has risen again to struggle for democracy, liberty, and justice for all Mexicans. Although he has indigenous blood, Votán Zapata is not just fighting for the indigenous, he is also fighting for those who are not indigenous but who live in the same misery, without rights, without justice for their work, without democracy for their decision-making, and without liberty in their thoughts and words. (EZLN cited in Stephen 2002: 169)

What, though, is the story of Votán Zapata's emergence and how might this story frame an understanding of the EZLN's appropriation of iconic photographic images?

In a letter dated December 1994, Marcos describes how, some time in the 1980s, he came to encounter 'el viejo Antonio'/old Antonio, the Tzeltal village elder who acted as a conduit for the urbanite rebels into the Indian communities, and to whom he attributes the origins of the mythical figure Votán Zapata. Asked by old Antonio to explain who he is and what he is doing in the highlands of Chiapas, Marcos states: '"It's a long story," I say, and start to tell about Zapata and Villa and the revolution and the land and the injustice . . . I end with "And so we are the Zapatista Army of National Liberation"' (cited in Stephen 2002: 160). Old Antonio asks Marcos to tell him more about Zapata, allowing him to run through the historical chronology – from birth in Anenecuilco to death in Chinameca – before he declares that this was not how it was. Old Antonio then proceeds to recount the story of the two gods, Ik'al and Votán, who 'were two as one' and who, through the process of questioning, learned to walk 'together but separated and in agreement' (ibid.: 161).

Learning his lesson, Marcos asks old Antonio 'And Zapata?' to which his interlocutor replies:

> It's *that* Zapata that appeared here in the mountains. He wasn't born here, they say. He appeared just like that. They say that he is Ik'al and Votán, that they came here to end their long journey . . . And this Zapata said that he had arrived here and here he was going to find that answer to where the long road led. And he said that

sometimes there would be light and sometimes there would be darkness, but that they were all the same, Votán Zapata, Ik'al Zapata, white Zapata, and black Zapata, and that the two were the same road for all real men and women. (ibid.)

At this point in his narrative, Marcos describes Old Antonio's next action and, in so doing, produces a detailed verbal portrait of an iconic photograph of Zapata:

Old Antonio takes a plastic bag out of his *morral*, or carrying bag. Inside the plastic bag is a picture from 1910 of Emiliano Zapata. Zapata's left hand is grabbing the hilt of his sword, at the height of his waist. In his left hand, he has a pistol; two belts of bullets are crossed on his chest – a two-tone band of black and white crossing from left to right. He has his feet placed like someone who is remaining calm or walking, and his gaze says something like "I am here" or "Now I am going." There are two stairways. On one of them that ends in darkness, more Zapatistas with brown faces can be seen, as if they are coming out of the background; on the other stairway, which is lighted, there is no one and you can't see where it is going or where it comes from. (ibid.: 161–2)

The photograph in question is clearly an uncropped version of the famous, full-body portrait of Zapata, captured by the German photographer Hugo Brehme sometime between 1911 and 1913 (Figure 8.2).[6] It is significant to note, however, that if Marcos is able to produce a fine-grained if essentially flawed description of the Casasola photograph of Zapata – in the photograph he is in fact carrying a *rifle* in his *right* hand[7] – it is thanks to the interpretive skills of old Antonio, who guides and frames his viewing of the photograph:

I would be lying if I said I saw all of these details. It was old Antonio who called my attention to them. On the back of the photo it read:

Gral Emiliano Zapata, Jefe del Ejército Suriano

Gen. Emiliano Zapata, commander in Chief of the Southern Army.

Le Général Emiliano Zapata, Chef de l'Armée du Sud

*c.*1910. Photo by: Agustín V. Casasola.

Old Antonio said to me, 'I have asked this picture a lot of questions. That's how I got this far.' He coughed and flicked the ashes off of his cigarette. He gave me the photo. 'Take it,' he said, 'so that you can learn to question . . . and to walk.' (ibid.: 162)

To be sure, this narration of his encounters with old Antonio and the invention of Votán Zapata are emblematic of a mode of lyrical story-telling for which Marcos is renowned and which has given rise to a significant corpus of written communiqués, in addition to other forms of literary output. Nevertheless, as a verbal account of an iconic visual image, it illustrates the process whereby Marcos comes to see Zapata through the eyes of old Antonio, grounded in the local conditions of indigenous experience, and whereby Zapata, in turn, is transformed into Votán Zapata. In a figurative sense, Marcos does indeed 'take' the

8.2 Emiliano Zapata en su cuartel de Cuernavaca, retrato / Emiliano Zapata in his
Cuernavaca barracks, portrait

reproduction of Brehme's photograph with him, learning through old Antonio's
mentoring to ask questions and also to make photographic images ask questions. In fact, the exchange with old Antonio as it relates to the transformation of
Brehme's image represents a form of template that prefigures the transformation

by the EZLN of key photographic images made during the 1914 occupation of Mexico City that have been the subject of earlier chapters, namely *Villa en la silla* and *Zapatistas en Sanborns*. The sections that follow explore the EZLN's mobilisation of these photographs in order, on the one hand, to forge links and establish dialogue with civil society and, on the other, at the same time to engage performatively with the demands for 'coeval participatory democracy' (Nash 2001: 244) that stand at the centre of the movement's struggle.

TODOS A LA CONVENCIÓN NACIONAL DEMOCRÁTICA

Long ago, as we saw in Chapter 3, Porfirio Díaz recognised that in 'an authoritarian country, public opinion and national sentiment were both concentrated in and represented in the national capital' (Lomnitz 2001: xii). Although remote from the epicentre of the rebellion, the nexus of power, the media and national and international communities, Mexico City – in Díaz's parlance, the 'balcony of the Republic' – has been an important strategic coordinate in the EZLN's struggle from the outset. It is widely acknowledged, for example, that thanks to the actions of the some 10,000 people who, on 7 January 1994, marched on Mexico City's main square, the Zócalo, representing the Zapatistas in absentia, a massacre by government troops was averted. With the rebels' cause placed in the media spotlight, the government had no choice but to call a ceasefire with the Zapatistas and start negotiations. When, in February 1995, government agents unmasked the EZLN's spokesperson, Subcomandante Marcos, on national television, revealing his privileged, middle-class background, the anti-Zapatista publicity stunt back-fired. Civil society mobilised in the Zócalo once again, chanting the slogans '¡Todos somos Marcos!' and '¡Todos somos indios!' (We are all Marcos! We are all Indians!).[8]

The capital was, then, an important location in which to call civil society to attend the first CND in August 1994, one in which *Villa en la silla* had particular historical resonances. It should by now be obvious, but nevertheless worth underlining, that the poster announcing the CND invoked *Villa en la silla* quite simply because it was instantly recognisable to those who encountered it on the streets of the capital. An image-event that occurred shortly after the historic 1914 Convention of Aguascalientes – an effort by warring factions to reach a common accord using means other than arms – the appropriation of *Villa en la silla* established a visual link between past and present attempts to foster debate and dialogue. But there was more to the mobilisation of *Villa en la silla* than simple ready recognisability.

The transformation in 1994 of the 1914 image was staged at a moment when official appropriation of revolutionary iconography had reached new heights of irony during the presidency of Carlos Salinas de Gortari. In his brief discussion of the EZLN's deployment of the photograph, Brunk (2008: 3) suggests that 'Salinas answered the EZLN with political theatre of his own. Although he was not ready to surrender the PRI's claim to Zapata, shortly after the outbreak of the Chiapas insurgency he chose to proclaim amnesty for the rebels and express his desire for dialogue in front of an image of Carranza – the man ultimately responsible for Zapata's death. The threat was not lost on Marcos.' In effect, although Salinas might have selected Carranza as an appropriate sinister symbol in front of which to make the offer of dialogue, as his regime dismantled Article 27, sounding the death knell to the agrarian and social ideals of the revolution, it was in fact Zapata who became Salinas's cultural symbol of choice. Indeed, Stephen (2002: 72) underlines a fundamental irony: namely if Zapata had always been synonymous with land ownership, in his new neoliberal reincarnation, he was now invoked as 'the defender of individual property rights'. In short, circa 1994, Zapata became a more ideologically charged figure than ever before.

To invoke *Villa en la silla* in 1994 is, then, to contest the official appropriation of revolutionary iconography and to tap into the political affect of that pivotal moment at which 'the peasantry was actually able to capture the social life of the whole nation' (Williams 2005: 101). It is to restage that capturing of social life, forging visual – and real – links between the southern rebels and a powerful urban grass-roots movement with considerable local, national and international momentum. In this poster, Subcomandante Marcos's head has been superimposed onto the body Zapata. Meanwhile, the smiling Villa has undergone a radical, full-body transformation, donning the mask, boots, lamé tights and cape of Superbarrio. With his roots in the flowering of civil society that took place in the aftermath of the devastating earthquake that struck Mexico City on 19 September 1985, Superbarrio emerged in June 1987 as a representative of the Asamblea de Barrios (Neighbourhood Assembly). A coalition of scores of neighbourhood organisations, the Asamblea formed to force the government to accelerate housing-relief plans, protesting against the property speculators, who owned real estate that stood semi-abandoned in the centre of the capital, while thousands of the barrio's poor remained homeless.[9] In the popular hero Superbarrio, the Asamblea gained a symbolic figurehead who led street protests and, refusing to remove his mask, became a deft media manipulator, forcing public officials to negotiate in front of cheering crowds and TV cameras. Superbarrio's activism has not, however, been limited to the sphere of local, Mexico City politics. In 1987, the Asamblea proposed his candidacy for the national presidential elections scheduled to take place the following 6 July 1988. And in 1989, he made his first sortie to the United States, campaigning on behalf of the millions of undocumented workers north of the border.

Placing Superbarrio on the presidential chair alongside Marcos to his left, the poster advertising the CND brings together two representatives of grass-roots movements with broad national and international reach and appeal. All evidence indicates that Villa's occupation of the presidential chair with Zapata beside him was an impromptu act – as we have seen, to relieve the tedium of watching the

passing parades – nevertheless, viewed through a retrospective optic, the unpre-
meditated performativity of this photographic gesture becomes a precursor for
the sophisticated theatricality of popular struggle that has become such a successful tactic in the arena of contemporary politics. Both Marcos and Superbarrio
incorporate a dynamic element of performativity into their political activism, not
least in the form of the 'charisma' associated with the mask, with its attendant
'deferment of the moment of unmasking' (Levi 1997: 64) and in the symbiotic
relationship with the mass media. But perhaps most importantly, the poster, like
the original photograph, with its sea of faces and now including masked figures,
conjoins geographically distinct regions, in the process enacting a claim to ethnic
citizenship. That claim, as we will see in the section that follows, turns on the
demand to 'ethnic citizenship': the right to occupy a place in the nation – materialised in photographic performances at key sites in the capital – and by extension
to be included in the definition of the nation; and also the right to look out-of-
place, the right to difference within the national space.

THE CONSULTA

The Zapatistas have not only been represented in the city in absentia in the
form of their mediated image on the one hand, and by their most effective ally,
civil society, on the other. Zapatista representatives have made their way to and
staged their presence in the nation's capital at a number of points during the
movement's history.[10] Notably, in the present context in March 1999, when 5,000
delegates from the EZLN set forth from the Lacandón jungle en route to multiple points throughout the republic. The object of their journey was to promote
the Consulta Nacional por los Derechos de los Pueblos Indios y por el Fin de
la Guerra de Exterminio (National Consultation for the Rights of Indigenous
Peoples and the End of the War of Extermination). Scheduled to take place on 21
March, the *Consulta*, or referendum, asked Mexican citizens to cast their vote on
four basic questions related to the rights and place of indigenous peoples in the
space of the modern nation:

> 1 Do you agree that indigenous peoples should be included in all their diversity in the
> national project and take an active part in the construction of a new Mexico?
>
> 2 Do you agree that indigenous rights should be incorporated into the national
> Constitution in accordance with the San Andrés Accords and the corresponding pro-
> posal of the Commission for Harmony and Pacification of the Congress of Union?
>
> 3 Do you agree that we should attain real peace by means of dialogue, demilitarising
> the country with the return of soldiers to barracks, as established by the Constitution
> and its laws?
>
> 4 Do you agree that the people should organise and demand that the government
> 'rule by obeying' in all aspects of national life?[11]

Given the nationally-inflected orientation of the questions and, concomitantly, the movement that formulated them, as symbolic centre of the nation the capital was an important hub in activities related to the *Consulta*. Buses transporting EZLN delegates from Chiapas converged on the heart of Mexico City before fanning out to the more far-flung corners of the country; meanwhile promotional events in the capital itself received considerable media coverage which documented activities in a series of photographs, perhaps more accurately described as photo opportunities.[12] In these images, Mexico City is not simply a scenic backdrop to the Zapatista incursion into the 'urban leviathan' (Davis: 1994). Rather, it represents a densely layered and intensely mediated historical site in which to stage 'performances of democratic participation' (Saldaña-Portillo 2002: 297) in state-sanctified spaces of civic ritual: Reception of Zapatista Delegates in the Capital's Zócalo (Opposite the National Palace) (Figure 8.3); Zapatistas in the Centro Histórico (the Templo Mayor and the Metropolitan Cathedral visible in the background); Zapatistas visit the Museo Nacional de Antropología.

In an essay published in the journal *Desacatos* in 1999, De la Peña (23) defines ethnic citizenship as the 'the call to maintain a different cultural identity and social organization within a given state, which in turn should not only recognize but also protect and legally sanction those differences'.[13] For the Mexican anthropologist, then, ethnic citizenship is a concept that holds in delicate equilibrium the notion of universal citizenship and equality before the law alongside an emphasis on cultural and social specificity as manifest, for example, in the right to maintain different languages, customs, religious and medical practices. The demand for ethnic citizenship also lies at the heart of the 1999 *Consulta* and the four simple questions posed by the referendum. Thus when voters were asked: Do you agree that indigenous peoples should be included in all their diversity in the national project and take an active part in the construction of a new Mexico?', the weight of the question rested on the counterpoint between indigenous people's right to inclusion and participation in the nation, at the same time as having their right to difference recognised. Meanwhile, question two, with its reference to the San Andrés Peace Accords negotiated between the EZLN and the government in February 1996, inserts the indigenous right to difference within the legal framework of proposed changes to the national Constitution. Finally, questions three and four call for the rejection of intensified military activity, and the kind community-based, consensual democracy practiced by the Zapatistas – grounded on the principle of 'mandar obedeciendo'[14] – to be embraced at a national level. Crucially, where indigenous difference has traditionally been registered in temporal terms in official narratives, as at once integral to the definition of and yet temporally behind the modernising nation, the Zapatistas call for a reconfigured understanding of the temporal and spatial status of indigenous identity: Indians exist inside the space, and are coeval with time of the modern nation. How, though, might the *Consulta* and especially its emphasis on ethnic citizenship translate into photographic performances and what, moreover, of the city as a spatial and temporal locus for such performances?

Analysis of the Zapatistas' itinerary in the city, above all else, reveals a keen sense of the photo opportunities that their presence in the capital had to offer. It is no coincidence that the Zócalo, at the heart of the *Centro Histórico*, marked their point of arrival and the strategic point of departure from which to launch the *Consulta* in the city and in the wider context of the nation. Writing of the *Centro Histórico* – the official name for the zone of some ten square kilometres with a high density of monuments of historical significance, designated by presidential decree in 1980 –Jérôme Monnet (1995: 25) has the following to say: 'When what is at stake is the centre of the capital of a great country, all discourses and practices enter into the arena of national politics, putting into play and manifesting the tensions that underpin all Mexican society and its relations with the world.'[15] Their route through the city demonstrates that the Zapatistas were clearly alert to the profoundly national resonances of the *Centro Histórico*, overlain successively with Aztec, colonial and post-independence foundations. As June Nash (2001: 241) observes, during the *Consulta* the Zapatistas 'experienced what it was to join in the production of national popular spaces in the Zócalo . . . the huge public space that has been the center of many storms of protest especially since the debt crisis of 1982'.

The symbolic occupation and production of nationally inflected space is increasingly evident as the Zapatistas circulated in a range of different sites and situations in which they were photographed. Sometimes, the resulting images are the products of contingency, whereby the photographer and his/her subject happen to have been in the right place at the right time. Such is the case of the high-angle shot of masked visitors in the entrance to the Legislative Assembly; and the photograph depicting a lone Zapatista who is snapped, seated on the bus that has carried him or her – the *pasamontañas* or ski mask makes it impossible to determine – from Chiapas to the Zócalo, his/her masked face juxtaposed beside a reflection of the national flag, occupying the right-hand two-thirds of the frame. Elsewhere, there is evidence of more active collusion between photographer and subjects. Such images include the row of seven Zapatista men and women, their backs to the camera as they salute assembled delegates in the Zócalo, the Palacio Nacional visible in the background, with the silhouette of the Mexican flag outlined above the central balcony (Figure 8.3); or the photograph of the opening ceremony of the football match against ex-professional players for the national team. Featuring masked, saluting Zapatistas, sporting matching tops emblazoned with a star and the initials EZLN, and outsized white shorts over mismatched footwear, this photograph appeared on the front cover of *La Jornada* on 16 March 1999 (Figure 8.4).

That these performances for the camera are highly theatrical bordering on the self-reflexive, while on one level self-evident, nevertheless requires further elaboration in relation to the photo opportunity in which the Neo-Zapatistas like

8.3 Zapatistas en el Zócalo / Zapatistas in the Zócalo.

8.4 Zapatistas en partido de futbol soccer amistoso / Zapatistas in friendly football match.

their forebears in 1914 before them, partook of light refreshment in the famous restaurant of Sanborns, the event captured by scores of waiting photographers and TV camera operators (Figure 8.5). In short, what we find here is a photo opportunity that re-stages a photo opportunity-turned-iconic photograph. What, though, is at stake in the recreation of this classic photograph and how might it inform our understanding of the sequence of images taken at key points in the

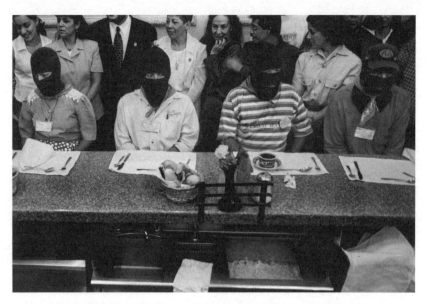

8.5 Zapatistas en el Sanborns de los Azulejos / Zapatistas in Sanborns.

capital during the Neo-Zapatistas' visit in 1994? To answer these questions, we must re-rehearse the meanings at play in the 1914 photo opportunity, in order to focus more fully on the play of race, space and time as they inhere in this image. As we saw in Chapter 6, when viewed in light of values of 1914, this sequence captures the transgressive irruption of indigenous peasants from the nearby state of Morelos into the 'civilised' and sacred space of the legitimate order represented by Sanborns. The incursion into the capital city was not something that the Zapatistas undertook with relish; their distrust and fear of urban values is well documented. Nor did the *capitalinos* greet the visitation by the armed rural masses with gusto, for their purported savagery and violent exploits had been vividly reported in the Mexico City press, in which the Zapatistas and particularly Zapata himself were consistently vilified throughout the armed conflict. These photographs, then, serve as visual evidence of the Zapatistas' encounter with the city: their lack of élan is clearly legible in the troops' faces; their rural apparel and demeanour are incongruous in the gentrified ambience of Sanborns.

In fact, as we saw, what arguably made the sight of Zapatistas in Sanborns such a compelling photo opportunity at the time of the production of this iconic sequence is its representation of a world turned (briefly) upside-down: in the turmoil of the revolution, the rightful occupants of the space behind the bar, frock-coated urban gentlemen, were usurped by gun-toting indigenous peasants. Significantly, if the original Zapatistas look out of place in Sanborns, that incongruity is predicated as much on a sense of temporal as spatial displacement: the city as bastion of modernity is no place for 'backward' indigenous peasants from the provinces.

By referencing the iconic (photographic) space occupied by their 1914 revolutionary namesakes and forebears, the contemporary Zapatistas engage in a complex rhetorical play of meaning. To metropolitan viewers in 1914, images in the 'Zapatistas in Sanborns' sequence connoted the irruption of the racial Other into the 'civilised' space of the modern city. In the aftermath of the conflict, however, the meanings associated with such images shifted fundamentally. The triumph of the conservative Constitutionalists brought with it the rehabilitation of both Zapata and Villa together with their popular, radical politics, as the post-revolutionary regime set out to establish or, more to the point, invent its revolutionary credentials.[16] With the redemption of these historical figures, and particularly Zapata, also came the valorisation of indigenous Mexico as a source of historical pride in the project of official *indigenismo* which, as we have seen, was merely a means to an end, the end being cultural *mestizaje*. In line with the official discourses of the post-revolutionary state, the meanings that accrued to images such as those in the 'Sanborns' sequence came to turn on a celebration of the popular forces unleashed by the revolution. What is more, nowhere was this visual rhetoric writ larger than across key public spaces of the capital, where the walls of the Palacio Nacional, for example, were filled to saturation with Diego Rivera's murals representing the nation's historical development: from the idyllic pre-Hispanic past, through the dark years of the conquest, to progress and bright future, products of the popular revolutionary struggle.

Temporarily taking the place of their wealthy, urbanite compatriots – who now pose in the back row, eager to form part of the photo opportunity – the contemporary Zapatistas skilfully signal that, despite the intervening eighty-five years between the production of the 1914 and 1999 photographs, like the original Zapatistas, as indigenous peasants – albeit masked indigenous peasants – they *still* look out of place at the bar of Sanborns.[17] In so doing, through this photographic staging, they call into question the post-revolutionary project of official *indigenismo*, revealing it to be a discourse of teleological development in which 'Indians may be Mexico's ideal ancestors, but mestizos are Mexico's ideal citizens . . . Indian difference is an essential precedent for this mestizo nation, even as Indians, with their difference, are the continuing targets of educational and cultural reform' (Saldaña-Portillo 2002: 295).

PHOTOGRAPHY AND METONYMY IN MEXICO CITY

The contemporary Zapatistas invariably still look out of place in Sanborns and, what is more, wherever they go in the city. Reporting one Tojolabal woman's experience of the metropolis during the *Consulta* in the pro-Zapatista daily newspaper *La Jornada*, respected EZLN commentator Hermann Bellinghausen (1999) recorded the following reaction: 'Accustomed to seeing cars very occasionally, one at a time, she found herself trapped in a traffic jam on the way to Magdalena Mixhuca, and asked with surprise: "why do they want so many cars?"' To the degree that the urban environment presented this indigenous woman with an array of unfamiliar and alien sensations, the Zapatistas in the city proved an equally strange sight to the capital's residents:

> But the surprises that they [the Zapatistas] get are equal to the surprises they give. Commotion on the corners of Iztacalco when a cattle truck passed by (which, for peasants, is for passengers) full of masked people looking at the passers-by who looked at them, stopped, pointed at them, commented on them to one another animatedly and greeted them with sympathy. (Bellinghausen 1999)[18]

To be sure, the encounter with *real-life* (rather than *mediated* Zapatistas) must have been disconcerting for these individual *capitalinos*, as evinced in the double-take described by Bellinghausen. The Zapatistas' masked faces and the simple detail of their mode of transport underlined the ideologically-charged gap separating rural and metropolitan Mexico and marked them as out-of-place in the urban environment.

To look out of place is, however, the point. The Zapatistas' struggle is about the simultaneous right to inclusion *and* ethnic specificity within the space of the modern nation. If, as I have suggested, the 'out-of-place-ness' of the original Zapatistas is both spatial and temporal, I now want to argue that the incongruity of the contemporary Zapatistas is an emphatically spatial displacement. Or to put this differently, the photographs produced during the *Consulta* are images that work performatively against the temporal logic that is inherent both in the photographic act and the city as a densely layered historical environment. There is, then, more to be said about the terms and conditions of the Zapatistas' incongruity in the city that sheds light not only the spatial dimensions of their staged photo opportunities, but also the temporal dynamics of these performances.

These dynamics come into focus through an exploration of the concept of metonymy and its relationship to photographic representation, and are crystallised in an essay by Eelco Runia, simply titled 'Presence'. Arguing against the dominance of metaphor in recent historiography, the philosopher of history asserts that presence – 'the unrepresented way the past is present in the present' (Runia 2006: 1) – as it is stored in metonymy may, in fact, constitute an equally, if not more compelling conceptual paradigm for thinking about what is at stake in the narration of history. Although a theoretical meditation on historiography, I suggest that Runia's reflections nevertheless offer an insight into the ontology of the photographic image and in particular, the relationship between space and time, presence and absence as they inhere in photographic images.

Runia situates his analysis as part of the contemporary turn to memory, remembrance and trauma, in which he argues that metonymy, the trope of 'presence in absence' (ibid.: 6) may prove an appropriate tool with which to grasp how the past continues to inhabit the present. In the first instance, Runia offers a dictionary definition of metonymy as 'a figure in which the name of an attribute or adjunct is substituted for that of the thing meant' (ibid.: 15), providing a range of specifically linguistic examples (i.e. sceptre for authority). However, he quickly clarifies that metonymy is not an exclusively linguistic occurrence, but can also inhere in objects – for example, in monuments or indeed cities themselves, in which '[s]ome parts are carefully restored, others are dilapidated. There are areas that once were destroyed by war (of which traces may or may not remain), areas that have been completely transformed by public works, areas in which "time has stood still"' (ibid.: 9). (Mexico City, it might be noted parenthetically, is a prime example of such a metonymic urban environment, manifesting traces of the Aztec and colonial pasts, as well as bearing the scars of conflict and indeed, natural disasters in the form of the 1985 earthquake.) To grasp the play of metonymy is then to reconsider historical time not in linear terms, but rather in terms of '"[c]ontinuity" and "discontinuity," that is not in a historical, temporal, "vertical" sense, but in the spatial, "horizontal" sense of "being thoroughly interwoven" and "radically contiguous"'(ibid.). It is ultimately to translate time into space. Furthermore, context is crucial to an understanding of the way in which metonymy functions, where it might be described as the '"wilfully inappropriate transposition of something from one context to another" and in its new context looks "slightly out of place"'(ibid.: 16).

With one brief exception, to be sure, Runia has nothing explicitly to say about photography. That exception is an allusion to the work of German writer W.G. Sebald, in whose novels, illustrations, in the form of photographs, train tickets, receipts, postcards, etc., which look strangely incongruous on the printed page, represent '[c]urious specimens of nonverbal metonymies in a linguistic context [where they] function as fistulae or holes through which the past discharges into the present'(ibid.).[19] Although he may have nothing directly to say about photography, it is striking that Runia's analysis of metonymy or 'presentism' could almost be a description of the ontology of the photographic image, in which the past lies in the object, whereby the photograph materialises presence in absence. Indeed, Runia invokes fossils and relics (ibid.) as examples of the kind of phenomenon under scrutiny which, like photographs, are precisely indexical signs, the trace of contact with the real inscribed on their surface. This is, of course, a terrain well-trodden by theorists of film and photography, from André Bazin (1967) to Roland Barthes (1981) and beyond. But where Runia's reflections on metonymy and its relationship to photography have particular explanatory force in the current discussion is in his emphasis, first, on the translation of time into space; second, on his understanding of the city as a densely layered space; and third, on his notion of metonymy as incongruity. How, then, might Runia's reflections on the trope of metonymy have a bearing on what is at stake in the Zapatistas' production of photographic space in the city?

Among the destinations on the Zapatistas' schedule in the capital are two we have not yet had occasion to comment upon more fully, depicting visits to the Templo Mayor and the Museo Nacional de Antropología (see Figure 8.6).[20] As even the casual visitor to Mexico City will recognise, these repositories of

CULTURA 33 LaJornada

VIERNES 19 DE MARZO DE 1999

■ Recorrido por el Museo Nacional de Antropología

Quince zapatistas descubrieron parte de sus raíces mayas

■ El grupo se sorprendió al ver a los voladores de Papantla

Ángel Peguero □ En tierra azteca, 15 zapatistas –procedentes de los Aguascalientes de La Realidad y Roberto Barrios– descubrieron parte de sus raíces mayas.

Al Museo Nacional de Antropología, el grupo llegó directo a la cafetería para tomar un refresquito para aminorar el calor de medio día y el altercado que tuvieron con el cuerpo de seguridad de la Basílica de Guadalupe que insistía en que se quitaran sus pasamontañas para entrar a la iglesia de la Cuauhtémoc que, como parte de las actividades previas a la consulta, los fueron a conocer la casa de la Virgen morena, el museo y el Metro. Al primer [...] uniformada que, finalmente, permitió el paso.

[...] de chiquitos de primaria se [...] la sorpresa de los turistas que visitan el museo cuando entraron al recinto [...] fue más, cuando desplegaron la manta [...] identifica como miembros de la brigada "Pancho Villa" que enarbola un sonriente y colorido *Speedy González*. Visitaron la sala maya y la de etnografía, [...] aprovecharon para intercalar su propia lección ayer temprano, a padecer la ciudad [...].

En ese jardín –que calmó los ánimos del pequeño Nicolás, bebé de once meses encaramado en la cintura de su madre zapatista– se toparon con estudiantes de la secundaria México, quienes los rodearon para preguntarles, primero con sorna y luego con curiosidad, el porqué estaban ahí.

"Por la consulta, para invitarlos a que participen", respondió un zapatista. "¿Y por qué luchan?", se aventó otra chavita, "por la pobreza que vivimos, porque el gobierno nos ha traído siempre entre ellos sin ayudarnos y ya nos cansamos, por eso nos organizamos, hicimos papelitos, los trajimos a ver si así puede haber una solución", les dijeron unos de dirigirse hacia la sala etnográfica para firmar el libro de visitantes distinguidos. Ahí, dos hombres y dos mujeres estamparon con letra chica y clara una frase que se repitió tres veces: "Bases de apoyo del EZLN".

Salieron sin recibir aplausos ni vivas, sólo alguna sonrisa de complicidad. Afuera, los voladores de Papantla se aprestaban a surcar los aires, "quiénes son, qué van a hacer", preguntaron los zapatistas que siguieron su camino sin detenerse. "Hubiera estado bonito verlos", dijo uno. Otra vez será.

Las bases del EZLN, en el Museo Nacional de Antropología ■ Foto: Cristina Rodríguez

■ **LA VIDA BREVE**

■ Cuatro embajadores rebeldes, en el CNA

La voluntad individual debe analizar su propio corazón

■ Cada uno debe luchar por un México nuevo, mensaje a los asistentes

Ángel Vargas □ Si algo caracteriza al movimiento zapatista desde su irrupción en 1994 es la palabra, aun aquella que está tando en silencio dice. Con ella mantiene su desigual lucha desde hace un lustro. Con ella vive esperanzado a que sus demandas sean escuchadas y cumplidas.

"Queremos decirles que nunca nos cansaremos y que seguiremos exigiendo", exclamaron *Arbey, Niel, Cristina y Yanet*, cuatro de los 5 mil delegados que el Ejército Zapatista de Liberación Nacional (EZLN) comisionó para promover en el país la consulta por el reconocimiento de los derechos de los pueblos indios y por el fin de la guerra de exterminio, que ha de celebrarse el próximo domingo.

Llegados al Distrito Federal desde la noche del domingo pasado, con poco más de un centenar de embajadores rebeldes, estos cuatro personajes se reunieron el mediodía de ayer con la comunidad artística del Centro Nacional de las Artes.

En el aula magna del CNA, investigadores, profesores, estudiantes y trabajadores administrativos y público escucharon durante dos y media horas la voz más profunda y llana de la realidad chiapaneca.

Luego de entonar el himno zapatista y un par de canciones para promover la consulta, *Cristina* leyó un comunicado de la dirigencia del EZLN, firmado por el *comandante Tacho*, en el que se plasman las razones por las que ese grupo envió delegados a todo el territorio nacional: nuestra "misión es dialogar con la sociedad civil, escuchar sus palabras y pedir que se escuchen las nuestras".

Arbey agregó: "No venimos a exigir a nadie. Es la voluntad de cada quien la que debe analizar su propio corazón". El diálogo había comenzado".

Con dificultades para expresarse en español, el hablar sencillo del cuarteto de delegados hizo poesía la mayoría de su decir. Por ejemplo, cuando *Arbey* definió el concepto de autonomía para el EZLN:

"Significa ser independiente al gobierno. Mandar obedeciendo. Atender el sentir del pueblo. No depender de ningún partido. No distinguir a la gente. Aquí nos estamos mandando y obedeciendo. Por eso a nadie se le obliga. Ser autónomo se vive respetando a los demás, pues todos somos iguales."

Luego de indicar que la fuerza para proseguir con su lucha está no en el cuerpo, sino en el espíritu, los zapatistas hicieron un llamado a la sociedad civil para romper el silencio que permite al gobierno apoderarse de todo México.

"El país entero está casi vendido, ya nos tienen vendidos. A cada uno nos toca algo que hacer para un México nuevo, con justicia, igualdad y libertad (...) Estamos sosteniendo todo el peso de aquellos que están bien plantados. Debemos luchar, tomados de las manos, para vivir mejor y que nuestros hijos sean felices en un mundo donde todos quepan."

Temas varios se desprendieron del corazón del grupo. Lo mismo expresaron la necesidad de que los indígenas sean incluidos en la Constitución, que definieron que *Marcos* es la suma de todos los que creen y pugnan por la libertad y la justicia; "es ser revolucionario".

Reiteraron su invitación a participar en la consulta y enfatizaron que continuarán con su consigna de "vivir por la patria o morir por la libertad".

■ *Eloísa, Erika, Saulo, Rodolfo, Claudio y Nicodemo dijeron su palabra*

8.6 Zapatistas visit the National Museum of Anthropology. *La Jornada*, 19 March 1999.

---

national cultural heritage are key sites not only on the tourist circuit, but also of civic ritual. The ruins of the foundations of Tenochtitlán's ceremonial centre and the national museum dedicated to the indigenous peoples of Mexico respectively, both are prime examples of sites that manifest Indians' status in national culture as Mexico's 'ideal ancestors' (Saldaña-Portillo 2002: 295), a status that does not, however, confer upon them the right to coeval citizenship. This dichotomy, as critics have noted, is reinforced in the Museo Nacional de Antropología's layout, where the displays have: 'consistently stressed the grandeur of the pre-Conquest past on the ground floor while promoting a stagnant, superficial profile of present-day indigenous communities on the top floor'. This has 'served to reinforce the notion that living indigenous communities are stuck in a cycle of reproducing a fixed "traditional" and "authentic" set of cultural practices, instead of actively producing culture' (Taylor 2005: 76). That is to say, the museum reproduces a temporal understanding of contemporary indigenous peoples as inhabiting a 'premodern' space prior to the present of the modern nation. In short, it denies their presence as coeval subjects within that national space.

Represented at the capital's key locations of cultural heritage, during the *Consulta* the city becomes a site in which the Zapatistas photographically perform the absence of contemporary Indians from the official spaces of the modern nation which, so to speak, only has room for an idealised, archaic construction of indigenous difference. What is more, the Zapatistas register this absence and the right to inclusion through the masked incongruity of their presence at these sites. What, after all, is a photo opportunity by one definition, if not a sight worthy of recording for posterity for its unique or unusual quality? Presence, absence and, indeed incongruity are, as we have seen, key attributes of not only metonymy but also photography. The photographic image, with its properties of preservation, fixes its referents in a time always prior to the click of the shutter.[21] In the context of the dominant teleological understanding of reality, the trace of an encounter with the real which is materialised as a presence in absence in the photograph is always incongruous. We just do not see it as such. This is because, metonymies, as Runia (2006: 17) reminds us, have 'careers': 'These careers come in two modalities. In most cases metonymy is absorbed by the context in which it is placed. What starts as an eye-catching, disconcerting, and ineluctable presence ends up as something so inconspicuous that it cannot even be called a cliché.' Here again, we might ask, in modern culture, what is a photograph by one definition, if not the ultimate inconspicuous object?

So, what of metonymy's second career? A conspicuous metonymy, says Runia (ibid.: 19), 'disturbs places. When fresh, it questions meanings, awakens us from what we take for granted, and draws attention to what we don't like to be reminded of: that the implicit rules of the place are far from natural and self-evident, are indeed a system of habits and conventions'. Herein, I suggest, lies the key to understanding the Zapatistas' photographic performances in the city, and particularly another inflection of their incongruity in that environment. If photography, like metonymy, functions by materialising presence in absence, at a discursive level, the performative thrust of these images works *against* this logic. The Zapatistas signal absence in presence and in so doing, assert their right to presence in the nation as coeval citizens. That is, these images strategically reverse the temporal logic of the photographic image and in so doing insist not on temporality, but on spatiality. The Zapatistas may be out of place in the city – because they belong in another space – but they are not out of its time.

NOTES

1 For an analysis of Monsiváis's chronicle see Jörgensen (2004), who notes that the chronicle was first published in the weekly news magazine *Proceso* on 15 August 1994. See also Saldaña-Portillo (2002 and 2003) for excellent accounts of the EZLN's use of silence at a similar event. In August 2003, the EZLN Command announced the end of the Aguascalientes and the creation of Caracoles. A continuation of the communitarian, consensus-based model of democracy espoused by the Zapatistas and enshrined

in the notion of 'mandar obedeciendo' (lead by obeying), Caracoles involve the formation of like-minded localities and communities into autonomous governments which in turn, conjoin with similar networks to form wider networks of autonomous rule.

2 'El turno en el podio es de Marcos. El instante es eléctrico, o así lo proclaman los rostros iluminados al ver que, por lo menos en esta magna alegoría, se cumple lo esperado desde 1914, o alguna otra fecha legendaria.'

3 I would like to thank Samuel Brunk for his generosity in sending me a copy of this poster.

4 The contextualising section below is indebted to the work of De la Peña (2006); Harvey (1998); Nash (1995 and 2001); and Saldaña-Portillo (2003).

5 In addition to Knight (1990) and Brading (1988), see Dawson (2004) for an excellent account of the efforts to integrate the Indian into post-revolutionary society and Lomnitz (2001) for a critical history of the development of anthropology in Mexico.

6 Based on convergences with another photograph made of the surrender of Cuernavaca which took place on 29 May 1911, Ariel Arnal (1998: 65) suggests that Brehme's image was taken sometime between May and June 1911. And as he notes, it was certainly taken before 1913, for it was used as a template for an engraving by José Guadalupe Posada, who died on 20 January 1913. An uncropped version appeared on the front cover of *El Imparcial*, dated 16 April 1913. See Escorza (2005) for an analysis. On Brehme, see Nungesser (2004).

7 I thank George Pitcher for pointing this out to me. This photograph is normally reproduced with brown-faced Zapatistas to the left of the frame cropped out.

8 See Guillermoprieto (2002) for an account of the unmasking and Henck (2007) for a biography of Marcos.

9 On Superbarrio see Schwarz (1994), Cadena-Roa (2002), Jottar (2004) and Levi (2008: 128–33).

10 In addition to the Consulta, other examples include the *Caravana de la Dignidad Indígena* (Caravan for Indian Dignity), which took place between February and April 2001. Visiting a range of communities along the way, the *Caravana* – popularly dubbed the *Zapatour* – culminated in Mexico City, where Zapatista delegates made a historic address before the Federal Congress. More recently, on 1 January 2006, the EZLN launched *La Otra Campaña* (The Other Campaign). Timed to coincide with the launch of the official political parties' campaigns for the presidential elections of July 2006, delegates embarked upon the first leg of a six-month journey through the thirty-one states that comprise the Republic, during which they consulted with labour, peasant, indigenous, student and civil organizations with the aim of forging a united opposition to neo-liberal capitalism. Like the *Caravana* before it, *La Otra Campaña* culminated in Mexico City, just as the capital's residents went to the urns to vote in the presidential election. On the address to parliament by Subcomandanta Esther, see Carbó (2003); on La Otra Campaña see *Contrahistorias: La otra Mirada de Clío* (2006) and Williams (2007).

11 '¿Estás de acuerdo en que los pueblos indígenas deben ser incluidos con toda su fuerza y riqueza en el proyecto nacional y tomar parte activa en la construcción de un México Nuevo?

    ¿Estás de acuerdo en que los derechos indígenas deben ser incorporados en la Constitución nacional conforme a los acuerdos de San Andrés y a la propuesta correspondiente de la Comisión de Concordia y Pacificación del Congreso de la Unión?

¿Estás de acuerdo en que debemos alcanzar la paz verdadera por la vía del diálogo des-militarizando al país con el regreso de los soldados a sus cuarteles, como lo establecen la Constitución y sus leyes?

¿Estás de acuerdo en que el pueblo debe organizarse y exigir al gobierno que "mande obedeciendo" en todos los aspectos de la vida nacional?'

12 Coverage of the *Consulta* can also be found in a range of national dailies, including *Excélsior*, *El Universal* and *Reforma*. See Adatto (2008) on the idea of the photo opportu-nity in a US context.

13 'reclamo de mantener una identidad cultural y una organización societal diferenciada dentro de un Estado, el cual a su vez debe no sólo reconocer, sino proteger y sancionar jurídicamente tales diferencias'.

14 Valeria Wagner and Alejandro Moreira (2003: 190) opt to diverge from the conven-tional translation of this concept and, in a helpful explanatory footnote, unpack its associated meanings: 'A word should be said about the translation of mandar obede-ciendo as "to order with obedience" instead of as "to rule by obeying", which often appears in English. First, the shades of meaning between mandar obediently, with obedience, or by obeying, is irrelevant to our argument (perhaps wrongly so), so we chose the formulation that sounded best to our non-Anglophone ears. The translation of mandar as "to order" rather than "to rule" or "to command" needs an explanation. The Zapatista concept of mandar obedeciendo covers all three senses of mandar: commanders should command with obedience (or in obedience, or obediently, or by obeying), as in an army; rulers should rule with obedience, as in governments; and everyone should order (give orders), in the sphere of daily life, with obedience. Commanders and rulers are to "obey" the people's will, the decisions taken demo-cratically, to attend ("to obey" comes from the Latin audire, to hear, listen) to what these rules and commands express. In the case of "everyone", orders should be given in the same spirit of attention to the collectivity and to the other. The oxymoron aims at neutralizing the authoritarianism associated with all forms of organization and the implicit model of power as domination (whoever commands/rules/orders dominates those she or he commands) that pervades all relations of power. This is why "order-ing with obedience" seems to us preferable to the other two translations: whereas "to command" evokes the military too strongly, and not everyone has occasion to rule, "ordering" and "giving orders" are carried out by commanders, rulers, and everyone else in daily life. In other words, the translation of mandar obedeciendo as "to order with obedience" is meant to include all levels at which authority and power are exercised.'

15 'Cuando se trata del centro de la capital de un gran país, cualquier discurso y cualquier práctica entran en la arena política nacional, ponen en juego y manifiestan las ten-siones que estructuran toda la sociedad mexicana y sus relaciones con el mundo.'

16 See Rajchenberg and Héau-Lambert (1998) on the relationship between the contem-porary Zapatistas and revolutionary symbolism.

17 The 1914 and 1999 images can be viewed together on the front page of *La Jornada* at www.jornada.unam.mx/1999/03/17/primera.html (accessed 29 May 2010).

18 'acostumbrada a ver carros muy ocasionalmente, de uno en uno, se vio atrapada en un embotellamiento camino a la Magdalena Mixhuca, y preguntó sorprendida: "¿Y para qué quieren tanto carro?"'/'Pero las sorpresas que [los zapatistas] se llevan se

emparejan con las sorpresas que dan. Revuelo en las esquinas de Iztacalco al pasar un camión de redilas (que para los campesinos es de pasajeros) lleno de encapuchados mirando a los transeúntes que los miraban, se detenían, los señalaban, comentaban animadamente entre sí y les decían adiós con simpatía'.

19 The work of W.G. Sebald has become a ubiquitous touchstone in contemporary theoretical debate where, beyond the sphere of strictly literary analysis, it has acquired an emblematic status in scholarship concerned with questions of memory and trauma. This is certainly the status of Sebald's novel, *Austerlitz* in Runia's essay.

20 We should note as an aside that the photograph, which appears under an article titled 'Fifteen Zapatistas discovered part of their Mayan roots', in fact features a Zapatista reaching out to touch the rattle of a figure performing a 'danza del venado' (deer dance), a ritual associated with the Mayos and Yaquis of the northern states of Sonora and Sinaloa.

21 I am adapting here Catherine Russell's (1999: 5) notion about the relationship between film and James Clifford's definition of the 'salvage paradigm'. Where the latter is a denial of coevalness of the ethnographic subject, for Russell this denial is 'especially true of film, which feeds on photographic properties of preservation, fixing its referents in the prior time of shooting. In the cinema, the pastoral allegory becomes exaggerated by the role of technology in the act of representation, further splitting the "modern" from "the premodern"'.

9
Conclusion

In an analysis of the results of two public opinion surveys conducted by MORI de México in 1997 and 1998, regarding the place of the revolution in the minds of the Mexican people, Vincent Gawronski maintains that, despite an ongoing democratic deficit:

> Mexican feelings about the Revolution are strong . . . Apparently most Mexicans still cherish many of the Revolution's basic principles. It also seems that Mexicans comprehend that the Mexican Revolution has been quasi-officially ended without ever being completed. Nonetheless, the Revolution still carries enormous rhetorical and symbolic value. It seems doubtful, however, that it will continue as an ideological and symbolic national adhesive, which means that it will be difficult to keep the Many Mexicos cobbled together based on the Revolution's basic principles. (Gawronkski 2002: 389)

If, in the era of globalisation, Mexican feelings about the revolution are still strong, it is thanks to the conflict's persistence in the national cultural imaginary, with iconic photographs alongside other material manifestations – monuments, museums, and so forth – contributing to its enduring presence in everyday lived reality. This select handful of photographs carry important rhetorical and symbolic value, coordinating patterns of identification with, and structuring feeling about this foundational historic event, whose very event-ness is, in part, constituted through these artefacts. Had the respondents of the survey been canvassed regarding which photographs encapsulated for them the revolution's basic principles, which would they have selected? Would they have chosen the same as those that have been the subject of this book?

The study of iconic photographs, it should by now be clear, like a MORI poll, is far from an exact science. If iconic photographs are those images which, through repeated, subjective – and as we have seen, sometimes serendipitous – processes of selection and dissemination, acquire cultural saliency, then any analysis by definition participates in this process, potentially augmenting a given image's iconic status. My study is not exempt from this dynamic, and while I would assert with some confidence – albeit in the absence of empirical data – that the majority of the photographs I have chosen to explore will be widely recognised by a broad community of citizens and students of Mexico, my corpus is not devoid of exclusions, biases and idiosyncrasies. What, the reader might ask, of the visually stunning photograph, taken on 18 May 1914, depicting the *Rurales* herding their horses onto a train that will take them to Aguascalientes? Or where is the striking 1913 image of the President of the Republic, Victoriano Huerta and his Estado Mayor?[1] These two images – randomly chosen – are not included here for the simple reason that the study of icons, like the phenomenon itself, is selective.

Nevertheless, by tracing the social biographies of a handful of these ubiquitous yet overlooked artefacts across time and media, we can gain insights not just into photographic iconicity as a phenomenon in Mexican cultural history and memory; in turn, open to successive appropriations and rearticulations, the trajectories of these socially salient images provide a fresh optic through which to explore the accommodations and negotiations for power between the masses and the authoritarian post-revolutionary state.

There are a number of points that we can establish with certainty regarding the repertoire of iconic photographs of the Mexican revolution. At the moment of the photographic event – that is, at the moment when the photographer framed his shot and released the shutter – there could be no predicting whether the ensuing image would have an enduring resonance beyond its immediate newsworthiness. What is more, while those images that made it into the print media during the armed conflict did so because they conformed to acceptable standards of framing and composition, according to the press conventions of the time, professional camerawork did not bring with it authorial recognition. Although more often than not attributed to the Casasolas by virtue of their astute agency and archival management, many of the iconic images that have been the subject of these chapters are of uncertain authorship. Other core features of iconic photographs are less certain and vary from image to image.

In some cases, it is possible to discern the onset of iconic status during the war years. Such is the case of Brehme's famous photograph of Zapata. Long before a reproduction ended up, wrapped in its plastic bag, in the *morral* of old Antonio, versions of this image had not only been used frequently in the press to illustrate stories about the figurehead of that 'imagined dark, rural, unruly, Indian Mexico' (Gilbert 2003: 127); by 1912, it had already crossed media, serving as a template for José Guadalupe Posada's much-reproduced engraving. In other cases, such as *Adelita / Soldadera*, photographs were published, buried deep inside the pages of the press, in formats that in no way foreshadowed their significant iconic afterlife. When Fortino Sámano faced the firing squad assembled to carry out his execution, to be sure he had a defiant eye to his personal posterity as he stood before the camera's lens. But as we saw, the future anterior that is so poignantly captured in this photographic unit of space and time – he is dead and he is going to die – is also the tense of iconicity. The post-revolutionary valorisation of the death cult, in which stoic masculinity is a prized quality, provides the sociocultural conditions that endow this about-to-die photograph with enduring relevance. At the same time, however, *Fortino Sámano*, like *Cadáver de Emiliano Zapata*, is an image that equally meshes with iconographic traditions that precede its making. In short, the study of photographic iconicity requires that we are attentive to multiple temporal registers, ideological tendencies and iconographic codes. The considerable visual eloquence of *Cadáver de Emiliano Zapata*, for example, derives from its composition, which on closer examination, reveals an uncanny repetition of the gestural conventions associated with scenes from the Passion of Christ.

Photographic images of the 1910 revolution do so much more than simply illustrate. Nevertheless, this is the role that they have conventionally been assigned in historical work, where visual evidence plays a subordinate, minor role in analyses based largely on textual sources. Just as old Antonio advises Marcos to take the photograph of Zapata so that he can learn to question, my aim in this book has been precisely to foreground and interrogate photographs of the revolution: what role do they play in its visual constitution as a historical event? What forms of affect and knowledge do they produce about the revolution? In learning to question, I have drawn on an interdisciplinary range of methodological approaches – from photography, memory, gender studies, through psychoanalysis, anthropology, to art and cultural history and the philosophy of history. As 'special acts of display' (Hariman and Lucaites 2007: 30), iconic photographs evoke affective responses from their viewers, inviting identification, for example, with the geographically and ethnically diverse figures who assembled around the presidential chair in December 1914. Framed within official discursive structures, such acts of identification produce hegemonic knowledge about the revolution as a socially radical event, where iconic images function as a form of ideological and symbolic adhesive. Here it is worth recalling Nancy Wood's (1999: 2) formulation, when she states that '[if] particular representations of the past have permeated the public domain it is because they embody an intentionality – social, political, institutional and so on – that promotes or authorizes their entry.' At the same time, however, photographic meaning always exists in excess of that intentionality. Careful scrutiny of the 'unconscious optics' of the photographic iconography of Porfirio Díaz reveals the limits of presidential vision. Similarly, to the conservative eyes of those who seized the levers of power after the revolution, many of the images that were authorised to circulate in the public domain to shore up a particular narrative about the struggle, contain within them anxiety-inducing knowledge of what might have been had the socially radical peasant armies triumphed.

CODA

If selection is one of iconicity's key tropes, then another is repetition, where repetition to the point of saturation arguably leads to our tendency to overlook iconic photographs. It is therefore fitting to close with a coda in the form of two further

9.1 *Plantones*, Mexico City, August 2006.

sightings of an image that has surfaced at several points in this study. In the aftermath of the controversial 2 July 2006 presidential election, the unsuccessful left-wing candidate for the Partido de la Revolución Democrática (PRD), Andrés Manuel López Obrador (widely known as 'AMLO') and supporters mounted a campaign of civil resistance contesting the result that saw the election of PAN candidate Felipe Calderón.[2] Demanding a vote-by-vote recount of the results, the coalition set up *plantones* (or 'tent cities') not only in the Zócalo and surrounding streets, but also in the capital's major thoroughfares, effectively closing them to vehicular traffic. Wandering through the *plantones* that summer with my camera, I encountered a stall selling photographs related to AMLO's campaign and to campaigns of an older vintage (Figure 9.1). On the one hand, the juxtaposition of AMLO and *Villa en la silla* makes rhetorical sense. Its eloquence in 2006 is aspirational, for the 1914 image conjures a moment when the 'old oligarchy had lost its

9.2 'Conclave revolucionario'/Revolutionary conference. José Carlo González.

power forever, together with much of its property – nothing like this had happened before in Latin America, nor would it again for many decades' (Gilly 2005: 148). On the other, however, the juxtaposition of the two photographs is shot through with irony: unlike AMLO, neither Villa nor Zapata had a programme for national power; both men, moreover, were assassinated by agents of the conservative revolution.

Later that same year, on 15 December 2006, the front page of *La Jornada* featured a photograph (Figure 9.2) of guerrilla leaders, from four of the six groups that make up the Coordinación Revolucionaria y Unión de Todos los Pueblos/'Revolutionary Coordination and Union of all Peoples'.[3] Taken at a press conference with *La Jornada*, the guerrillas claimed responsibility for the six bombs that had exploded in Mexico City the preceding 6 November: two bombs went off in the Plutarco Elías Calles auditorium in the national headquarters of the PRI; two in the Tribunal Electoral del Poder Judicial de la Federación (TEPJF); and two more in branches of Scotia Bank. Against the backdrop of the contested outcome of the July 2006 presidential elections and political unrest in Oaxaca, the guerrilla leaders declared that the recent bombs were '"a sign, a warning, an alert in the face of the escalation of governmental violence", as well as a warning so that painful episodes are not repeated, episodes which we thought had been left behind in history, but are present once again' (Aranda 2006).[4] The photograph taken at the press conference features the leaders Manuel, José Arturo, Gertrudis and Javier, their faces masked in bandanas with slits for eyes, seated in a row at a white-clothed table. Behind them on the wall are two Mexican flags, between which is a sepia photograph of *Villa en la silla*. These manifestations of *Villa en la silla* demonstrate that, to this day, this photograph – alongside other iconic images produced nearly one hundred years ago – has not ceased to bear emotional and ideological freight. Indeed, such images will undoubtedly continue to assert their iconic presence in twenty-first-century Mexico, engendering compelling new narratives as they go.

NOTES

1 Cuerpo de rurales, Ciudad de México (COL. SINAFO-FN-INAH #6345); *El Sr. Presidente de la República y su Estado Mayor*, 1913 (COL. SINAFO-FN-INAH #5764). On the Huerta photograph, see Escorza (2005: 40), who notes that this photograph has been multiply reproduced, emblematising the oscuranticism of Huerta's regime.
2 See Kesner (2007) for an overview.
3 The armed groups involved include: Movimiento Revolucionario Lucio Cabañas Barrientos (MRLCB), Tendencia Democrática Revolucionaria-Ejército del Pueblo (TDR-EP), Brigadas de Ajusticiamiento 2 de Diciembre (BA 2D), Organización Insurgente 1 de Mayo (OI 1M), Brigadas Populares de Liberación (BPL) and Unidad Popular Revolucionaria Magonista (UPRM). Thanks to Laura Campbell for drawing my attention to this image.
4 '"una señal, una advertencia, una alerta, frente a la escalada represiva del gobierno", además de una alerta para que no se repitan episodios dolorosos "que pensamos que habían quedado atrás en la historia, pero que nuevamente están presentes".'

Bibliography

Acevedo, Esther (2001) 'Entre la ficción y la historia: La denegación del perdón a Maximiliano', *Anales del Instituto de Investigaciones Estéticas*, 78: 235–48.

Adatto, Kiku (2008) *Picture Perfect: Life in the Age of the Photo Op*, Princeton: Princeton University Press.

Aguilar Camín, Héctor and Meyer, Lorenzo (1992 [1968]) *Historia Gráfica de México*, Tomo 7, México, D.F.: Editorial Patria/INAH.

—— (1993) *In the Shadow of the Mexican Revolution: Contemporary Mexican History, 1910–1989*, trans. Fierro, Luis Alberto, Austin: University of Texas Press.

Aguilar Ochoa, Arturo (1996) *La fotografía durante el imperio de Maximiliano*, México, D.F.: Universidad Autónoma de México/Instituto de Investigaciones Estéticas.

—— (2004) (ed.) 'François Aubert en Mexico', *Alquimia*, 21.

Ancira, Eduardo (2005) 'Fotógrafos de la luz aprisionada. Asociación de fotógrafos de la prensa metropolitana de la Ciudad de México, octubre–diciembre de 1911' in Aguayo, Fernando and Roca, Lourdes (eds) *Imágenes e investigación social*, México, D.F.: Instituto Mora.

Anderson, Benedict (2006 [1983]) *Imagined Communities: Reflection on the Origin and Spread of Nationalism*, Rev. edn, London: Verso.

Appadurai, Arjun (ed.) (1986) *The Social Life of Things: Commodities in Cultural Perspective*, Cambridge: Cambridge University Press.

Aranda, Jesús (2006) 'La fuerza social debe parar la violencia de estado', *La Jornada*, 15 December 2006. www.jornada.unam.mx/2006/12/15/index.php?section=politica&art icle=012e1pol (accessed 20 July 2007).

Archivo Casasola (1942) *Historia gráfica de la Revolución. México. 1900–1940*.

Arnal, Ariel (1998) 'Construyendo símbolos – fotografía política en México: 1865–1911', *Estudios Interdisciplinarios de América Latina y el Caribe* 9(1): 55–73.

Arriola, Enrique (1983) *La rebelión delahuertista*, México, D.F.: Martín Casillas/SEP.

Arroyo, Sergio Raúl and Kuri, Viviana (2000) 'La caja de Pandora', *Alquimia* 3(9): 4–5.

Arroyo, Sergio Raúl and Casanova, Rosa (2002) 'Los Casasola, La épica cotidiana' in Ortiz Monasterio, Pablo (ed.), *Mirada y memoria: Archivo fotográfico Casasola, México: 1900–1940*, México, D.F.: Consejo Nacional para la Cultura y las Artes/Instituto Nacional de Antropología e Historia.

Azoulay, Ariella (2001) *Death's Showcase: The Power of Image in Contemporary Democracy*, Cambridge, MA: MIT Press.

Azuela, Mariano (2007 [1915]) *Los de abajo: Novela de la revolución mexicana*, ed. Luis Leal, Buenos Aires: Stockcero.

Baldwin, Gordon (1991) *Looking at Photographs: A Guide to Technical Terms*, Los Angeles: The J. Paul Getty Museum and British Museum Press.

Bantjes, Adrian A. (1994) 'Burning Saints, Molding Minds: Iconoclasm, Civic Ritual, and the Failed Cultural Revolution', in Beezley, William H., Martin, Cheryl, English and French, William E. (eds) *Rituals of Rule, Rituals of Resistance: Public Celebrations and Popular Culture in Mexico*, Wilmington: SR Books.

—— (2006) 'Saints, Sinners, and State Formation: Local Religion and Cultural Revolution in Mexico', in Vaughan, Mary Kay and Lewis, Stephen E. (eds) *The Eagle and the Virgin: Nation and Cultural Revolution in Mexico, 1920–1940*, Durham, NC and London: Duke University Press.

Barbosa, Carlos Alberto Sampaio (2006) *A fotografia a service de Clio: Uma interpretação da história visual da Revolução Mexicana (1900–1940)*, São Paolo: Editora UNESP.

Barrios, José Luis (2001) 'Iconography Past and Present: Visual Constructions of Power in Post-PRI Mexico', *Discourse* 23(2): 26–43.

Barthes, Roland (1993 [1981]) *Camera Lucida*, trans. Howard, Richard, London: Vintage.

Bartra, Armando (1997) 'Ver para descreer', *Luna Córnea* 13: 11–15.

Bartra, Roger (ed.) (2002) *Anatomía del mexicano*, México, D.F.: Plaza y Janés.

Bazin, André (1967) *What is Cinema?* Trans. Gray, Hugh, Berkeley: University of California Press.

Beezley, William H. (2004) *Judas at the Jockey Club and Other Episodes of Porfirian Mexico*, 2nd edn, Lincoln: University of Nebraska Press.

Bell, Steven M. (1992) 'Contexts of Critical Reception in *El laberinto de la soledad*: The Contingencies of Value and the Discourse of Power', *Siglo XX/20th Century: Critique and Cultural Discourse* 10(182): 101–24.

Bellinghausen, Hermann (1999) 'Engullidos en el caos citadino, los zapatistas promueven la consulta', *La Jornada*, 16 March, www.jornada.unam.mx/1999/03/16/promeuven. html (accessed 17 January 2010).

Benjamin, Thomas (2000) *La Revolución: Mexico's Great Revolution as Memory, Myth and History*, Austin: University of Texas Press.

—— (2003) *La Revolución Mexicana: Memoria, mito e historia*, México, D.F.: Ediciones Taurus.

Benjamin, Walter (1970) *Illuminations*, trans. Zohn, Harry, London: Jonathan Cape.

Blasio, José Luis (1934) *Maximilian Emperor of Mexico: Memoirs of his Private Secretary*, trans. and ed. Murray, Robert Hammond, New Haven, CT: Yale University Press.

Bourdieu, Pierre et al. (1990) *Photography: A Middle-brow Art*, trans. Whiteside, Shaun, Cambridge: Polity Press.

Braddy, Haldeen (1960) 'The Head of Pancho Villa', *Western Folklore* 19(1): 25–33.

Brading, David A. (1988) 'Manuel Gamio and Official *Indigenismo* in Mexico', *Bulletin of Latin American Research* 7: 75–89.

Brenner, Anita and Leighton, George R. (1996 [1943]) *The Wind that Swept Mexico: The History of the Mexican Revolution of 1910–1942*, Austin: University of Texas Press.

Brink, Cornelia (2000) 'Secular Icons: Looking at Photographs from Nazi Concentration Camps', *History and Memory* 12(1): 135–50.

Bronfen, Elisabeth (1992) *Over Her Dead Body: Death, Femininity and the Aesthetic*, Manchester: Manchester University Press.

Brothers, Caroline (1997) *War and Photography*, London: Routledge.

Brunk, Samuel (1993) 'Zapata and the City Boys: In Search of a Piece of the Revolution', *Hispanic American Historical Review* 73(1): 33–65.

—— (1995) *¡Emiliano Zapata! Revolution and Betrayal in Mexico*, Albuquerque: University of New Mexico Press.

—— (1998) 'Remembering Emiliano Zapata: Three Moments in the Posthumous Career of the Martyr of Chinameca', *The Hispanic American Historical Review* 78(3): 457–90.

—— (2004) 'The Mortal Remains of Emiliano Zapata', in Johnson, Lyman, L. (ed.) *Death, Dismemberment and Memory: Body Politics in Latin America*, Albuquerque: University of New Mexico Press.

—— (2006) 'The Eyes of Emiliano Zapata', in Brunk, Samuel and Fallaw, Ben (eds) *Heroes and Hero Cults in Latin America*, Austin: University of Texas Press.

—— (2008) *The Posthumous Career of Emiliano Zapata: Myth, Memory, and Mexico's Twentieth Century*, Austin: Texas University Press.

Buffington, Robert M. and French, William E. (2000) 'The Culture of Modernity' in Meyer, Michael C. and Beezley, William H. (eds) *The Oxford History of Mexico*, Oxford: Oxford University Press.

Cadava, Eduardo (1997) *Words of Light: Theses on the Photography of History*, Princeton, NJ: Princeton University Press.

Cadena-Roa, Jorge (2002) 'Strategic Framing, Emotions, and *Superbarrio*: Mexico City's Masked Crusader', *Mobilization: An International Journal* 7(2): 201–16.

Carbó, Teresa (2003) 'Comandanta Zapatista Esther at the Mexican Federal Congress: Performance as Politics', *Journal of Language and Politics* 2(1): 131–74.

Cartier-Bresson, H. (1995) *Henri Cartier-Bresson: Mexican Notebooks*, London: Thames & Hudson.

Caruth, Cathy (ed.) (1995) *Trauma: Explorations in Memory*, Baltimore: Johns Hopkins University Press.

Casanova, Rosa (2001) 'Memoria y registro fotográfico en el Museo Nacional', *Alquimia* 4(12): 7–16.

Casanova, Rosa and Konzevik, Adriana (2006) *Luces sobre México: Catálogo selectivo de la Fototeca Nacional del INAH*, México, D.F.: CNCA/INAH/Editorial RM.

Casasola, Agustín Víctor (ed.) (1921) *Álbum histórico gráfico: contiene los principales sucesos acaecidos durante las épocas de Díaz, de la Barra, Madero, Huerta y Obregón*, México, D.F.: Agustín Víctor Casasola.

Casasola, Gustavo (1966) *Seis siglos de historia gráfica de México, 1325–1925*, 3 vols, México, D.F.: Ediciones Gustavo Casasola.

Casasola, Juan Manuel (1977) *Pueblo en armas*, México, D.F.: Editorial Libros de México.

Castañeda, Jorge (2000) *Perpetuating Power: How Mexican Presidents were Chosen*, New York: The New Press.

Cockcroft, James D. (1998) *Mexico's Hope: An Encounter with Politics and History*, New York: Monthly Review Press.

Contrahistorias: La otra mirada de Clío, Dossier: La Otra Campaña, 3(6), 2006.

Coronil, Fernando (2004) 'Seeing History', *Hispanic American Historical Review* 84(1): 1–4.

Craven, David (2002) *Art and Revolution in Latin America, 1910–1990*, New Haven, CT: Yale University Press.

Creelman, James (1908) 'President Díaz: Hero of Mexico', *Pearson's Magazine* 19(9): 231–82.

Cuevas-Wolf, Cristina (1996) 'Guillermo Kahlo and Casasola: Architectural Form and Urban Unrest' *History of Photography*, 20(3): 196–207.

Davis, Diane E. (1994) *Urban Leviathan: Mexico City in the Twentieth Century*, Philadelphia: Temple University Press.

Dawson, Alexander S. (2004) *Indian and Nation in Revolutionary Mexico*, Tucson: University of Arizona Press.

Debroise, Olivier (1998) *Fuga Mexicana: Un recorrido por la fotografía en México*, México, D.F.: Consejo Nacional para la Cultura y las Artes.

—— (2001) *Mexican Suite: A History of Photography in Mexico*, trans. and revised in collaboration with the author by de Sá Rego, Stella, Austin: University of Texas Press.

De la Colina, José (2000) 'Breve lectura de la fotografía *Villa en la silla presidencial*', *Alquimia* 3(9): 12–13.

De la Peña, Guillermo (1999) 'Territorio y ciudadanía étnica en la nación globalizada', *Desacatos*, primavera: 13–27.

—— (2006) 'A New Mexican Nationalism? Indigenous Rights, Constitutional Reform and the Conflicting Meanings of Multiculturalism', *Nations and Nationalism* 12(2): 279–302.

Del Castillo Troncoso, Alberto (2005) 'La historia de la fotografía en México, 1890–1920: La diversidad de los usos de la imagen', in Casanova, Rosa, Castillo Troncoso, Alberto del, Monroy Nasr, Rebeca and Morales, Alfonso (eds) *Imaginarios y Fotografía en México, 1839–1970*, México, D.F.: CONACULTA-INAH/Lunwerg Editores.

De los Reyes, Aurelio (1985) *Con Villa en México: Testimonios sobre camarógrafos norteamericanos en la revolución, 1911–1916*, México, D.F.: Universidad Nacional Autónoma de México/Instituto de Investigaciones Estéticas.

De Orellana, Margarita (1992) *La mirada circular: El cine norteamericano de la revolución mexicana*, México, D.F.: Joaquín Mortiz.

Doane, Mary Ann (1982) 'Film and the Masquerade: Theorising the Female Spectator', *Screen* 23: 74–87.

—— (2002) *The Emergence of Cinematic Time: Modernity, Contingency, the Archive*, Cambridge, MA and London: Harvard University Press.

Dubois, Philippe (1983) *L'Acte photographique*, Paris: Nathan.

Edwards, Elizabeth (2001) *Raw Histories: Photographs, Anthropology and Museums*, Oxford and New York: Berg.

Edwards, Elizabeth, and Hart, Janice (eds) (2004) *Photographs Objects Histories: On the Materiality of Images*, London: Routledge.

Edwards, Holly (2007) 'Cover to Cover: The Life Cycle of an Image in Contemporary Visual Culture', in Reinhardt, Mark and Edwards, Holly (eds) *Beautiful Suffering: Photography and the Traffic in Pain*, Chicago: Williams College Museum of Art/ University of Chicago Press.

Elkins, James (2005) 'Critical Response: What Do we Want Photography to Be? A Response to Michael Fried', *Critical Inquiry* 31: 938–56.

Escorza Rodríguez, Daniel (2005) 'Las fotografías de Casasola publicadas en diarios capitalinos durante 1913', *Alquimia* 9(25): 35–40.

Etherington, Shelly (1993) 'Progressivist Stories and the Pre-Columbian Past: Notes on Mexico and the United States', in Hill Boone, Elizabeth (ed.) *Collecting the Pre-Columbian Past*, Washington DC: Dumbarton Oaks Research Library and Collection.

Ethington, Philip J. and Schwartz, Vanessa R. (2006) 'Introduction: An Atlas of the Urban Icons Project', *Urban History* 33(1): 5–19.

Florescano, Enrique (1993) 'The Creation of the Museo Nacional de Antropología of Mexico and its Scientific, Educational, and Political Purposes', in Hill Boone, Elizabeth (ed.) *Collecting the Pre-Columbian Past*, Washington DC: Dumbarton Oaks Research Library and Collection.

—— (1998) *La bandera mexicana: Breve historia de su formación y simbolismo*, México, D.F.: Fondo de Cultura Económica.

Folgarait, Leonard (2008) *Seeing Mexico Photographed: The work of Horne, Casasola, Modotti, and Álvarez Bravo*, New Haven: Yale University Press.

Foucault, Michel (1977) *Discipline and Punish: The Birth of the Prison*, trans. Sheridan, Alan, New York: Vintage Books.

Franco, Jean (2004) 'The Return of Coatlicue: Mexican Nationalism and the Aztec Past', *Journal of Latin American Cultural Studies* 13(2): 205–19.

French, William E. (1999) 'Imagining and the Cultural History of Nineteenth-Century Mexico', *Hispanic American Historical Review* 79(2): 249–67.

Freud, Sigmund (2003 [1920]) *Beyond the Pleasure Principle and Other Writings*, trans. Reddick, John, intro. Edmundson, Mark, London: Penguin.

Gaonkar, Dilip Parameshwar (2002) 'Toward New Imaginaries: An Introduction', *Public Culture* 14(1): 1–19.

Garner, Paul (2001) *Porfirio Díaz*, London: Longman.

Gautreau, Marion (2003) 'Questionnement d'un symbole: Agustín Víctor Casasola, Photographe de la Revolution Mexicaine', MA thesis, Université de Paris IV, Sorbonne.

Gawronski, Vincent T. (2002) 'The Revolution is Dead. ¡Viva la revolución!: The Place of the Mexican Revolution in the Era of Globalization', *Mexican Studies/Estudios Mexicanos* 18(2): 363–97.

Gilbert, Dennis (2003) 'Emiliano Zapata: Textbook Hero', *Mexican Studies/Estudios Mexicanos* 19(1): 127–59.

Gilly, Adolfo (1971) *La revolución interrumpida, México, 1910–1920: una guerra campesina por la tierra y el poder*, México, D.F.: Ediciones El Caballito.

—— (2005) *The Mexican Revolution*, trans. Camiller, Patrick, New York: The New Press.

Gómez Morin, Mauricio (2000) 'La mirada de Zapata sin silla', *La Jornada Semanal*, 31 December, www.jornada.unam.mx/2000/12/31/sem-morin.html (accessed 17 January 2010).

González Rodríguez, Sergio (2009) *El hombre sin cabeza*, Barcelona: Editorial Anagrama.

Grosz, Elizabeth (1989) *Sexual Subversions*, St Leonards: Allen & Unwin.

Gruzinski, Serge (2001) *Images at War: Mexico from Columbus to Blade Runner (1492–2019)*, trans. MacLean, Heather, Durham, NC: Duke University Press.

Guerra, François Xavier (2007) 'Mexico from Independence to Revolution: The Mutations of Liberalism' in Servín, Elisa, Reina, Leticia and Tutino, John (eds) *Cycles of Conflict, Centuries of Change: Crisis, Reform, and Revolution in Mexico*, Durham, NC: Duke University Press.

Guillermoprieto, Alma (2002) 'The Unmasking', in Hayden, Tom (ed.) *The Zapatista Reader*, New York: Thunder's Mouth Press/Nation Books.

Gunning, Tom (1995) 'Tracing the Individual Body: Photography, Detectives, and Early Cinema', in Charney, Leo and Schwarz, Vanessa R. (eds) *Cinema and the Invention of Modern Life*, Berkeley: University of California Press.

—— (2008) 'What's the Point of an Index? Or, Faking Photographs', in Beckman, Karen and Ma, Jean (eds) *Still Moving: Between Cinema and Photography*, Durham, NC and London: Duke University Press.

Gutiérrez Ruvulcaba, Ignacio (1996) 'A Fresh Look at the Casasola Archive', *History of Photography* 20(3): 191–5.

Guzmán, Martín Luis (1991 [1928]) *El águila y la serpiente*, México, D.F.: Editorial Porrúa.

Hagopian, Patrick (2006) 'Vietnam War Photography as Locus of Memory', in Kuhn, Annette and McAllister, Kirsten Emiko (eds) *Locating Memory: Photographic Acts*, London: Berghahn.

Halbwachs, Maurice (1980) *The Collective Memory*, New York: Harper and Row.

Hamnett, Brian (1994) *Juárez*, London: Longman.

Hariman, Robert and Lucaites, John Louis (2002) 'Performing Civic Identity: Iconic Photograph of the Flag Raising in Iwo Jima', *Quarterly Journal of Speech* 88(4): 363–92.

—— (2007) *No Caption Needed: Iconic Photographs, Public Culture, and Liberal Democracy*, Chicago: University of Chicago Press.

Hart, John Mason (2000) 'The Mexican Revolution, 1910–1920', in Meyer, Michael C. and Beezley, William H. (eds) *The Oxford History of Mexico*, Oxford: Oxford University Press.

Harvey, Neil (1998) *The Chiapas Rebellion: The Struggle for Land and Democracy*, Durham, NC and London: Duke University Press.

Henck, Nick (2007) *Subcommander Marcos: The Man and the Mask*, Durham, NC and London: Duke University Press.

Hirsch, Marianne (1997) *Family Frames: Photography and Narrative and Postmemory*, Cambridge, MA: Harvard University Press.

—— (2001) 'Surviving Images: Holocaust Photographs and the Work of Postmemory', *The Yale Journal of Criticism* 14(1): 5–37.

Historia. Cuarto Grado, Secretaría de Educación Pública, 1994.

House, John (1992) 'Manet's Maximilian: History Painting, Censorship and Ambiguity' in Wilson-Bareau, Juliet (ed.) *Manet: The Execution of Maximilian: Painting, Politics and Censorship*, London: National Gallery Publications.

Ibsen, Kristine (2006) 'Spectacle and Spectator in Éduoard Manet's Execution of Maxmilian', *Oxford Art Journal* 29(2): 213–26.

Jay, Martin (1995) 'Photo-unrealism: The Contribution of the Camera to the Crisis of Occularcentrism', in Melville, Stephen and Readings, Bill (eds) *Vision and Textuality*, London: Macmillan.

Jörgensen, Beth E. (2004) 'Making History: Subcomandante Marcos in the Mexican Chronicle', *South Central Review* 21(3): 85–106.

Joseph, Gilbert M. and Nugent, Daniel (eds) (1994) *Everyday Forms of State Formation: Revolution and the Negotiation of Rule in Modern Mexico*, Durham, NC and London: Duke University Press.

Joseph, Gilbert M., Rubenstein, Anne and Zolov, Eric (eds) (2001) *Fragments of a Golden Age: The Politics of Culture in Mexico Since 1940*, Durham, NC and London: Duke University Press.

Jottar, Berta (2004) 'Superbarrio Gómez for US President: Global Citizenship and the "Politics of the Possible"', http://hemi.nyu.edu/journal/3.1/eng/en31_pg_corbin.html (accessed 17 January 2010).

Katz, Friedrich (1998) *The Life and Times of Pancho Villa*, Stanford, CA: Stanford University Press.

Kesner, Joseph L. (2007) 'The 2006 Mexican Election and its Aftermath: Editor's Introduction', *PS Political Science and Politics* 40(1): 11–14.

Knight, Alan (1986) *The Mexican Revolution*, 2 vols, Lincoln: University of Nebraska Press.

—— (1990) 'Racism, Revolution, and Indigenismo: Mexico, 1910–1940', in Graham, Richard (ed.) *The Idea of Race in Latin America, 1870–1940*, Austin: University of Texas Press.

—— (1992) 'The peculiarities of Mexican History: Mexico Compared to Latin America, 1892–1992', *Journal of Latin American Studies* 24: 99–144.

—— (1994) 'Popular Culture and the Revolutionary State in Mexico, 1910–1940', *Hispanic American Historical Review* 74(3): 393–444.

—— (1999) 'Political Violence in Post-Revolutionary Mexico', in Koonings, Kees and Kruijt, Dirk (eds) *Societies of Fear: The Legacy of Civil War, Violence and Terror in Latin America*, London: Zed Books.

—— (2001) 'Democratic and Revolutionary Traditions in Latin America', *Bulletin of Latin American Studies* 20(2): 147–86.

—— (2002) 'Subalterns, Signifiers, and Statistics: Perspectives on Mexican Historiography', *Latin American Research Review* 37(2): 136–58.

—— (2007) 'Mexico's Three Fin de Siècle Crises', in Servín, Elisa, Reina, Leticia and Tutino, John (eds) *Cycles of Conflict, Centuries of Change: Crisis, Reform, and Revolution in Mexico*, Durham, NC and London: Duke University Press.

Koetzle, Hans-Michael (2005) *Photo Icons: The Story behind the Pictures 1827–1991*, Köln/London: Taschen.

Krauze, Enrique (1987) *Emiliano Zapata: El amor a la tierra*, México, D.F.: Fondo de Cultura Económica.

—— (1997) *Biografía del poder: Caudillos de la Revolución mexicana (1910–1940)*, México, D.F.: Tusquets Editores.

Lalucq, Virginie and Nancy, Jean-Luc (2004) *Fortino Sámano (Les débordements du poème)*, Paris: Galilée.

Laplanche, J. and Pontalis, J.-B. (1988) *The Language of Psychoanalysis*, London: Karnac Books.

Lara, Jaime (2008) *Christian Texts for Aztecs: Art and Liturgy in Colonial Mexico*, Notre Dame, IN: University of Notre Dame Press.

Lara Klahr, Flora (1986) *Jefes, héroes y caudillos*, México, D.F.: Fondo de Cultura Económica.

Lear, John (2001) *Workers, Neighbors and Citizens: The Revolution in Mexico City*, Lincoln: University of Nebraska Press.

Legrás, Horacio (2003) 'Martín Luis Guzmán: El viaje de la revolución', *Modern Language Notes* 118: 427–54.

Lempérière, Annick (1995) 'Los dos centenarios de la independencia mexicana (1910–1921): De la historia patria a la antropología cultural', *Historia Mexicana* 14(2): 317–52.

Lerner, Jesse (2001/02) 'Imported Nationalism', *Cabinet*, 5. www.cabinetmagazine.org/issues/f/importednationalism.php (accessed 17 January 2010).

—— (2007) *El impacto de la modernidad: Fotografía criminalística en la ciudad de México*, Mexico: Turner/INAH/CONACULTA.

Levi, Heather (1997) 'Sport and Melodrama: The Case of Mexican Professional Wrestling', *Social Text* 50: 57–68.

—— (2008) *The World of Lucha Libre: Secrets, Revelations, and Mexican National Identity*, Durham, NC and London: Duke University Press.

Lévi-Strauss, Claude (1966) *The Savage Mind*, London: Weidenfeld & Nicolson.

Linhard, Tabea Alexa (2005) *Fearless Women in the Mexican Revolution and the Spanish Civil War*, Columbia, MO and London: University of Missouri Press.

Lomnitz, Claudio (2001) *Deep Mexico, Silent Mexico: An Anthropology of Nationalism*, Minneapolis: University of Minnesota Press.

—— (2005) *Death and the Idea of Mexico*, New York: Zone Books.

—— (2006) 'Final Reflections: What was Mexico's Cultural Revolution?' in Vaughan, Mary Kay and Lewis, Stephen E. (eds) *The Eagle and the Virgin: Nation and Cultural Revolution in Mexico, 1920–1940*, Durham, NC and London: Duke University Press.

Marien, Mary Warner (2002) *Photography: A Cultural History*, London: Laurence King Publishing.

Martínez Assad, Carlos (2005) *La patria en el Paseo de la Reforma*, México, D.F.: UNAM / Fondo de Cultura Económica.

Matabuena Peláez, Teresa (1991) *Algunos usos y conceptos de la fotografía durante el porfiriato*, México, D.F.: Universidad Iberoamericana.

Mbembe, Achille (2003) 'Necropolitics', *Public Culture* 15(1): 11–40.

McCaa, Robert (2003) 'Missing Millions: The Demographic Costs of the Mexican Revolution', *Mexican Studies / Estudios Mexicanos* 19(2): 367–400.

McCauley, Elizabeth Anne (1985) *A. A. E. Disdéri and the Carte de Visite Portrait Photograph*, New Haven, CT: Yale University Press.

Medina Peña, Luis (2004) 'Porfirio Díaz y la creación del sistema político en México' *Istor* 5(176): 60–94.

Metz, Christian (1990) 'Photography and Fetish', in Squiers, Carol (ed.) *The Critical Image: Essays on Contemporary Photography*, London: Lawrence & Wishart.

Meyer, Jean (2004) *La Revolución Mexicana*, trans. Pérez-Rincón, Héctor, México, D.F.: Tusquets.

Meyer, Michael C. and Beezley, William H. (eds) (2000) *The Oxford History of Mexico*, Oxford: University of Oxford Press.

Mitchell, Stephanie and Schell, Patience A. (eds) (2006) *The Women's Revolution in Mexico, 1910–1953*, Lanham, MD: Rowman and Littlefield.

Mitchell, W.J.T. (2005) *What do Pictures Want: The Lives and Loves of Images*, Chicago and London: University of Chicago Press.

Monk, Lorraine (1989) *Photographs that Changed the World:The Camera as Witness: The photograph as Evidence*, Toronto: Macfarlane Walter and Ross.

Monnet, Jérôme (1995) *Usos e imágenes del centro histórico de la Ciudad de México*, México, D.F.: Departamento del Distrito Federal / Centro de Estudios Mexicanos y Centroamericanos.

Monroy Nasr, Rebeca (2006) 'Las entrañas de la imagen', *Alquimia* 9(27): 6–23.

Monsiváis, Carlos (1970) *Días de guardar*, México, D.F.: Biblioteca Era.

—— (1977) '(Prólogo a manera de foto fija)', in Casasola, Juan Manuel, *Pueblo en armas*, México, D.F.: Editorial Libros de México.

—— (1980) 'Notas sobre la historia de la fotografía en México', *Revista de la Universidad de México* 35(5/6), unnumbered pages.

—— (1984) 'Continuidad de las imágenes: Notas a partir del Archivo Casasola', *The World of Agustín Víctor Casasola*, travelling exhibition catalogue.

—— (1987) '"Look Death, Don't be Inhuman": Notes on a Traditional and Industrial Myth', in Pomar, María Teresa (ed.) *El Día de los Muertos: The Life of the Dead in Mexican Folk Art*, Texas: The Fort Worth Art Museum.

—— (1994a) 'Crónica de una convención (que no lo fue tanto) y de un acontecimiento muy significativo', *EZLN: Documentos y comunicados 1*, México, D.F.: Ediciones Era.

—— (1994b) 'La foto testimonial: La historia se hace a cualquier hora', www.fotoperiodismo.org/FORO/files/fotoperiodismo/source/html/textos/carlos.htm (accessed 17 January 2010).

—— (2006) *Imágenes de la tradición viva*, México, D.F.: Universidad Autónoma de México/ Fondo de Cultura Económica.

Morales, Miguel Ángel (2006) 'La célebre fotografía de Jerónimo Hernández', *Alquimia* 9(27): 68–75.

Morales Moreno, Luis Gerardo (2001) 'El primer museo nacional de México (1825–1857)', in Acevedo, Esther (ed.) *Hacia otra historia del arte en México: De la estructuración colonial a la exigencia nacional (1780–1860)*, México, D.F.: CONACULTA.

Mraz, John (1990) 'Objetividad y democracia: Apuntes para una historia del fotoperiodismo en México', *La Jornada Semanal*, 25 February.

—— (1992) 'Más allá de la decoración: Hacia una historia gráfica de las mujeres en México," *Política y cultura*, 1.

—— (1997) 'Photographing Political Power in Mexico', in Pansters, Will (ed.) *Citizens of the Pyramid: Essays on Mexican Political Culture*, Amsterdam: Thela.

—— (2000) 'Historia y mito del Archivo Casasola', *La Jornada Semanal*, 31 December: www.jornada.unam.mx/2000/12/31/sem-john.html (accessed 17 January 2010).

—— (2001) 'Envisioning Mexico: Photography and National Identity', Duke University of North Carolina Program in Latin American Studies, Working Paper #32.

—— (2003) *Nacho López: Mexican Photographer*, Minneapolis: University of Minnesota Press.

—— (2004) 'Picturing Mexico's Past: Photography and *Historia Gráfica*', *South Central Review* 21(3): 24–45.

—— (2005) 'Historiar la fotografía', *Estudios Interdisciplinarios de América Latina y el Caribe* 16: 2.

—— (2007) '¿Fotohistoria o historia gráfica? El pasado mexicano en fotografía', *Cuicuilco* 14(41): 11–41.

—— (2009) *Looking for Mexico: Modern Visual Culture and National Identity*, Durham, NC and London: Duke University Press.

Mulvey, Laura (2006) *Death 24x a Second: Stillness and the Moving Image*, London: Reaktion.

Nagel, Alexander (2000) *Michelangelo and the Reform of Art*, Cambridge: Cambridge University Press.

Nash, June (1995) 'The Reassertion of Indigenous Identity: Mayan Responses to State Intervention in Chiapas', *Latin American Research Review* 30(3): 7–41.

—— (2001) *Mayan Visions: The Quest for Autonomy in an Age of Globalization*, New York and London: Routledge.

Noble, Andrea (2004) 'Photography, Memory, Disavowal: The Casasola Archive', in Andermann, Jens and Rowe, William (eds), *Images of Power: Iconography, Culture and the State in Latin America*, New York and Oxford: Berghahn.

—— (2005) *Mexican National Cinema*, London: Routledge.

Nungesser, Michael (2004) *Hugo Brehme 1882–1954: Fotograf; Mexiko Zwischen Revolution und Romantik/Hugo Brehme 1882–1954: Fotógrafo: México entre Revolución y Romanticismo*, Berlin: Arenhövel.

Ochoa Sandy, Gerardo (1997) 'Historia de un archivo', *Luna Córnea* 13: 11–15.

O'Kane, Martin (2005) 'Picturing "The Man of Sorrows": The Passion-Filled Afterlives of a Biblical Icon', *Religion and the Arts* 9(1/2): 62–100.

Olcott, Jocelyn (2005) *Revolutionary Women in Postrevolutionary Mexico*, Durham, NC and London: Duke University Press.

O'Malley, Ilene (1986) *The Myth of the Revolution: Hero Cults and the Institutionalization of the Mexican State: 1920–1940*, New York: Greenwood.

Ortiz Gaitán, Julieta (2003) *Imágenes del deseo: Arte y publicidad en la prensa ilustrada mexicana (1894–1939)*, México, D.F.: UNAM.

Ortiz Monasterio, Pablo (2000) 'María Zavala "La destroyer", ayudó a bien morir a los soldados', *Alquimia* 3(9): 24–5.

—— (ed.) (2002) *Mirada y memoria: Archivo fotográfico Casasola, México: 1900–1940*, México, D.F.: Consejo Nacional para la Cultura y las Artes/Instituto Nacional de Antropología e Historia.

Pacheco, Cristina (2005 [1988]) *La luz de México: Entrevistas con pintores y fotógrafos*, México, D.F.: Fondo de Cultura Económica.

Pani, Erika (2002) 'Dreaming of a Mexican Empire: The Political Projects of the "Imperialistas"', *Hispanic American Historical Review* 82(1): 1–31.

Paz, Octavio (1988 [1950]) *El laberinto de la soledad*, México, D.F.: Fondo de Cultura Económica.

Pollock, Griselda (1988) *Vision and Difference: Femininity, Feminism and the Histories of Art*, London: Routledge.

—— (1995) 'The "View from Elsewhere": Extracts from a Semi-Public Correspondence about the Politics of Feminist Spectatorship', in Florence, Penny and Reynolds, Dee (eds) *Feminist Subjects, Multi-Media Cultural Methodologies*, Manchester: Manchester University Press.

—— (1999) 'Killing Men and Dying Women: Gesture and Sexual Difference', in Bal, Mieke (ed.), *The Practice of Cultural Analysis: Exposing Interdisciplinary Interpretation*, Stanford, CA: University of Stanford Press.

Poniatowska, Elena (1969) *Hasta no verte Jésus mío*, México, D.F.: Ediciones Era.

—— (1999) *Las Soldaderas*, México, D.F.: Ediciones Era/CONACULTA/INAH.

Przyblyski, Jeannene (1995) 'Moving Pictures: Photography, Narrative and the Paris Commune of 1871', in Charney, Leo and Schwarz, Vanessa R. (eds) *Cinema and the Invention of Modern Life*, Berkeley: University of California Press.

Radstone, Susannah (ed.) (2000a) *Memory and Methodology*, Oxford: Berg.

—— (2000b) 'Screening Trauma: *Forrest Gump*', in Radstone, Susannah (ed.) *Memory and Methodology*, Oxford: Berg.

Rajchenberg, Enrique and Héau-Lambert, Catherine (1998) 'History and Symbolism in the Zapatista Movement', in Holloway, John and Peláez, Eloína (eds) *¡Zapatista!: Reinventing Revolution in Mexico*, London: Pluto Press.

Riley, Luisa (1997) 'La piedra sin sosiego', *Luna Córnea* 13 (septiembre/octubre): 17–23.

Ruiz, Luis F. (2007) 'From Marxism to Social History: Adolfo Gilly's Revision of *The Mexican Revolution*', *A Contra corriente* 4(2): 243–53.

Runia, Eelco (2006) 'Presence', *History and Theory* 45(1): 1–29.

Russell, Catherine (1999) *Experimental Ethnography: The Work of Film in the Age of Video*, Durham, NC and London: Duke University Press.

Salas, Elizabeth (1990) *Soldaderas in the Mexican Military: Myth and History*, Austin: University of Texas Press.

Saldaña-Portillo, María Josefina (2002) 'Reading a Silence: The "Indian" in the Era of Zapatismo', *Nepantla* 3(2): 287–314.

—— (2003) *The Revolutionary Imagination in the Americas and the Age of Development*, Durham, NC and London: Duke University Press.

Scharf, Aaron (1968) *Art and Photography*, London: Penguin.

Scherer García, Julio and Monsiváis, Carlos (2002) *Parte de Guerra: Los rostros del 68*, México, D.F.: Nuevo Siglo / Aguilar.

—— (2004) *Los patriotas: De Tlatelolco a la guerra sucia*, México, D.F.: Nuevo Siglo / Aguilar.

Schwarz, Mauricio-José (1994) *Todos somos Superbarrio: La verdadera y asombrosa historia del luchador social más enigmático de México*, México, D.F.: Planeta.

Segre, Erica (2005) 'The Hermeneutics of the Veil in Mexican Photography: of *rebozos, sábanas, huipiles* and *lienzos de Verónica*', *Hispanic Research Journal* 6(1): 39–65.

—— (2007) *Intersected Identities: Strategies of Visualisation in Nineteenth- and Twentieth-century Mexican Culture*, New York: Berghahn Books.

Servín, Elisa, Reina, Leticia and Tutino, John (eds) (2007) *Cycles of Conflict, Centuries of Change: Crisis, Reform, and Revolution in Mexico*, Durham, NC and London: Duke University Press.

Sherman, John W. (2000) 'The Mexican "Miracle" and its Collapse', in Meyer, Michael C. and Beezley, William H. (eds) *The Oxford History of Mexico*, Oxford: University of Oxford Press.

Solomon-Godeau, Abigail (1991) *Photography at the Dock: Essays on Photographic History, Institutions and Practices*, Minneapolis: University of Minnesota Press.

—— (1997) *Male Trouble: A Crisis in Representation*, London: Thames & Hudson.

Sorell, Victor (1987) 'The Photograph as a Source for Visual Artists: Images from the Archivo Casasola in the Works of Mexican and Chicano Artists', in *The World of Agustín Víctor Casasola, Mexico: 1900–1938*, travelling exhibition to galleries in US and Canada, 27 November 1984–November 1987.

Stanton, Anthony (2001) 'Models of Discourse and Hermeneutics in Octavio Paz's *El Laberinto de la Soledad*', *Bulletin of Latin American Research* 20(2): 210–32.

—— (2008) (ed.) *El laberinto de la soledad*, Manchester: Manchester University Press.

Stein, Sally (2003) 'Passing Likeness: Dorothea Lange's "Migrant Mother" and the Paradox of Iconicity', in Fusco, Coco and Wallis, Brian (eds) *Only Skin Deep: Changing Visions of the American Self*, New York: International Center of Photography / Harry N. Abrams.

Stephen, Lynn (2002) *¡Zapata Lives! Histories and Cultural Politics in Southern Mexico*, Berkeley, Los Angeles and London: University of California Press.

Tagg, John (1982) 'The Currency of the Photograph', in Burgin, Victor (ed.) *Thinking Photography*, London: Macmillan.

Taylor, Analisa (2005) 'The Ends of Indigenismo in Mexico', *Journal of Latin American Cultural Studies* 14(1): 75–86.

Tejada, Roberto (2009) *National Camera: Photography and Mexico's Image Environment*, Minneapolis: University of Minnesota Press.

Tenorio-Trillo, Mauricio (1996a) *Mexico at the World's Fairs: Crafting a Modern Nation*, Berkeley: University of California Press.

—— (1996b) '1910 Mexico City: Space and Nation in the City of the *Centenario*', *Journal of Latin American Studies* 28: 75–104.

—— (2009) *Historia y celebración: México y sus centenarios*, México, D.F.: Tusquets Editores.

Tierney, Dolores (2007) *Emilio Fernández: Pictures in the Margins*, Manchester: Manchester University Press.

Van Young, Eric (1999a) 'Making Leviathan Sneeze: Recent Works on Mexico and the Mexican Revolution', *Latin American Research Review* 34(3): 143–65.

—— (1999b) 'The New Cultural History Comes to Old Mexico', *Hispanic American Historical Review* 79(2): 211–47.

—— (2007) 'Of Tempests and Teapots: Imperial Crisis and Local Conflict in Mexico at the Beginning of the Nineteenth Century', in Servín, Elisa, Reina, Leticia and Tutino, John (eds) *Cycles of Conflict, Centuries of Change: Crisis, Reform, and Revolution in Mexico*, Durham, NC and London: Duke University Press.

Vaughan, Mary Kay and Lewis, Stephen E. (eds) (2006) *The Eagle and the Virgin: Nation and Cultural Revolution in Mexico, 1920–1940*, Durham, NC and London: Duke University Press.

Vaughan, Mary Kay (2006) 'Introduction. Pancho Villa, the Daughters of Mary, and the Modern Woman: Gender in the Long Mexican Revolution', in Olcott, Jocelyn, Vaughan, Mary Kay and Cano, Gabriela (eds) *Sex in Revolution: Gender, Politics, and Power in Modern Mexico*, Durham, NC and London: Duke University Press.

Wagner, Valeria and Moreira, Alejandro (2003) 'Toward a Quixotic Pragmatism: The Case of the Zapatista Insurgence', *Boundary 2*, 30(3): 185–212.

Wasserman, Mark (2000) *Everyday Life and Politics in Nineteenth Century Mexico: Men, Women, and War*, Albuquerque: University of New Mexico Press.

Weeks, Charles A. (1987) *The Juárez Myth in Mexico*, Tuscaloosa: The University of Alabama Press.

Widdifield, Stacie (1996) *The Embodiment of the National in Late Nineteenth-Century Mexican Painting*, Tucson: The University of Arizona Press.

Williams, Gareth (2005) 'Sovereign (In)hospitability: Politics and the Staging of Equality in Revolutionary Mexico', *Discourse* 27(2/3): 95–123.

—— (2007) 'The Mexican Exception and the "Other Campaign"', *South Atlantic Quarterly* 106(1): 129–51.

Wilson, Colette E. (2007) *Paris and the Commune, 1871–78: The Politics of Forgetting*, Manchester: Manchester University Press.

Wilson, Michael L. (2004) 'Visual Culture: A Useful Category of Historical Analysis?' in Schwarz, Vanessa R. and Przyblyski, Jeannene M. (eds) *The Nineteenth-Century Visual Culture Reader*, London: Routledge.

Wilson-Bareau, Juliet (1992) *Manet: The Execution of Maximilian: Painting, Politics and Censorship*, London: National Gallery Publications.

Womack, John, Jr. (1968) *Zapata and the Mexican Revolution*, New York: Alfred A. Knopf.

Wood, David (2009) 'Memorias de una mexicana: La Revolución como monumento fílmico', *Secuencia* 75 (septiembre–diciembre): 147–70.

Wood, Nancy (1999) *Vectors of Memory: Legacies of Trauma in Postwar Europe*, Oxford: Berg.

Zelizer, Barbie (2005) 'Death in Wartime: Photographs and the "Other War" in Afghanistan', *Harvard International Journal of Press/Politics* 10(3): 26–55.

Newspaper sources

El Correo Español
El Demócrata
El Diario
Excélsior
El Globo
El Imparcial
El Independiente
La Jornada
El Liberal
El Monitor: Diario de la Mañana
Nueva Era
El Popular
El Pueblo
Reforma
La Semana / La Semana Ilustrada
Semanario Rotográfico
El Tiempo / El Tiempo Ilustrado
El Universal

Film sources

El compadre Mendoza, Fernando de Fuentes, 1933.
Enamorada, Emilio Fernández, 1946.
Flor silvestre, Emilio Fernández, 1943.
Memorias de un mexicano, Carmen Toscano de Moreno Sánchez, 1950.
El prisionero trece, Fernando de Fuentes, 1933.
El signo de la muerte, Chano Urueta, 1939.
Los últimos Zapatistas: Héroes olvidados, Francesco Tabone Taboada, 2002.
¡Vámonos con Pancho Villa! Fernando de Fuentes, 1935.

Exhibitions

¡Tierra y Libertad! Photographs of Mexico from the Casasola Archive, Museum of Modern Art Oxford, 16 June–28 July 1985.

The World of Agustín Víctor Casasola, Mexico: 1900–1938, travelling exhibition to galleries in US and Canada, 27 November 1984–November 1987.

Mexico 1910–1960: Brehme-Casasola-Kahlo-López-Modotti, Galerie im Treffpunkt Rotebühleplatz Volkshochschule Stuttgart, 29 May–26 July 1992.

Internet sources

A Nation Emerges: Sixty-Five Years of Photography in Mexico, Getty Research Institute: www.getty.edu/research/conducting_research/digitized_collections/photography_mexico/photographers.html (accessed 17 January 2010).

Bi100: Bicentenario de la Independencia y Centenario de la Revolución en la Ciudad de México: www.bi100.df.gob.mx/ (accessed 17 January 2010).

Colección Mexicana de Tarjetas Postales Antiguas Universidad Autónoma de Ciudad Juárez: bivir.uacj.mx/postales/ (accessed 17 January 2010).

Facsimile of the Creelman-Díaz interview, March 1908, *Pearson's Magazine*: www.bibliotecas. tv/zapata/bibliografia/indices/entrevista_diaz_creelman01.html (accessed 17 January 2010).

Florescano, Enrique (2006) 'La imagen de Benito Juárez', www.jornada.unam.mx/2006/03/21/juarez.php (accessed 17 January 2010).

Manet and the Execution of Maximilian, Museum of Modern Art: www.moma.org/exhibitions/2006/Manet/index.htm (accessed 17 January 2010).

México 2010: Bicentenario Independencia/Centenario Revolución: www.bicentenario. gob.mx/ (accessed 17 January 2010).

Mexico: From Empire to Revolution, Getty Research Institute: www.getty.edu/research/conducting_research/digitized_collections/mexico/html/index.html (accessed 17 January 2010).

No Caption Needed: Iconic Photographs, Public Culture, and Liberal Democracy: www. nocaptionneeded.com/ (accessed 17 January 2010).

Sistema Nacional de Fototecas: www.sinafo.inah.gob.mx/ (accessed 17 January 2010).

Index

Note: 'n.' after a page reference indicates the number of a note on that page.